Praise for
SLOW TRAIN TO SWITZERLAND

For my parents, Jenny & David,

who started me off on this journey

SLOW TRAIN TO SWITZERLAND

One Tour, Two Trips, 150 Years –

and a World of Change Apart

DICCON BEWES

NICHOLAS BREALEY
PUBLISHING

London • Boston

First published in 2016 by Nicholas Brealey Publishing
An imprint of John Murray Press

An Hachette company

5

Published in hardback by Nicholas Brealey Publishing in 2013
Previous paperback edition published by Nicholas Brealey Publishing in 2014
Copyright © Diccon Bewes 2013, 2014, 2016

British Library Cataloguing-in-Publication Data
A catalogue record for this book is available from the British Library.

ISBN 978-1-85788-651-1
eBook ISBN (UK) 978-1-85788-976-5
eBook ISBN (US) 978-1-47364-491-5

Printed and bound by Clays Ltd, Elcograf S.p.A.

John Murray Press policy is to use papers that are natural, renewable and
recyclable products and made from wood grown in sustainable forests.
The logging and manufacturing processes are expected to conform to
the environmental regulations of the country of origin.

Nicholas Brealey Publishing
John Murray Press
Carmelite House
50 Victoria Embankment
London, EC4Y 0DZ, UK
Tel: 020 3122 6000

Nicholas Brealey Publishing
Hachette Book Group
Market Place Center, 53 State Street
Boston, MA 02109, USA
Tel: (617) 523 3801

www.nicholasbrealey.com
www.dicconbewes.com

CONTENTS

FOREWORD

Change is a funny thing to try to assess. Often it passes by without being noticed, but equally often it hits you in the face when you least expect it. And what can be hardest is getting enough distance from events to look back and see what actually happened. Fortunately, fate sometimes plays a helping hand, giving you the chance to see into a world or time other than your own. In my case, fate came in the form of a long-forgotten travel journal that was but a footnote in some English guidebooks on Switzerland.

And that is exactly where I discovered the journal while researching my first book four years ago. It didn't take long to track down a copy online, in a second-hand bookshop in Amsterdam, of all places. A few days and some euros later, a small package arrived in my post box: inside, a little hardback book, 126 pages long, its sky-blue dust jacket decorated with edelweiss. Not the original, of course, but an edition printed 50 years ago for the centenary of a landmark tour, one that would change a country and launch a new form of leisure activity into the world. This was a trip where women in huge dresses hiked across glaciers, where trains were a slow but exciting novelty, and where the landscape left the author almost speechless with wonder.

In a moment of inspiration or madness (or both), I decided to follow the trail that author had left behind. Guided by a woman who had been dead for well over a century, I would set off across Europe to try to see it through her eyes. Along the way, I hoped to make a personal connection with her, despite all the differences and distance between us. She had gone in search of adventure; I would go in search of her. I had her journal, so I could follow her words, but I also wanted to find some trace of her in the places both of us were visiting. It was more than about having proof that she had been there before me; it was about making the link between her tour and mine, between tourism then and tourism now – between the two of us.

And of course, I wanted to see how much had really changed since she made the same journey: not only the obvious aspects, such as journey times, but the changes you don't really think about. After years as a travel writer, would I see what travelling was like for those package pioneers? After years as a tourist, would I learn how it all began? After years as a Brit in Switzerland, would I discover how my fellow countrymen and women helped transform that country? And had Switzerland really been so different back then? I would soon find out.

It was a tour that changed the world of travel.

It was a journey that launched mass tourism.

It was an invasion that created modern Switzerland.

It was a trip I simply had to do.

So I did.

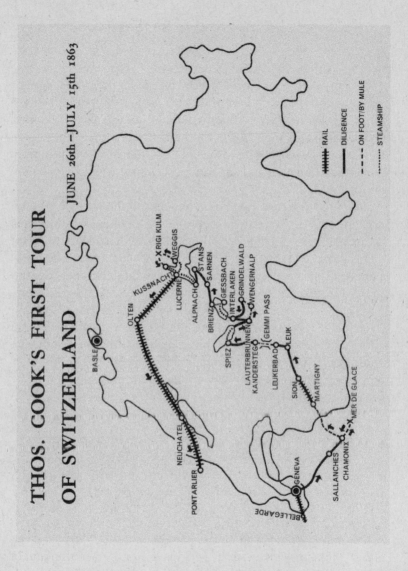

The route of the original tour in Switzerland

INTRODUCTION

They were found in a battered tin box in the post-war rubble of London's East End: two large books with scuffed red leather covers that had contrived to survive the Blitz intact, thanks to their sturdy container. Even then, they were almost lost, tossed aside with all the other debris from the nightly bombings. Fortunately, someone discovered them before they disappeared for ever.

Together, the two volumes make up a complete journal, an account of a trip across Europe that took place many decades before. They are written in longhand, in a lovely sloping script that is perfectly legible but delightfully old-fashioned, and occasionally illustrated with pen-and-ink drawings of foliage curling round the text. More frequent are faded black-and-white pictures and colourised postcards that have been stuck in, making it as much a scrapbook as a diary. But there is very little personal information about the author, not even her full name, or how the books could have ended up in a bombed building 80 years after they were written. As for where she went, that sounded like a challenging destination for any Victorian lady:

> "We landed at Weggis, and if each man, boy and mule-keeper who attacked us had been a wasp and each word a sting, Weggis had possessed our remains. We were literally infested by, dogged and danced around by these importunates!"

After those "wasps" she encountered "parasites" and "goitred ogres", none of which exactly springs to mind when thinking of Switzerland. Yes, Switzerland, now one of the wealthiest, healthiest countries in the world. Her trip was a three-week tour of the Alps; to be more exact, the journal was an account of Thomas Cook's First Conducted Tour of Switzerland. Not that it was the country we now know. In today's Switzerland trains, chocolate and money are so typically Swiss that they have become shorthand for the whole country. These clichés are, however, based on fact. The Swiss are world champions in all three – per head they travel more by train, eat more chocolate and store more gold than any other country.

But 150 years ago none of them would have conjured up an image of Heidi's homeland, as none of them existed in the same way (least of all Heidi, who made her first appearance in 1880). The Swiss arrived late to the idea of railways, so that back then there were only 650km of tracks in operation compared to over 5000km now; milk chocolate, Switzerland's gift to the sweet-toothed everywhere, didn't appear until 1875; and as for money, that was in short supply in a nation where many still lived off the land or from which they emigrated in search of a better life. A century and a half ago Switzerland was a very different place, where large parts of the country festered in rural poverty, and where the daily wage of an average factory worker was the same as the price of breakfast in a tourist hotel. One English guidebook from that time offered this advice to its readers:

> *A sou or any small coin is sufficient for the legions of beggars besetting one's way. Make a rule of never going out without a supply of small coins, however, but never use them lavishly.*

For British visitors, who were used to slums in their cities and Oliver Twists on the streets, this didn't quite match the popular romantic image of Switzerland. It was a far-away country, although not exactly unknown territory. For decades the Alps had been bewitching writers, painters and climbers, all of whom helped transform the mountains from a daunting barrier at the heart of Europe into the natural wonder of the nineteenth century, albeit a slightly wild and dangerous one. But neither was Switzerland overrun with hordes of tourists: European travel was still largely the preserve of the rich and reckless, those with both time and money. So while Byron, Turner, Dickens and Wordsworth had all made lengthy inspirational visits to Switzerland, such a trip was beyond the aspirations of most British people, being simply too far and too expensive. The Alpine Republic was the geographical equivalent of European royalty: dazzling, beautiful and intriguing, but out of reach for normal folk, only to be appreciated from a distance. That all changed in 1863, thanks to the British middle classes and their appetite for adventure.

It would be these visitors, these bankers and lawyers, who would help revolutionise Switzerland. Their peaceful invasion provided the financial and social means for turning rags into riches. Tourism made Switzerland the Cinderella of Europe. And every Cinderella needs a fairy godmother, or in this case, godfather. That was Thomas Cook, a man who would change the world in the most leisurely way possible – through holidays.

For over 150 years the name Thomas Cook has been synonymous with travel and adventure, but before he became a global brand, he was a man with a mission. A Baptist minister from Derbyshire, he wanted the world to give up alcohol and take up travelling. While his first step down the road to worldwide recognition was organising a train trip in the English Midlands, it was Switzerland that provided him with the success needed to create the new industry of tourism. Although Thomas Cook didn't start the trend for foreign holidays, he broadened their appeal, made them readily available and expanded their scope far beyond northern France. What until then had been a trickle became a steady stream that quickly turned into a flood that has never truly subsided – a case of all abroad!

Cook made Switzerland accessible and affordable. Trains reduced travel times and going in groups reduced the costs, so that the new middle class in Britain were able to enjoy a holiday in the Alps. His first conducted tour of Switzerland was so successful that another soon followed, then another, and another and another, until British visitors were almost as commonplace as brown cows. And the Swiss were not slow to realise the potential of this incoming tide and to capitalise on its possibilities. Hotels were built, souvenirs created and railways raced up the mountains, all for the benefit of the visitors from over the Channel. It was a relationship that suited both sides. The British got to see the Alps from the comfort of a train, sleep in a proper bed each night and go home with a nice new watch. The Swiss got to make money. It's a love affair that has lasted 150 years and counting.

However, this book isn't just the story of how foreign travel stopped being a luxury or of how one trip started the trend for holidays abroad. It is the story of the relationship between two nations, a tale of two countries that could not have been more different: the powerful monarchy whose empire stretched around the globe, and the small republic only just recovering from a civil war. Without Switzerland, the British may never have travelled merely for the sake of it, rather than to conquer the locals or convert them. Without the British, Switzerland might never have developed into one of the world's richest countries.

Cook's first Swiss tour was an engine for development in Switzerland as much as were the trains that brought him. It is thanks to him that a party of intrepid British travellers landed in France one Friday in June. It is thanks to the railways that this group could reach Switzerland in two days not two weeks. And it is thanks to both Thomas and the trains that travelling was transformed. This was the start of mass tourism and one of its participants recorded every detail.

Fast forward around 140 years and I'm standing in Newhaven on a warm summer's day. The journal's author didn't have anything positive to say about the place – "There is not a drearier port anywhere than Newhaven" – but it was the departure point for Cook's group. I could have flown to Geneva and been there in time for lunch, or taken the Eurostar via Paris and arrived in time for supper, but I wanted to follow in the tracks of that first conducted tour, and that meant taking the slow train to Switzerland. It's no longer the easiest option but it is the original one.

I am going to retrace the journal's route from London to Lucerne, following the same itinerary and staying in the same places (even in the same hotels if possible). Ahead lie three weeks of travelling by boat, train and bus through France and Switzerland, doing what the original tourists did each day.

I also know which guidebook my Victorian lady friend used, so both that and her diary are in my bag instead of my mobile phone and iPad. It might prove frustrating not to have the latter two, but I don't want instant access to maps, timetables and taxis. I'll have just the books as guides, although even with them to hand I have no idea what to expect on this modern version of that historic trip. My tour will be her tour with two crucial differences: clothing and transport. Even though she hiked over the mountains in a crinoline, I'm not going to be dressing up in *Gone with the Wind* gowns.

As for trains, I'll use them where possible, even if that hadn't been an option for her. Riding a donkey over an Alpine pass is unnecessary now that there's a perfectly good train to take the strain; this isn't an attempt to re-enact the trip, but to re-trace it. Indeed, railways are a crucial element of the whole picture: trains made the first trip possible and they are still an integral part of the Swiss landscape, as iconic as the mountains they conquer. Visitors take them up to get the views from the top; locals use them to come down after a day's hiking. Switzerland without trains would be like America without cars – unthinkable.

This is a chance to step back in time and experience what it was like to be a tourist before tourism was an industry, before being a tourist became a negative concept in some people's eyes. Grand tourists were once the greatest travellers, but now the two words have gone far beyond loose synonyms. As Evelyn Waugh said, "The tourist is the other fellow", summing up the perception that many people have of themselves and others when abroad. In the culture war of arrogance versus ignorance, travellers (as in people who travel rather than gypsies) and tourists view each other with such disdain that they reduce the other side to caricatures.

Travellers are seen as pretentious and patronising, looking down on anyone who stoops so low as to choose Disneyworld over riding across Mongolia in a truck full of goats. They are obsessed with going off the beaten track in the search for authenticity, but get annoyed if others do the same. Tourists are viewed as sheep who only travel in groups and rarely interact with the locals. They stick to their tick lists of sights, don't look beyond the camera lens and usually ruin the charm of wherever they go simply by being there. Their idea of being daring is having paella with their chips.

But what if we could go back to the point when travellers became tourists – back to a time long before TripAdvisor and travel agents, when taking a train across Europe was an intrepid adventure, the trip of a lifetime for its excited participants? What if we could go where they went, see what they saw, do what they did and hear what they thought? Maybe that would change our perception of them, and us, as tourists – and of the man who started it all.

This is the tale of how Thomas Cook changed the world that summer of 1863 with his winning concept of quality travel at an affordable price: "We make no provision for Third Class travelling. Our object has been to give Second Class comforts at Third Class rates." It is also the story of one man's dream – my own. Thanks to an old diary, I am able to follow in the footsteps of Mr Cook and his rail-blazers. Almost 150 summers later, I'm about to discover how much today's travellers – and the Swiss – owe to the tourists of yesterday. And in the process, I'm about to get a surprise of my own.

This is one tour, two trips, 150 years – and a world of change apart.

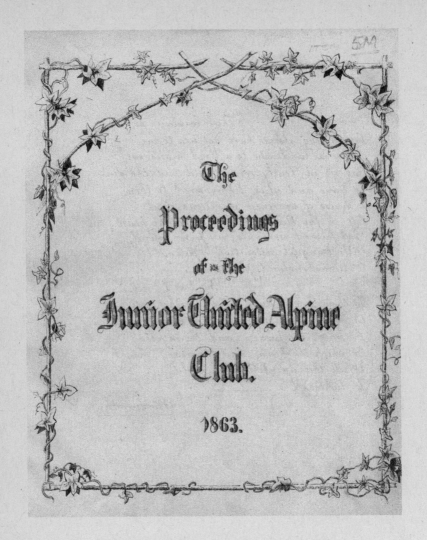

The
Proceedings
of the
Junior United Alpine
Club.
1863.

Title page from Miss Jemima's original diary

ONE

THE JUNIOR UNITED ALPINE CLUB

It is our intention to accompany a party to Geneva, Lucerne and other principal places in the Alpine and Lake Districts.
              —*Thomas Cook,* The Excursionist, *June 1863*

Junior United Alpine Club group photo:
Miss Jemima is third from left

Her name was Jemima, or Miss Jemima, to be more precise. For decades little more than that was known about her, not even her surname. But she was real, that much was sure, because she wrote a diary. Hers isn't as historical as Anne Frank's or as hysterical as Bridget Jones's, and it doesn't even cover a whole year, but this diary marks an important moment in the history of travel. For Miss Jemima was one of the participants in Thomas Cook's First Conducted Tour of Switzerland in 1863. She was present at the birth of modern international tourism, and she recorded every detail.

Since it was written, *Miss Jemima's Swiss Journal* has been lost, found, reprinted and forgotten again, so many people have never heard of it. I hadn't, until I started researching Swiss history and tourism back in 2009. A small aside in the *Rough Guide to Switzerland* was all that was needed for me to go online in search of this unique account of a nineteenth-century tour and it only took a few clicks to find a copy of the 100th anniversary edition. Even once I'd read it, I had no idea who Miss Jemima really was or that her diary would become so significant for me – but I wanted to find out.

And that's how I ended up in Newhaven two years later with her book in my bag, along with *A Handbook for Travellers in Switzerland, and the Alps of Savoy and Piedmont* (1861 edition), the guidebook she used. I was ready to follow Mr Cook and his extended party of 130 or so tourists who crossed the Channel with him to see what was on the other side. Half of them would only go as far as Paris, others would leave after Geneva or Mont Blanc, so that by the time the whole tour was complete barely a handful remained: the Junior United Alpine Club, as they christened themselves. Here's how they are introduced in the front of the journal:

"Miss Eliza	'Guide, Philosopher, Friend', Hon. Physician to the Expedition (Allopathic)
Miss Mary	French Interpreter
Miss Jemima	Artist
Miss Sarah	Continental Traveller

Mr William	Paymaster
Mr Tom	Professeur (ætat 28), Complete Letter Writer, Interpreter in the German Cantons, Hon. Physician to the Expedition (Homeopathic)
Mr James	French Interpreter and Pœt Laureate"

While the journal describes the journey in detail, it reveals nothing about its author. Miss Jemima was a complete mystery for many years. Her diary was written solely as "a record of the wanderings" of the Club and was never really intended for mass public consumption, so it effectively disappeared as soon as it was written. No one remembered its existence and things would have remained that way without Herr Hitler and Herr Göring: it was one of their raids on London that led to the two books later being found in a blitzed warehouse. However, the author was known only as Miss Jemima until 1963, when the journal was published for the centenary celebrations of the tour. Then the connection was finally made, thanks to the ensuing publicity and to author Anne Vernon, who was researching a book about a prominent Yorkshire family. Among the many papers were some letters written in the summer of 1863 during a trip to Switzerland, and a quick visit to Thomas Cook's archives clarified that it was the same trip as in the diary. Miss Jemima gained a surname – and a life.

Jemima Anne Morrell was born in Selby, Yorkshire, on 7 March 1832, the daughter of Robert and Anna Morrell. Her father was a bank manager in the town and they were a well-to-do middle-class family with enough money for a cook, a housemaid and private schools for the children. The 1841 census shows that Jemima had three siblings: Robert (aged 11), Anna (6) and the youngest William (then aged 4); by the 1861 census, Anna had died and Jemima was the only one still living with her parents. So at the time of her great adventure, she was 31, single and an aspiring artist – and, clearly, an adventurous spirit.

Although Jemima's father could have afforded to pay for the Swiss trip, the journal makes it clear that it was in fact her brother William, a banker like his father, who did so, "having to

William Morrell and Jemima Morrell

his surprise come into possession of a *very* small fortune through a literary venture on the delightful subject of Income Tax". And it's that brother, William Wilberforce Morrell, who is the Mr William listed above as the Paymaster of the Junior United Alpine Club. It was his letters back to "My dear father" during the trip that helped solve the mystery of the journal's author, and they provide a second eyewitness account, albeit much briefer, of that trip. Some of his comments are deliciously dry, such as the one from Geneva: "The highest mountain we have climbed is to the top of the hotel, fourth landing." Others are interestingly mundane: "Will Mother enquire of Mrs Mark-Hutchinson the size of her gloves she wishes me to get her?" And they are all signed in style: "with dear love from us both, I remain your affectionate son, W.W.M."

Of the other Club members little is known, except that "Miss Sarah" was the Morrells' cousin, Sarah Ayres. It is interesting to note that women outnumbered men by four to three, and Miss Jemima herself wrote that she only "consented to join, if suitably accompanied". That was one factor in the early success of Cook's Tours: single women could travel as part of a group, without any

Jemima Morrell and her parents in their garden

fear for their safety or damage to their honour. It was both practical and proper. The days of chaperones and restrictions were over.

The Junior United Alpine Club set off on their great adventure with over 120 others on Friday, 26 June 1863, having got up at 4am in London to catch a train south. I set off at 7.30am but 148 years and 28 days later, with only four people joining me, three of them dead: Miss Jemima, Mr Cook, Mr John Murray, publisher of travel guidebooks, and my mother, Jenny. Both trips started with a train journey to Newhaven, although theirs was considerably longer and harder than mine.

Train travel in 1863 was popular but not particularly pleasant. Carriages were wooden and divided into small compartments, with no corridor running between them and no connecting doors. Each compartment had its own external door, meaning that the guard had to use outdoor footboards to move down the train. There was no heating and the dim lighting came from a single oil lamp per compartment; the windows did open, although that usually let in all the steam, soot, grit and sparks bellowing out of the engine. First class was relatively luxurious, with plushly upholstered seats, foot warmers for hire and only six people to a compartment. Third class was more squashed, with more compartments per carriage and more people per compartment, which were fitted with hard wooden bench seats and a roof; early third-class carriages were open, and even in 1863 Thomas Cook was still at pains to advertise that his British trips were in "covered carriages". Second class was usually better, with upholstery as a minimum. Of course prices reflected the level of comfort: in 1863 Cook advertised a return trip from Lincoln to London for 18 shillings (or about £70 today) in first but only 9 shillings in the "covered car"; the 120-mile journey took six hours each way no matter which class you travelled in.

The padding in first class also helped absorb the shocks and jolts of rail travel. Carriages typically only had four wheels, were badly sprung, travelled on imperfect tracks, had handbrakes and were linked by chains rather than buffers. None of that made for a seamless, bumpless ride. In effect, the carriages were like a few stagecoaches jammed together and clattering along as one unit. No wonder some passengers behaved as they had done in a coach: riding on the roof, sticking their head out the window and trying to disembark while still moving.

Furthermore, crossing the Channel has never been easier than it is today. You can go under it by train, over it by plane (if you must) or still do it the old-fashioned way, by boat. While Thomas Cook had only that last option in terms of transport, there was more than one port on offer. He chose the one that was closest to London and also served by railway companies with which he could negotiate favourable terms. The direct train connections on both sides of the sea made the Newhaven–Dieppe route a feasible option, but the overall journey was not short. Although the 4½-hour boat trip was only 30 minutes longer than today, it had to be endured as part of an 18-hour journey from London to Paris – a tiring day in any century. Newhaven might have been less than attractive, but in economic terms it was convenient and cost-effective; aesthetics would have to wait until France.

Miss Jemima wasn't the only one to be less than charitable about the Sussex port. Eleven years of ever-increasing traffic seemingly did little to improve Newhaven, given that an 1874 Thomas Cook guidebook described it as "A place where there is nothing to see and nobody to see it." That description could still apply today; in fact, as I walk along the straggling High Street I begin to think it's a bit on the generous side. Between the pound shops and bookies are empty windows and To Let signs. It's a depressing place that clings on to existence thanks to the harbour, which itself needs a bit of TLC. It's hard to imagine a less appealing port in Britain or a less inspiring spot to start a holiday. No wonder Newhaven's biggest claim to fame is that it's where Lord Lucan's car was found when he disappeared without trace in 1974.

Newhaven no longer has a direct train service from London, so to be at the docks for the morning ferry we have to stay the night before. It is surprisingly hard to find a room for a Saturday night in July, so perhaps everyone else is also staying just long enough to catch the ferry to France. With no room at the Premier Inn, which was booked out weeks ahead, we have to decamp a few miles along the coast to Newhaven's alter ego, Seaford. This is Beauty to Newhaven's Beast, with some of the charm that its nearby ugly sister lacks; most impressively, it sits beside the finest coastal landscape in southern England, the Seven Sisters. Forget Dover, these white cliffs are the ones worthy of a song, looking like they're brushed every day with Colgate.

There's not enough time for the beautiful walk up onto the cliffs and along to Britain's No. 1 suicide spot, Beachy Head, so we make do with a bracing stroll along the shingly seafront, past the painted beach huts and a solitary angler, then retire to the B&B.

Before we set off in earnest, this is a good time to introduce my other travelling companions properly, in chronological order. First, Thomas Cook. Born on 22 November 1808, he was many things before becoming a travel agent *extraordinaire*. He started as an apprentice cabinet maker, then was an itinerant Baptist preacher, became a husband and father, and was finally a determined advocate of temperance (not drinking alcohol, to you and me). It was his opposition to drinking that led him to organise temperance tours by train, the first being for 500 people along the 11 miles from Leicester to Loughborough in July 1841. Cook's road after that trip wasn't always easy, not just because Loughborough isn't exactly the dream destination with which to start a travel agency. He went bankrupt in 1846, though the cause of the collapse remains unclear, but bounced back quickly with tours to Scotland, the Lake District and Wales. He followed that with immensely popular excursions to see the Great Exhibition of 1851 in London: 150,000 people travelled with him to view the gigantic Crystal Palace with its 300,000 panes of glass.

That success coincided with the launch of *The Excursionist*, the company newspaper that sold for a penny and was Cook's primary form of sales and marketing. In modern terms, it was part travel brochure (but without the glossy photos), part travel blog. The size of a broadsheet newspaper, its pages were crammed with details of forthcoming trips, reports of previous ones, readers' letters, train timetables and adverts for anything and everything a traveller might need. The stage was set for Cook to go overseas.

In August 1855, Thomas Cook thought that the British public couldn't wait to explore Belgium and the Rhine, so he organised four routes in an ambitious first foray onto the Continent. In his engrossing biography of Cook, Piers Brendon remarks that for the customers the trip was a success. They were charmed by Brussels and enjoyed the romance of the Rhine, though they were less impressed with the inferior German trains and open gutters in Cologne (one participant claimed to have identified 73 different smells, presumably none of them pleasant). While a second tour followed, both "involved much cost of labour, time and money and both were attended with a loss", as Cook himself wrote. Even so, he proposed more trips the following year, with the proviso that a minimum of 50 passengers paid a deposit. In the event the tours never took place, and it was back to square one, and Blighty, for Cook.

An official portrait of Thomas Cook, taken in 1863

Despite the financial failure, he had learned from his European misadventures: the need for bilingual guides, the unpredictability of hotel standards, the problems of transporting people and luggage abroad en masse. He was amassing knowledge and experience that would be useful in the future, not least, as Brendon so neatly puts it, "He could advise English tourists to equip themselves with soap and tea." Such advice is still followed today by many Brits abroad, although the soap has probably been replaced by Marmite in many cases.

Undaunted, Cook carried on with domestic tours while waiting for the next opportunity to dazzle the masses with dreams of travelling overseas. That came in May 1861 with his £1 return ticket to Paris, in third-class carriages. What is incredible is not that he made a loss, again, but that 1673 people went with him on that six-day trip. Imagine the extraordinary challenge of organising a tour for so many people at the same time, not least because many of them would never have left their own county, let alone the country. It was another milestone along Cook's bumpy road to becoming a household name with a clear aim of affordable quality.

Nevertheless, it wasn't all plain sailing. An editorial in *The Times* foamed against "excursion mania" while, most damaging of all, Cook's successful tours to Scotland came to an abrupt end when the Scottish train companies declined to renew his cheap tickets. By 1863, he needed to find the Big New Thing if he were to survive. And it came in the shape of a small notice in *The Excursionist* on 6 June, the one quoted at the beginning of this chapter. Switzerland was to be the new Scotland, although with bigger mountains and better cheese. Cook took a chance on the Alps being a big enough draw to entice the British off their island, and he was right. That first announcement brought a "deluge of letters of enquiry". Less than three weeks later, the journey began.

The first Murray Handbook came into the world four years after Miss Jemima, with the alarmingly general title of *A Handbook for Travellers on the Continent*, although in fact it only covered "Holland, Belgium, Prussia, and Northern Germany, and Along the Rhine from Holland to Switzerland". Individual countries had to wait a bit longer, so the first edition of Switzerland (with the Alps of Piedmont and Savoy lumped in with it) appeared in 1838. The series was the brainchild of John Murray III, grandson of the original John Murray who had started the publishing house in 1768. The company also published Jane Austen, Charles Darwin and Lord Byron, but it was for the trademark red guidebooks that Murray became famous. It was the English Baedeker (or maybe Baedeker was the German Murray; the two men were once collaborators rather than competitors).

Whereas Baedeker's guide to Switzerland first appeared in English only in 1863, by the time Miss Jemima took Murray's Swiss guide with her it was in its ninth edition and was full of advice on the strong sun – "Most travellers in the upper regions lose the skin from every exposed part of the face and neck" – travel – "[By railway] is now the quickest mode of reaching Berne from Lucerne, and takes about 5 hours" – and drinks – "Swiss wine is generally condemned". There were practical tips, too – "The Englishman should present his name printed or very legibly written, as our pronunciation is frequently unintelligible to foreigners" – and words of caution – "The luggage arrangements on the Swiss railways are if possible more inconvenient than on the French or German railways; and there is a system of extortion for conveyance to and from the stations which the traveller should be on his guard against." In essence, such guides were a cheaper replacement for the courier, who up until then had been an essential part of a foreign trip; he found hotels, organised carriages and was generally useful, if expensive.

Miss Jemima went with her brother; I am going with my mother. It was mostly down to her that our family holidays were spent driving across Europe, usually in search of the perfect picnic spot. No matter which route we took, the goal was always the same, which isn't a surprise given that her mother, my grandmother, was Italian. My memories of childhood revolve around that annual dose of organised chaos known as Italy. As for my father, he always seemed happy to be there, although I suspect that, given the choice, he might at some point have been content to settle for two weeks in Cornwall. But by bundling their three kids into the car every Easter and setting off across the Channel, both my parents sowed the seeds of my love of travel and dislike of cars.

Since leaving university I have been a bookseller, traveller, bookseller (again), travel writer, bookseller (yet again) and traveller (again). I finally decided to combine the two and write travel books that I could sell, if not myself then through other bookshops. I have lived in Bern, the Swiss capital, for the past eight years and can't see any reason to leave just yet: the chocolate is far too good to say goodbye to. The success of my first book, *Swiss Watching*, meant that I could give up being a bookseller (although probably not for ever, if the past is anything to go by) and concentrate on writing – and speaking. An Englishman in Switzerland is no real novelty, but one who likes to talk knowledgeably about the Swiss (and make them laugh) is not that usual, especially if he does it in German, or as close to German as possible. I am the accidental expat expert.

So that's our group of travellers: Jemima, Jenny, John, Thomas and me. Granted, we're not the most normal of groups, but then this isn't the most normal of trips. In the days of easyJet and Eurostar, who travels through Europe the hard way? We had no car or coach, no transfers or tour guides, and no real goal other than to follow in the footsteps of a travel giant. If it sounds a bit too unplanned to be a package tour, it's how that first tour was as well. Looking back from this distance, it's all too easy to impose on it our modern expectations and prejudices.

That first trip wasn't organised to within an inch of its life, didn't have planned excursions and wasn't an exercise in group bonding. Thomas Cook admitted as much in *The Excursionist*:

> It is not possible for us to mark out the exact course of travel from day to day after the arrival in Geneva. This must depend on local circumstances, the number of the party who choose to travel together, the modes of conveyance and other matters which cannot be foreseen.

The same applied to expenses – "it is impossible to give any accurate statement".

Nevertheless, the tour was conducted, in the sense that Thomas Cook accompanied the participants, even if the conductor was more of an organiser than a guide. It was intended "to explore and examine, with a view to future and more enlarged operations". Essentially, it was a recce, a fact-finding mission that happened to have paying guests as its guinea pigs. It could have been a total disaster, *Carry On Heidi* without the innuendo, but luckily it was a success. Those "future and more enlarged operations" turned out to be not a disturbing medical diagnosis but the travel industry as we know it. Without that tour it's possible that we wouldn't now have all-inclusive hotels in Jamaica, coach tours of Italy, stag parties in Tenerife or cruises down the Nile; not forgetting travel agencies, sleeping cars, brochures and traveller's cheques. It all started with the Swiss.

A nd so, on with the trip. After living in Switzerland for so long, I do realise that I've become used to punctuality on public transport. Everything running on time is normal for the Swiss. So it's odd to be back in a country where trains often have a mind of their own; odd but somehow rather comforting, the transport equivalent of beans on toast or *Doctor Who*. British rail timetables are evidently still more guideline than gospel, if the three-mile train ride between Seaford and Newhaven is anything to go by. But at least we get to the ferry terminal in time for the boat and can enjoy watching Newhaven slip away as we sail out of the harbour, past the marina and the breakwater, along the coast to admire the Seven Sisters and then out into the open sea. Next stop France – only four hours away.

Despite the sea crossing being longer than from Dover, the fact that Newhaven is only 56 miles from London made it a natural choice for a ferry link to France. A regular steamer service began in 1824 when the General Steam Navigation Company started sailing twice weekly in both directions. Once the train from London arrived in 1847, under the auspices of the London, Brighton and South Coast Railway, passenger numbers soared; by the 1860s 50,000 people a year were sailing this route across the Channel. In addition, Dieppe is much closer to Paris than is Boulogne or Calais (92 miles not 133), a distinct advantage in the days when travelling on land was as slow as at sea; a train ride through the fields of Normandy is also infinitely preferable to one through the flat expanse of northern France. No wonder Cook chose this route.

The Newhaven harbour records for 26 June 1863 show that the paddle steamer in operation that day was the *Dieppe*, and that the weather was fine with a fresh breeze, much as it is for our crossing 15 decades later. Apart from that, the two journeys could not be more different. First and second classes, tea and biscuits, sitting on coils of rope, sleeping under umbrellas – that was the essence of Miss Jemima's crossing. It sounds uncomfortable but peaceful. Today, with 51 cabins, 5 lounges, a bar, a restaurant, a shop, a kids' play area and up to 650 passengers and crew, ours is not a small ship. Most likely it's more comfortable, and more hectic, than the old one, but it's not particularly memorable. It could be any one of the giant car ferries that ply the Channel, taking bargain hunters to the French hypermarkets and holidaymakers to the sun. However, it does have touches of Gallic flair. The name – *Côte d'Albâtre*, or Alabaster Coast – refers to the coastline of Normandy, our destination today; the restaurant has couscous and lamb tajine on the menu; and the staff are as friendly as in any shop along the Champs-Elysées. It feels like France already.

One thing that hasn't changed, and probably never will, is the temptation to indulge in some people-watching. Ferries are great places for that, as indeed is any form of public transport; Joanna Trollope once said that one of the best places for an author to research human behaviour, conversations and relationships is on board a London bus. And alongside the watching is the judging, something to which Miss Jemima was not immune:

> "The members of the Junior United Alpine Club, remembering the German proverb that 'None but Englishmen and madmen travel first class', were all second-class passengers. ... The swells being all in the fore cabin, we were driven to criticising those in the aft; who, but for the redeeming presence of those in the Club, would have been on the whole, voted second class in more senses than one. Yes, those two brown-hatted ladies sitting opposite, on the shady side of fifty, do not their features tell of endurance and patience? ... Can you not picture their home? Thrifty but faded."

Today there isn't a hat of any colour to be seen among the female passengers, possibly due to the gusty wind as much as changes in fashion, although a few men are sporting a baseball cap. The stylistic rigours of nineteenth-century travellers are as alien to us as our communication methods would be to them. Men have, thankfully for me, ditched stiff collars and tweed jackets in favour of jeans and fleeces, cargo shorts and trainers. Women have exchanged their full-length dresses and sensible shawls for similar jeans and fleeces, cargo shorts and trainers.

As curious as our modern unisex clothes would be to Miss Jemima, it is the public displays of flesh, both male and female, that would shock her into stunned silence. Such scandalous behaviour was not the done thing in polite society. Perhaps that's not such a bad thing. Seeing acres of pasty skin slowly roasted to lobster red is bad enough on a beach in Spain; having to endure it on a ferry to France could induce sea-sickness. There is some on display today, but the windy conditions have made all but the hardiest few cover up, me included. Still, I'm enjoying every breath of salty air prickling my face. Having grown up near the Hampshire coast, the thing I miss most in Switzerland is the sea; as stunningly beautiful as they are, mountains simply don't smell or feel the same.

Clothes aside, one other big difference between then and now is the presence of children. Our boat echoes to the sounds of their clattering feet and chattering voices, even outside their designated fun zones. An upstanding Victorian lady like Miss Jemima would probably blanch at youngsters being seen and heard in such numbers. As for travelling with your offspring in tow, such behaviour was actively discouraged by Thomas Cook himself:

> Children in arms, under three years of age, travel free in both England and France, and from three to seven years of age they travel at half-price. We hope that the infantile race will stop in the nurse's arms and that the next grade above them, under seven, will not be taken to Switzerland.

The Continent was indeed a dangerous place for children, where men in black tempted them with lollipops and witches fattened them up for roasting. If not that, then they froze to death selling matches or were lured away for ever by pied pipers. Much better to stay in Britain, where they could be trained as pickpockets, chimney sweeps and factory workers. The past was definitely not a nice place to grow up.

Four hours of drinking, eating, chatting, reading, playing, screaming and (in my case) deep breathing later, the coastline of France drifts onto the horizon. These cliffs are not as high or as white as their English counterparts, but they are clearly cut from the same stone. The two ports, on the other hand, could not be more different: Dieppe is the cheese to Newhaven's chalk. The closer we get, the more appealing it looks, with a wide beach, seafront promenade, castle and smart rows of houses.

Deboarding (which apparently is a word, if we believe the ship's captain) seems so easy until our bags, which we had to check in when we boarded, do not arrive in the terminal with us. There's no choice but to sit and wait. We have 25 minutes before the bus leaves for the town centre, but the longer we wait, the greater our chances are of missing it, and our direct train to Paris. To make things feel much worse, the terminal is enclosed by 2m high metal fences topped by rolls of barbed wire. A few passengers trade forlorn greetings and finger touches with relatives waiting for them on the other side, and I half expect a food parcel to come sailing over the top at any moment.

The bonus of being trapped in Camp Dieppe is that we have a chance to chat to our fellow inmates, and my mother is soon exchanging sighs and stories with an elegant but formidable woman in charge of a husband and two grandchildren. Listening to her reminisce, I learn how wonderful it was to arrive in Dieppe in the 1980s. The ship docked right in the middle of town and you disembarked straight into the Gare Maritime and a waiting train. But the French are never ones to let perfection stand in the way of progress, so the old ferry terminal was dismantled in the 1990s and

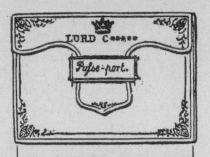

PASSPORTS

Obtained through the medium of Bankers' Letters, carefully mounted and inserted in morocco cases, with name lettered in gold.

Ambassadors' Signatures obtained to British Secretary of State's and American Passports, at One Shilling each.

Advert from Murray's Handbook, May 1861

this new one built out of town, without a station. Using this ferry is definitely not a good idea for two people with no transport, no transfer and no tour guide.

We can see the bus stop on the other side of the wire fence, so near but so far. The bus arrives on time, but it doesn't wait for anyone or anything; while it might be here purely for ferry passengers, it departs with no one on board, exactly as our bags arrive. Welcome to France!

Cook chose this route precisely because of its good train connections. His customers would have been able to change from boat to train with no hassle, but 150 years later we can't, and nor can eight or nine others who also missed the bus. After a few minutes of common incredulity at our predicament, we all start walking into town.

Miss Jemima's first brush with the Continent was very different. First, she had no passport. Such a document was not required for travel to most of the Continent, although Cook advised his customers to take one. Applicants simply had to write to Her Majesty's Secretary of State for Foreign Affairs, and two shillings and two days later the passport would arrive in the post. Even then, one passport was enough for all those travelling together: "the names of all male persons must be stated, and the number of females given". As antiquated as that sounds, at least women eventually got passports before they got the vote: the individual British passport as we know it, with a photo and a cardboard cover, arrived in 1915, followed by the old blue one in 1920 and the modern burgundy in 1988.

Not that any of that concerned Miss Jemima. She was more vexed that Miss Sarah's Yorkshire tarts were subject to a tax of 50 cents by the *douaniers*, "more from disappointment that they were not invited to partake than from any right they had to levy it". Once in town, she notes that Dieppe's staple trade is "ivory carving, examples of which we saw in the shop windows". Although Yorkshire tarts are probably still viewed with some suspicion, both the levy and ivory have disappeared from today's Dieppe, as have the exuberant clothes Miss Jemima finds so captivating:

> "Nothing in our entire route struck us as wearing a more foreign aspect than the varied groups of figures in motley costume awaiting our arrival on the pier. There were artisans in their loose blue blouses, soldiers in many uniforms, some of them most laughable, their capacious bloomer costume reaching to the centre of the calf of the leg, then four inches of buff leather, then a white gaiter of ample dimensions fitting like a tureen cover over the boot, while a shako jauntily tips off the whole."

Throw in a gendarme in a cocked hat, a priest in a shovel hat and women in white mob caps and you can see what an impression the crowd made on her. No shakos to be seen today, although the French policeman's kepi is surely a subdued descendant of this tall military hat that nineteenth-century armies loved so much, rather like a top hat that's been pimped up with medals, bobbles and tassels.

At head height all might have been wondrous to behold, but down at shoe level it was not. The narrow streets "had the advantage of shade, but not of a local board of health, as their open gutters testified". You can almost see Miss Jemima's nose turning up in disgust. Don't forget that this was exactly the period when Victorian Britain was investing its imperial wealth in public works. After the cholera epidemic of 1853–54 and the "Great Stink" of 1858, London cleaned up the Thames and transported its waste along sparkling new sewers to treatment works.

Dieppe no longer has open sewers, but its streets are still plagued by one very unsightly problem: they are full of crap, of the canine kind. I have no idea what the French feed their pets but whatever it is, it produces the most prodigious after-effects known to man, or dog. This is at its most unwelcome when trying to wheel a suitcase at speed, a feat that involves much swerving and jumping. I thought the blobs of chewing gum that plague Swiss streets were bad, but I'd rather have one of those caught on my suitcase wheels than dog poo.

So it's with some relief that we arrive at the main station with clean wheels and a little time to spare. As we route-marched through town, we had but a passing glimpse of the old quayside where the boats used to dock, now restored to its picture-postcard prettiness. And we certainly had no time for tea, an obligatory stop for Cook's group, although the café of "thoroughly foreign appearance" served tea that was "pronounced to be truly peculiar". Maybe it's just as well we skipped the tea break.

We bought two singles to Paris and were straight onto the train. Thank God we weren't subjected to nineteenth-century French station etiquette:

> None but the passengers are allowed to enter, who are locked in the salle d'attente until the arrival of the train, when they are let out in order of first, second and third classes.

Now I know where the budget airlines got the inspiration for their boarding procedures.

"I don't care so much for Paris myself except as a place to see," wrote William to his father. I have a shocking confession to make: I agree with him. Paris isn't my favourite city, possibly only just making it into my Top Ten. I've been in springtime, in summer and in autumn, but I've failed to fall in love with it. It's always left me not wanting more, but I keep going back in the hope that one day I'll see the light in a city that everyone else loves (or says they do). Yes, there are parts of Paris that are wonderful: the windows of Sainte-Chapelle, the graves in Père Lachaise, brunch in the Marais, sunset at the Sacré Coeur. But despite these delightful ingredients, the overall dish leaves me as unsatisfied as some of the creations served in its bistros, where there's more plate than food – all style and no substance.

But for once, I'm glad to arrive in the French capital. It is the light at the end of the tunnel that was a long day of constant travelling. We'd been on the go for ten hours, which is still eight hours less than Miss Jemima & Co. had to endure. Having left at 6am, they arrived in Paris after midnight. Then again, they started in London, not Newhaven, and they stopped for a French cup of tea, so perhaps the timings aren't so different after all. They stayed for all of five hours in Paris, not because they shared my view of the city – on the way back they stayed for five days – but because another 18-hour marathon lay ahead of them to reach Geneva. We can at least take our time and enjoy 18 hours in one place.

Outside the monumental Gare Saint-Lazare, we have to pick our way past the commuters and beggars dotted along the steps and the pavement; not so different from most stations in any other big city. It's only a short walk to the hotel, and that couldn't be more appropriately located. Just around the corner is a travel agency with a very familiar name: Thomas Cook. They obviously knew we were coming.

Paris to Geneva now takes a little over three hours, assuming you take the TGV or *Train à Grande Vitesse*, a real high-speed train that makes British ones look like snails. Travelling at such speed would be enough to give Thomas Cook apoplexy; he was warning customers 150 years ago:

21

> *[Paris to Geneva] will require some effort ... but it is not*
> *really necessary for any to travel so fast if they feel it to*
> *be burdensome.*

He was talking of 20mph, not the 200mph that is normal today. That might seem pedestrian to us, but for the Victorians such speeds were nothing short of miraculous – and quite enough. Any faster and women might faint or body parts be disrupted.

I have no such fears, so we are going on the 13.09 to Geneva. It's the only train I pre-booked, mainly because train tickets have never been easier to book online, and never harder to understand. The price depends on how far in advance you book, how fast you go, where you sit, what day and time you travel, how old you are and if there's an R in the month. Internet booking has revolutionised personal travel, but it sometimes makes my head spin with its limitless choices. While it may well be a fatal threat to travel agents like Thomas Cook, I can understand why some people still avoid the DIY route.

Unlike Miss Jemima, we won't be returning to Paris on the last leg of our tour; I'll stay in Switzerland and my mother will go straight back to London. With only a few hours, rather than a few days, to play with, we decide to go and admire Baron Haussmann's city makeover, which was in full swing by 1863. The cramped Paris of Quasimodo and D'Artagnan was at that time being bulldozed into wide boulevards and public parks. As Thomas Cook noted in May of that year:

> *whole streets of close-crowded houses are gone, and*
> *not a trace of them can be found; whilst, as by the wand*
> *of some mighty magician, have sprung up on their*
> *sites lines of buildings – mansions or shops of great*
> *magnificence.*

Just such a shop is the Galeries Lafayette, which admittedly came after Haussmann but sits on the boulevard that bears his name and is the epitome of the Parisian *grands magasins*. Its interior is as opulent as most of the goods on sale, so we admire the art nouveau domes while ignoring the price tags. It apparently attracts 120 million visitors each year, and I think a good percentage of them are there with us. It's like playing a game of sardines with 1000 participants, none of whom can stand still.

Shopping was also on the 1863 Paris itinerary, with the ladies in particular succumbing to some retail therapy. They requested that their luggage restrictions be removed as "amid the attractions of the Parisian shops, it was found almost impossible to carry them out", while on departure "the entire available staff of the hotel" was needed to attend to the luggage. We are decidedly more restrained, although I can't resist indulging in a *pain au chocolat*. They always taste better in France.

Shopping aside, Miss Jemima's whistle-stop tour of Paris included a Sunday service at Notre-Dame, climbing to the top of the Pantheon, strolling down the Champs-Elysées and devouring the art in the Louvre: not so different from a modern visitor's wish list, although that would have the obvious additions of the Eiffel Tower and the Sacré Coeur (dating from 1889 and 1914 respectively). Instead of these two was one must-see of that era: Napoleon's tomb in the Hôtel des Invalides. These days the golden domed building itself is possibly more of a draw, but in Miss Jemima's time the imposing red quartzite tomb was only two years old. Boney died in 1821 while in exile on the island of St Helena, although he had to wait 19 years before his body was brought back to Paris, and another 21 for his tomb beneath the dome to be finished. For Victorian visitors, beside an appreciation of the monument – "its magnificence was dazzling" – there was most likely also some *Schadenfreude* in seeing the last resting place of the man who'd (almost) conquered Europe but was defeated by Nelson and Wellington (with a little help from their European friends).

Being closer in time to those events (the Battle of Waterloo was less than 50 years earlier), Miss Jemima probably had a relatively good grasp of contemporary French history. If your knowledge of that era relies on reading *A Tale of Two Cities* and watching *Les Misérables*, or even singing along to "Waterloo", then here's a quick guide to help you understand the France of 1863.

The storming of the Bastille on 14 July 1789 precipitated the revolution that ended with the execution of Louis XVI and the creation of the First Republic. Then came Napoleon. A general in the revolutionary army, by 1804 he had crowned himself emperor. The First Republic was dead; long live the First Empire. But once a general, always a general, so Napoleon couldn't resist invading most of Europe, only to lose it all in 1815; back to square one. The republic had failed, as had the empire, so the answer was obvious: bring back the monarchy, under another Louis (XVIII), although that also didn't last. In 1848 Revolution No. 3 (and you thought there'd only been one) ushered in the Second Republic for just four years, when it was a case of the empire strikes back.

Louis-Napoleon Bonaparte has a unique place in French history, managing to be both the first president of France and its last monarch. Having been legitimately elected, he proclaimed himself emperor in 1852, so creating the Second Empire. Napoleon III lasted much longer than his uncle (the first Napoleon), finally being overthrown in 1870 in favour of the Third Republic. However, he was very firmly in power when the Junior United Alpine Club arrived in Paris.

Despite the "fatigues of sightseeing in a great city", Miss Jemima enjoyed the French capital. She is most effusive about La Madeleine church – "Truly magnificent erection!" – and the Place de la Concorde – "one of the most magnificent squares in Europe" – but less impressed by the local work ethic:

> "It was a brilliant day, and we saw Paris in holiday attire. Indeed, when is Paris not keeping holiday? For what the Parisians call work, we would style recreation in England."

She left Paris happy, while I'm happy to leave.

Train rides need never be dull. Oscar Wilde made sure that he brought his entertainment with him – "I never travel without my diary. One should always have something sensational to read in the train" – whereas Miss Jemima was content to look out of the window – "And what armies of poplars intersected the meadows; undoubtedly the poplar is the tree of the country" – or watch the locals:

> "the semi-theatrical yet joyous meeting and greeting between Monsieur and Madame, ... as they kissed each cheek repeatedly then kissed again, the same repeated with compound interest on le petit enfant."

She and her companions even manage to "air our acquirements in la langue française" with "two very sensible and, of course, polite Frenchmen" sharing their carriage.

The poplars and people may not have changed in 150 years, but the level of comfort has improved as much as the speed of travel. Miss Jemima's account of their day-long trip – "these pent-up, stuffed carriages become a torment to us and in our parboiled condition, how we hailed every stoppage as a welcome opportunity to descend and cool" – sounds like a ride on the London Underground today. The regular stops back then were possibly as much about taking on fresh water for the engine as fresh air for the passengers. Electricity and air-conditioning have replaced both sorts of steam that train travel once produced, but the changed internal design of the carriage helped as well. In the 1860s French trains were similar to British ones, divided into compartments of different classes and levels of comfort, with no corridors or connecting doors. It was the same in French-speaking Switzerland, where Baedeker rated the lines as "far inferior in comfort" to those in the German-Swiss areas, which used the American design from the start: a central gangway with seats on either side and a door at each end of the carriage. That was much more comfortable, and better for accommodating large dresses or moving around to see the views.

Miss Jemima was certainly impressed when she finally got to ride on such a train:

> "The Swiss undoubtedly understand and believe in comfortable railway travelling. The carriages on the broad gauge are not cut

into compartments, but are large cushioned saloons with an aisle down the centre. Neither are the railway managers niggardly in space, nor bent on conveying strangers too swiftly through their lovely country, but transmit them from station to station with a measured dignity, at two-thirds of which we alighted to change carriages, but no bustle, fuss nor even steam, for the engines burn coal: consequently the funnels pour out a volume of smoke as black as any in Leeds or Lancashire."

Smoke outside, smoke inside. *Cook's Tourist's Handbook to Switzerland* makes it clear that smoking carriages were attached to every train, but indulging was not ladylike behaviour: "Gentlemen desiring to smoke should always seek a smoker's compartment, as the odour of tobacco, which will cling to a carriage for days, is very nauseous, and often even injurious to certain temperaments." When I first moved to Switzerland, the smoking compartments were still there on SBB trains – most carriages had a divider one third of the way down with smoking allowed in the smaller part. Swiss public transport, as well as stations, became smoke free in December 2005.

Our carriage is a sleeker, modern version of the same design; cool, comfortable, smoke free and first class. The oddities of modern ticketing being what they are, it was cheaper than second, so we gave ourselves an upgrade. However, our fellow travellers are neither sensible nor polite. We are surrounded by one man, three women, two children and a baby, though it's not clear if they're one big happy family. The youngsters are certainly less than happy, unless those screams are ones of pleasure, but they're clearly a family along with the women. Each of their three faces is a wiser, wrinklier version of the younger model: three generations of motherhood. Where exactly the man fits into the picture is hard to judge: father, grandfather, brother, uncle or maybe all four. I'm left thinking that Thomas Cook would not be amused – these are definitely children he would classify as not to be taken to Switzerland.

Salvation comes in the form of lunch, which brings peace to the carriage. Never having travelled first class in a TGV, I hadn't realised that food was included, so our preparation for the journey involved eating lunch near the station. But free food is free food, so we indulge in a second lunch. Then, helped by the gentle rocking of the train, the kids subside into snuffles of a post-prandial snooze, surrounded by their detritus strewn all over the carriage – messy, but blissfully quiet.

Lunch at your seat is a far cry from the bun fight that Cook & Co. had to experience when eating on the go. In his report of that first trip to Switzerland, Cook tells how the 62 passengers in his group were fed while waiting in Dijon station, which had Refreshment Rooms that were "pronounced by Bradshaw as one of the best Buffets in France". He had telegraphed ahead earlier that day, asking the proprietor "to provide dinner for fifty, if he thought they would have time to eat it". The menu was slightly more than a filled baguette:

> a most excellent dinner had been prepared, and so admirably was it served that in ten minutes a considerable party got a satisfactory repast. Soup, fish, meats, potatoes, peas, French beans, sweets and fruits were all served in rapid succession.

I only hope he had some indigestion tablets to hand out on the train afterwards.

The French countryside flashes past until Mâcon, where the train transforms from a hare into a tortoise. We rechristen it the TPV, or *Train à Petite Vitesse*, although it still goes at a speed that would give Miss Jemima a fit of the vapours. While she'd be happier with the even slower pace needed to wind along the Rhone valley, to be honest no one wants to go faster just when the scenery becomes more interesting. The cliffs grow higher as the river gets narrower and hills threaten to become mountains; a lumpier landscape means that Switzerland can't be far away. The closer we get, the more impatient I become, but, of course, we are running late. We may be travelling to Geneva, the birthplace of Swiss watchmaking, but we're on a French train, so the normal rules of punctuality don't apply. Finally we arrive in Switzerland, or *la Suisse* as it's called in these parts.

Hopping across the Channel has become the travel equivalent of a microwave ready meal, so quick and easy that we barely notice it any more. Visiting France is now commonplace for many Brits: a day trip to Calais supermarkets, a weekend at Disneyland Paris, a summer holiday in the Dordogne, a year in Provence – each of them seems normal, whether by car, train or plane. Even if some of us still don't really understand the language(s) or road rules, the Continent has long since lost its air of mystery. But 150 years ago, things were very different. Going to France was an adventure, not least because the country had been the enemy for most of the past 800 years; the Battle of Waterloo was closer in time to Miss Jemima than the Cuban Missile Crisis is to us today.

As for travelling onwards to see the Alps, it might as well have been Outer Mongolia in many people's minds, so distant and so alien, and yet almost familiar and welcoming through the poems and paintings of the incurable Romantics. Byron, Turner, Wordsworth and Shelley – they had made the Alpine scenery seem inviting to the British public, while adventurous mountaineers such as Leslie Stephen and Edward Whymper were making headlines by conquering peak after peak. The seaside was out, mountains were in. Nevertheless, as appealing and exciting as it was, most people had neither the time nor the money to go off on a Grand Tour; that was still largely something for rich young men whose rite of passage was to experience life in the bars and brothels of Europe. Still, the desire was there and holidays were becoming more normal for the almost-wealthy, the growing middle classes who were getting tired of British breaks. Miss Jemima's first words in her journal are telling:

> "What an anxious question this annual holiday is now becoming! Everyone has been to Scotland, some of us had done the Land's End, Ireland is not everybody's choice, the International Exhibition had tired us all of London, Scarbro' is only suitable for invalids and children, the Lake District done years ago, and Fleetwood is worse than Scarbro' – where shall we go next?"

Where indeed. The obvious answer was abroad – the Continent, as the British like to call the rest of Europe – but such a trip involved time and money, both of which had been in short supply for anyone other than the idle rich. Now, though, as the leader of the Industrial Revolution, Britain had become the wealthiest country in the world and the only one where more people lived in towns than the countryside. A whole new class was developing rapidly, one between factory workers and landowners, a middle class of doctors, lawyers, bankers and vicars. It was a group of people who had enough money and enough time to think of a holiday abroad; all that was needed was the means. Enter Thomas Cook.

There's no clear evidence of why he chose Switzerland for his next big trip. It was hardly an undiscovered country (the first Murray Handbook had appeared 25 years before), although Cook hadn't been there himself at that point, and as we've seen, his first forays across the Channel ten years before weren't so successful. When he announced the first trip on 6 June 1863, he tried to explain the delay:

> For many years we have been pressed to attempt a trip to Switzerland but two great difficulties always presented themselves in the face of this idea: First, we were so wedded to Scotland ... that we felt unable to give the time requisite for a Swiss excursion. ... In the second place, we always felt the difficulty of attempting to conduct anything like large parties where there were no complete links of railways or steamboat communication.

That changed with his trip to Paris in May of that year, where he got both new information on routes and a promise of cheap fares. A Swiss trip was now viable, and Cook obviously had an inkling that if he could provide a practical way for people to get to the Alps, they would want to follow in the footsteps of painters and mountaineers. He was the right man with the right plan at the right moment. Taking people by train made the idea feasible in terms of time; taking them in a group made it possible in terms of money.

He could offer a tour that was affordable and achievable within two or three weeks. It was the perfect solution, just as long as there were enough customers to make it profitable. That was impossible to predict, so he took the plunge to see what would happen.

While the lure of the mountains – fresh air, spectacular scenery, great cheese – has not changed, the means of reaching them has. I could have got to Geneva by plane, train or even automobile, but I took the boat–train combination, just as those first Cook's tourists did. That showed me one thing about my journey so far: not a lot has changed in the last century and a half, apart from speed.

My trip from Newhaven to Geneva was slow by modern standards but far faster than Miss Jemima's, mainly thanks to the TGV rather than the ferry, although it wasn't so different that she wouldn't recognise it. Just think how much more advanced we are in other areas, such as communication or warfare, compared to the nineteenth century. Railways were the revolution that made this trip possible, shrinking Europe to such an extent that going abroad for two weeks became a reality for the first time. Still, in the age of the plane the train is holding its own, at least in Europe. Fly from London to Paris and by the time you've got to the airport, queued for security, waited to board, gone up in the air, come down again, waited for your luggage and finally travelled back into the centre, you're probably better off getting on the train at St Pancras and relaxing all the way.

For 150 years the train has kept on running in the face of faster or more flexible competition. While it has faced cutbacks and delays, it has not gone the way of the VHS tape or the USSR and been consigned to the scrapheap of history. If anything, train travel is enjoying a revival in its fortunes as people seek either to do more than just get from A to B as quickly as possible or to reduce their carbon footprint. Slow travel is back, with the trip itself often now part of the holiday, both the means and the end. Miss Jemima and Mr Cook must be smiling in their graves.

TWO

THE CITY BY THE LAKE

It is a great mistake to suppose that travelling in Switzerland is so very difficult that it may not be undertaken by ladies, or by persons not of the strongest mental and physical calibre ... even delicate persons may, with tolerable ease, reach the famed scenes of Geneva.

—*Thomas Cook,* The Excursionist, *August 1863*

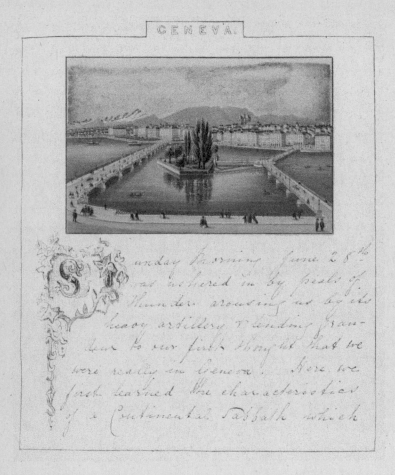

Sunday in Geneva was the first highlight of that first tour

One franc and fifty rappen a day. That's all an average Swiss factory or farm worker earned in 1863 – just enough to buy a bar of soap or three kilos of flour. In today's money, it's about 22 francs, or closer to a typical hourly wage. Switzerland was a relatively poor country in the mid-nineteenth century, certainly in comparison to Britain, where workers earned a lot more for shorter hours: three times as much money for a factory worker on 10 hours a day rather than the 12–13 hours in Switzerland, though both were at work 6 days a week. That included children in many cases; child labour was abolished in Switzerland only in 1877.

At least food in Switzerland was cheaper than in Britain – beef was 1 franc per kilo compared to 1.70 francs (8 pence a pound in old English money, or around £2.40 today) – but it ate up twice as much of the household budget, because that itself was substantially lower. Other goods were unbelievably expensive – a pair of shoes was 6½ pence in Britain but 5 francs (nine times as much) in Switzerland. Renting a three-room flat in Switzerland cost 275 francs a year, whereas a two-up, two-down house in Britain was only £8 (or 200 francs). Things that seemed cheap for visitors were often out of reach for most Swiss people – a second-class train ticket from Lausanne to Bern cost 7.20 francs, which is 100 francs in today's money but back then was more than two days' wages for even a skilled Swiss worker.

Such luxuries were almost impossible for a normal Swiss household in the 1860s, when 60 per cent of its money went on food, 20 per cent on rent and heating and 14 per cent on clothes. There wouldn't have been a lot left for doctor's bills, let alone train trips. Today, a typical Swiss household spends 10 per cent of its (much higher) budget on travel and only 9 per cent on food and drink; the biggest chunk (36 per cent) goes on taxes and insurance.

Rural poverty was a fact of life in nineteenth-century Switzerland, which had almost no natural resources other than water, wood and milk, a rugged landscape that wasn't particularly suited to arable farming, and poor internal transport. It relied heavily on imports to survive, which was made harder with no access to the sea, but at least it controlled the crucial Alpine passes, so could make a living from imports and exports. There was money in and around the prosperous cities of the north, such as Basel or Zurich, where textiles and watches, bankers and merchants were the generators of wealth, but not much trickled down into the countryside. Half of Switzerland's 2.5 million people were then living at a basic level and life expectancy was 40 years for men and 43 for women, or half what it is now. So while Miss Jemima would be content with the "famed scenes of Geneva", she would also be confronted with beggars and paupers in the countryside.

Famine, floods and fires made a hard life impossible for many, so they fled abroad. They didn't just go to neighbouring countries where they could maybe find a job, but overseas, where they could build a new life. In 1850 there were 50,000 Swiss living abroad; by 1880 this had shot up to 250,000; by 1914, over 400,000 Swiss had left their native country. For somewhere the size of Switzerland that is a significant percentage of the population, although in a few cases the emigrants were paid to leave. The situation in some places was so bad that they shipped the paupers to America so the community didn't have the cost of looking after them.

Switzerland had only been a country in the modern sense for a decade or so. For five centuries it had been a loose confederation of states (known as cantons), with almost no central government or national identity. Then in the space of 50 years, it endured invasion, famine, social unrest and civil war, and was reinvented three times until a new federation emerged in 1848. That federal state has survived until now, although that wasn't a foregone conclusion. The original three cantons united in 1291 to resist their Austrian overlords; as more cantons joined, the Swiss Confederation had grown to 13 cantons (and a motley collection of territories, protectorates and allies) by the time Napoleon invaded in 1798. He swept away the whole system and introduced a new Helvetic Republic, a single state with one government. It wasn't popular and was abolished before its creator could lose the Battle of Trafalgar. However, a return to a newer version of the old Confederation, this time with 22 cantons, proved equally untenable, thanks to the divisions between town and country, Protestants and Catholics, rich and poor. The inevitable civil war came in 1847, after the Catholic cantons formed a secret alliance (known in German as the *Sonderbund*) and tried to break away. War only lasted a month, with victory for the Protestants and a total of 98 fatalities – a very civil war.

That short conflict led to a long peace under a new constitution that created a federal government, a federal capital in Bern, a single market and a single currency. The Swiss nation and franc were born. Fifteen years later, the new republic was doing alright, especially in comparison to the previous five decades when it had been constantly divided or conquered. Nevertheless, progress was slow, with real development hampered by both geography and politics. However, change was just around the corner.

In the decades immediately after Cook's first tour, the Swiss railways, then in their infancy, would expand over and under the mountains; the pharmaceutical companies would explode (though not literally) into life; Daniel Peter would invent his milk chocolate and Karl Elsener would create his Swiss army knife; and, most importantly, Johanna Spyri would write a book about a little orphan girl who lived in the mountains with her grandfather and a worryingly large number of goats. The British would come in their thousands, bringing their money and their morals with them – an economic and social invasion that would affect Switzerland almost as much as any of the far-flung corners of the British Empire. Not that that was the intent: the Brits came simply for some fun and adventure in the playground of Europe.

What did the British think of the Swiss in Miss Jemima's day? Our heroine doesn't say much on the subject, but others did. Thomas Cook commented that "The Swiss are a kind, generous and appreciative people", while another travelling diarist, Miss M.J. Furby, noted that "They seemed poor but quite contented people". But it's Mr Murray who holds forth in wonderful style:

> On the subject of the moral condition of the Swiss, and their character as a nation, there is much variety of opinion. The Swiss with whom the traveller comes into contact, especially the German portion of them, are often

*sullen, obstinate, and disagreeable, and he is annoyed
by the constant mendicancy of the women and children,
even in remote districts, and on the part of those who
are not, apparently, worse off than their neighbours.
This disposes the traveller to dislike and to take very little interest in the people amongst whom he is travelling;
he has also heard much of their timeserving, their love
of money, and their readiness to fight for any paymaster
in former times.*

He goes on to praise Swiss guides – "For the most part, the guides
may be said to be obliging, intelligent, and hard-working men" –
while warning of the men in the coaches, "The conductors, especially with a small additional fee, are generally civil; the clerks &c,
at the diligence offices are occasionally insolent and disobliging."
In the end, he appreciates the ease of travelling in "the land of
liberty":

*There are no passports, no custom-houses, no tolls,
no gendarmes; none of those ridiculous restrictions
to prevent people from incurring danger which are so
annoying in France and Germany; and no interference
whatever with the individual freedom, whilst there are
nearly everywhere good inns, good roads, and tolerable
means of locomotion.*

The means of locomotion have only got better since then.

Geneva was one of the pockets of wealth in the Switzerland of
1863, and that's largely down to watches, banks and one determined man – a Frenchman at that – Jean Calvin. The man from
Picardy transformed Geneva into a Protestant Rome, making it a
place of nineteenth-century pilgrimage, although not for nuns and
kneeling worshippers. This city was top of the must-see list for
those who believed that hard work and proper behaviour were the
way to salvation, or at least to having a good life before enjoying
a good death. A newly industrialised Britain had discovered that

Gare Cornavin, Geneva, which only opened in 1858, was
Miss Jemima's first taste of Switzerland

the Protestant work ethic produced material and spiritual benefits in equal measure. So they came to see the city of Calvin, "that tried citadel of Protestantism" as Miss Jemima described it; although she also called him "the supreme Dictator", so this wasn't exactly hero worship. Naturally, on arriving in Geneva the first thing our travellers did was go to church. It was a Sunday morning, after all.

With its simple stone clock tower and A-frame nave, Holy Trinity Church would not look out of place in the Cotswolds or the Dales. It's an English village church that happens to sit in the middle of Switzerland's second city, halfway between the lake and the station. You might think that odd until you learn that Anglicans first fled to Geneva in the 1550s, not because they fancied living by the lake but because they feared dying at the stake. England under Mary I was not a safe place for those who thought the Pope was a charlatan in red shoes. Holy Trinity was founded in 1555 by Anthony Gilby and Christopher Goodman, two Marian exiles who went on to help create the Geneva Bible, an English translation that pre-dates the King James Version. This became the bible of choice for many

English-speaking Protestants, including the Pilgrim Fathers, who took it with them on the *Mayflower*. The current church building on Rue du Mont Blanc dates from August 1853, built where the city walls had stood until three years earlier. The roll call of chaplains shows that Miss Jemima would have listened to a sermon from Henry Dowton. Many chaplains later and the church is still there, with all its services in English.

Inside it feels just as English, not as bare as Swiss Protestant churches nor as fussy as Catholic ones: simple wooden pews with well-thumbed *New English Hymnals*, memorials to British Consuls long since gone, the hymn board showing this week's choices (398, "Lift up your hearts!" and 436, "Praise my soul, the King of Heaven") and a poster about weekly coffee mornings. I find churches fascinating places – not for their religious role, which leaves me cold in disbelief, but for their architecture, history, peacefulness and feeling of community. This church is no different. It may be lacking in architectural splendour, but that doesn't mean it's not at the heart of its own community. As for peace, there's plenty of that. Cocooned inside the tranquil, dark nave, you forget that one of Geneva's busiest streets is outside the door. For me, every church has something individual about it, something I remember long after stepping outside into the real world. At Holy Trinity, it's the wall memorial adorned with a small pickaxe: "In tender memory of Howard Neil Riegel who perished on Mont Blanc July 12 1898, offered by his loving friends Beatrice and Fanny Suckling." Those last two names are so English they're positively Dickensian.

Having nourished the soul, Miss Jemima and friends proceeded with their traditional English Sunday by sitting down to lunch. But this was no Sunday roast, it was a *table d'hôte*, a communal meal (eaten with Americans, Germans and French, no less) of multiple courses. The whole thing impressed her so much that she listed everything they ate:

> "Ten courses served in succession; it reads like an index to a cookery book ...

1 Vegetable soup (mild)
2 Salmon, with cream sauce
3 Sliced roast beef with brown potatoes
4 Boiled fowl, served on rice
5 Sweetbreads
6 Roast fowl with salad
7 Artichokes
8 Plum pudding, steeped in brandy
9 Sponge cakes and stewed fruit
10 Sweet pudding in iced custard
11 Two varieties of creams
12 Ripe cherries"

Artichokes and cherries aside, that doesn't sound like the lightest or healthiest meal around. No wonder they decided to spend the afternoon exploring the city, as much to walk off the food as see the sights. But what was there to see in Geneva back then? Today's tourists might come for the Jet d'Eau, one of the world's tallest fountains, or a tour of the United Nations building, but both those were a long time in the future in 1863. Time to consult the Murray Handbook:

> *Although Geneva is deservedly a great focus for trav-*
> *ellers of all nations, it possesses within it few objects of*
> *interest to the passing stranger. As a town, it is not very*
> *prepossessing; it has no fine public buildings; in short,*
> *scarcely any sights.*

Not the most glowing recommendation, but the book does goes on to praise the city's location beside the lake and near the mountains, and devotes eight pages to describing the sights that it had just declared not worth seeing, as well as giving a potted history and shopping tips. That is much like most guidebooks today, all of which can be viewed as direct descendants of this format, and of its German counterpart Baedeker. This is the grandmother of all guidebooks, so let's meet the old lady herself.

My *Handbook to Switzerland* is the ninth edition, published in May 1861 and most likely the one Miss Jemima used, since it was the latest edition available in June 1863. It's a small hardback with burgundy-red covers, 590 thin pages and small print. It has fold-out maps but no illustrations and is organised around different touring routes, rather than alphabetically or by region. So, for example, the Geneva section is part of Route 53, which falls about a third of the way into the book. In all there are 170 different routes, some of them quite short and all cross-referenced, so you sometimes have to leaf back and forwards. It's not always user friendly, at least not to a user from the twenty-first century.

Before the routes comes the advice, 66 pages of practical information on everything from money and modes of travelling to guides and local customs. So we can discover that horse-drawn carriages "at convenient hours and very moderate fares now traverse almost every road in Switzerland daily" or be warned that "In making purchases, as in the choice of inns, travellers should be cautious of following blindly the advice of the guide, who too often regards the percentage offered or the quantity of liquor supplied to him more than the interest of his employer". We can also get top survival tips, like "Many persons find relief from the intense thirst by keeping a pebble in the mouth." Tasty.

Best of all, given that many of the book's readers will never have been to Switzerland, there are five suggested Skeleton Tours for planning a trip. Wonderful idea, until you actually see what is being proposed:

> A: TOUR FOR PERSONS WHO DO NOT RIDE; about
> six weeks of easy travelling.

That covers almost the whole of Switzerland and beyond: Basel to Chur, Lugano to Schaffhausen, Constance to Mont Blanc, and everything in between. You'd essentially be on the go constantly for six weeks – in a carriage. If that wasn't enough, then Tour B was the same but with Zurich thrown in for good measure.

> *C: ROUTE FOR MODERATE PEDESTRIANS, OR FOR*
> *LADIES ABLE TO RIDE, including most of the remarka-*
> *ble scenery of the Central Alps. Three months.*

This was a serious tour suggestion, obviously for those with both time and money, and very good shoes. Much of the itinerary, which covers every corner of the country, is on foot (for the men, anyway), with over 70 stops and excursions listed. The description does at least recognise that not everyone is equally able: "Excursions rather too difficult and fatiguing for delicate ladies are given in italics." One such excursion is simply written as "Ascend the Aeggischhorn", omitting the fact that it's a mountain just under 3000m high.

For a shorter trip, consider this:

> *D: TOUR OF FOURTEEN OR SIXTEEN DAYS, hard*
> *travelling and fine weather.*

That might sound more doable to our modern time sensibilities, but they're not joking about the hard travelling. Day 1 is either Schaffhausen, Rhine Falls and Zurich, or Basel and Lucerne. Then it's walking and riding through central Switzerland, across the Bernese Oberland, over into Savoy, back to Lake Geneva, on to Bern and Basel. Every day somewhere new, a Victorian version of "If it's Tuesday it must be Grindelwald" but without the tour bus. And there's more:

> *E: TOUR FOR PRACTISED PEDESTRIANS, keeping to*
> *the higher parts of the Swiss and Savoy Alps.*

The crucial word here is "pedestrians", which doesn't mean someone walking along a street but someone hiking across country and up above 3000m. The handbook details 52 days of walks, but advises that "from 10 to 14 days additional should be allowed for rest and detention by bad weather". That's alright then: 10 days of rest dotted in between 52 days of exertion. It sounds like a great holiday for mountain goats.

Such suggested tours were obviously fairly impractical for most visitors, especially those who were only in Switzerland for a fortnight or so, but the book itself is more helpful when it comes to the details for each place. For example, in Geneva it has hotel suggestions with comments ("Hotel d'Angleterre, a new but second-rate inn, near the railway; Hotel du Rhone, clean and reasonable"), a map, a general overview of the city and its history, a short bio of Calvin, a quick run-through of the main sights – Cathedral, Zoological Museum, Public Library, Botanic Garden – and practical information about trains, the British Consul ("most obliging and anxious to be useful"), day trips and shopping. That last part is very much for the Englishman (and woman) abroad, listing where to buy English cutlery, good stationery, the best snuff, English books, and of course good tea.

Perhaps the most engaging part of the book for a modern reader isn't the lengthy descriptions of the hikes but the adverts at the back – 52 pages of ads touting hotels, portmanteaus, watches, passports, maps, telescopes, insurance and cough remedies. In case you're not entirely sure what a portmanteau is, it's nothing more than a mini-trunk with drawers, dividers and compartments. Rather oddly, the adverts cover everywhere from Munich and Florence to Paris and London, so maybe this section was the same in every Murray Handbook, not just the Swiss one. There are some Swiss advertisers, such as J. Grossmann, "manufacturer of Swiss wood models and ornaments in Interlacken" (sic), the Swiss Couriers' and Travelling Servants' Society, and first-class hotels in Villeneuve, Lucerne and Bern. There are also two pharmacies, one in Interlaken, who declares he is an English druggist, the other in Zurich, who "prepares and dispenses Medicines and Prescriptions according to the English Pharmacopœia". All rather ironic, given that many of today's medicines available in Britain are made in Switzerland.

Back to Geneva. In 1863 it was the largest city in Switzerland: the 1860 census shows it having 41,415 inhabitants, far more than Basel, Bern or Zurich. Its mighty city walls had been recently

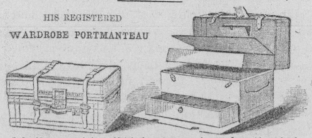
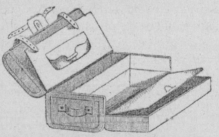
knocked down and the main train station built, but at its heart was still the old town up on the hill, as it is today. Since then Geneva has grown to 192,000 people (along the way losing its No. 1 status to Zurich) and become a centre for international finance and diplomacy, but walking around the historic centre is like stepping back in time. The narrow streets, the tall houses, the sloping squares, the steep steps all combine to create the illusion that the nineteenth century has yet to arrive, let alone the twenty-first. That is, until you see the prices in the chic antique shops along the Grande-Rue; they are definitely modern.

The living-museum atmosphere makes it very easy to follow Miss Jemima's walk around town, knowing that little has changed since she saw it. First to Calvin's house, these days marked by an engraved stone plaque, from which we learn that his actual house was demolished in 1706 and replaced with this one. So much for him being revered as the father and saviour of Geneva. It might be a very extreme case of the Swiss not idolising anyone (statues of the great and good are few and far between); or more likely, the citizens of Geneva got fed up with his restrictions on having a good time. Calvin believed that people should work, rest and pray, and Murray takes great delight in listing some of the more severe pronouncements from the "dictator of the republic":

> a dinner for ten persons was limited to five dishes; plush breeches were laid under interdict; violations of the sabbath were followed by a public admonition from the pulpit; adultery was punished with death; and the gamester was exposed in the pillory, with a pack of cards tied round his neck.

Not much fun for anyone. But once you see Calvin's chair in the cathedral, it all makes sense. No one who had to sit on that hard wood for hour after hour would be willing to tolerate anyone else having a good time, or indeed a life. As for the building that rang to the sound of his sermons, it's not Switzerland's finest specimen of religious architecture, externally at least. Prince Charles would no doubt have something carbuncular to say about St Pierre Cathedral, which has a strange Roman temple meets Bank of England look going on. Or, as Miss Jemima so succinctly puts it, "a fine old building it is, only barbarously disfigured by a mask of Corinthian columns on the West Front". The best view is from the top of the north tower, where all you can see is the city rooftops, the lake and the mountains; definitely worth climbing up the 157 steps. Inside the cathedral, it's stark and bare; beautiful in its way, but a typically puritanical Swiss Protestant church.

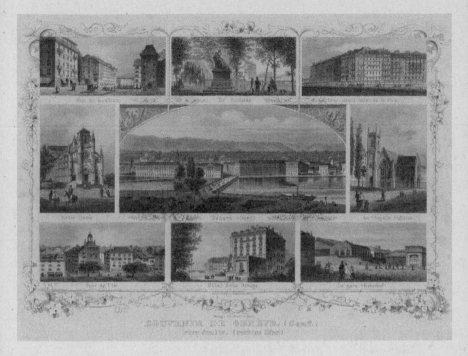

Souvenir of Geneva, including the English church (centre right)

After that we need sustenance. Our lunch is positively Calvinist in its frugality, but we make up for only managing two courses not ten by eating them in the most atmospheric square in the old town. In fact, it's about the only one that has any signs of real life, all the others being strangely empty and soulless. Even though it's more triangular in shape, Place du Bourg-de-Four is the sort of square that would be visited by every tourist if it were in France; it would probably star in countless Hollywood films that involved buckles being swashed or chocolate shops being opened. For me, it's enough that it has big umbrellas over the outdoor tables, more than two affordable cafés and a clutch of pretty houses round the edge. All that's missing is some men playing boules beside the fountain.

Then it's on past the birthplace of Geneva's most famous son, the philosopher Jean-Jacques Rousseau, to the sombre Hôtel de

Ville, where a metal plaque marks the birth of something altogether different: the signing of a convention that took the city's name. It's cited so often in war films and news reports that we probably all think we know what the Geneva Convention is about: helping the victims of battle and the fair treatment of prisoners of war. In fact, there are four separate conventions covering wounded soldiers, wounded sailors, prisoners of war and civilians in wartime. And they all began here in 1863.

Geneva has always been Switzerland's world city, partly because of its position, partly because of its politics. Foreigners came to trade and to be saved, meaning that for centuries the city was a meeting place for half of Europe, particularly the Protestant half. These days it's no longer French Huguenots or Scottish preachers who come here in exile, but international diplomats and English bankers. Geneva is now a city where almost half the population is not Swiss, largely thanks to its role as a centre for diplomacy and home to over 250 international bodies and non-governmental organisations. All that is down to one man, for whom 1863 was a very important year: Henry Dunant, local banker turned hero. There aren't many of those around in any century.

Dunant is one of those historical figures who wouldn't be credible if he were in a novel. Because his story is true and led to such a remarkable legacy, he deserves a mention, not least because at the time Miss Jemima visited Geneva, the wheels that would change the world were already rolling. The good idea that would become the Red Cross began four years earlier, with a battle between the French and the Austrians at Solferino in northern Italy. Dunant was stalking Napoleon III at the time, trying to get an audience with the supreme ruler of France, and he arrived as the fighting stopped. His efforts to help the 40,000 dead and dying changed his life, and ours. He wrote and then self-published a book in 1862, *Un Souvenir de Solferino*, in which he floated the idea of having qualified volunteers to care for the wounded in times of war. Humanitarian aid had arrived, at least in theory.

In practice, it took a while longer. Under the auspices of a local charity, the Geneva Society for Public Welfare, a committee was created on 9 February 1863, consisting of Dunant plus two doctors, a lawyer and a general. Its composition is not the cue for a bad joke but for good deeds in the shape of the International Committee for Relief to the Wounded, the forerunner of what we know as the International Committee of the Red Cross, ICRC for short – or simply the Red Cross. That first committee organised an international conference on 26 October 1863, oddly enough exactly the same day as the Football Association first met in London. Three days later the conference adopted Dunant's proposals and declared that voluntary medical personnel "shall wear in all countries, as a uniform distinctive sign, a white armlet with a red cross" (Article 8, Resolution of the Geneva International Conference). The following year the Conference became a Convention, the original Geneva Convention for the Amelioration of the Condition of the Wounded in Armies in the Field. Twelve states signed the Red Cross into being on 22 August 1864 in the Alabama Room of Geneva's Hôtel de Ville.

This was the high point of Dunant's life, which was downhill after that. In 1867 he bankrupted his bank with a disastrous venture in Algeria and was one of the few to have to leave Geneva in exile, having been kicked out of the Red Cross. He was officially *persona non grata* and never saw the city again. Wandering around Europe, penniless and hungry, he ended up a hermit in Heiden, eastern Switzerland. Shortly before his death, he was at last remembered by the world for his act of humanity, being awarded the first Nobel Peace Prize in 1901. He gave the prize money to charity.

In his home town there are a few reminders of the greatest Genevan since Rousseau. There is no grave, as that is in Zurich's Sihlfeld Cemetery, but there is, of course, a city street named after him and a small bust, discreetly placed at the end of Rue de la Croix Rouge, which runs beneath the old city ramparts. Up above, in the old town, there's a second plaque, this one on the sombre grey walls of Rue du Puits-Saint-Pierre 4, near the Hôtel de Ville:

This house saw the birth of the Red Cross, editing of Un Souvenir de Solferino *by Henri Dunant, first meeting of the International Committee of the Red Cross.*

Nothing too ostentatious, as befits the man, his Swiss heritage and the organisation he helped to found. Geneva is still the world headquarters for the Red Cross, and many of the international bodies that came after it.

In June 1863, all that was in the future. It was an event in the past that led Miss Jemima to a leafy terrace on the city ramparts, overlooking an even leafier park, once the Botanic Gardens and now the Parc des Bastions. It was here that a crucial piece of Geneva's history took place. I'm not talking about the installation of what is claimed to be the world's longest wooden park bench, which has been there since 1767; at 120m it's certainly long, although it is of course many armless benches linked together one after the other. No, this historic moment was the Escalade of 1602.

At 2am on the longest night of the year (12 December, old-style calendar), the Duke of Savoy's army sneakily tried to scale the city walls with ladders, thinking that everyone in Geneva was asleep. They hadn't counted on Mère Royaume being up early to make vegetable soup. She threw her *marmite*, or cauldron, of boiling soup over the invaders, killing one (presumably with the pot, not the carrots) and raising the alarm. Soldiers and citizens ran to the walls and Geneva was saved, although 18 locals died. The event is still celebrated every December with chocolate cauldrons full of sweets and a weekend of costumed processions.

If that all sounds rather bellicose for the famously neutral Swiss, you have to remember that Geneva has only been part of Switzerland since 1815. Before that it was an independent city-state that suffered from being sandwiched between Burgundy, France and Savoy, so it often ended up on the wrong side of one or other of them. Independence from Savoy in 1536 led to the Republic of Geneva being allied with, but not part of, the Swiss Confederation, a situation the Escalade invasion tried and failed to reverse. After that victory, the lowest point came when Geneva disappeared as a separate entity in 1798, having been conquered by Napoleon and reduced to a *département* in his empire. His defeat in 1815 restored Geneva's sovereignty in its newest incarnation, as the 22nd canton of Switzerland, although the past remains in its official title: the Republic and Canton of Geneva.

Once free from the strictures of the old town, Miss Jemima's sightseeing tour that afternoon was soon sidetracked by the very frivolous pastimes of concert booths and merry-go-rounds. And on a Sunday, if you please. No doubt it was the wrath of God that cut short all the fun with a storm:

> "a peal of thunder, not of British mildness, but of mountainous volume arrested us. ... We rushed to our hotel just in time to escape the fury of the storm."

Lake Geneva is famous for its cold wind, the Bise, which cuts through you all year round but is particularly harsh in winter, when it can whip up the water and then freeze the spray as it lands. The thunderstorms, which roll across the vast expanse of water that is western Europe's largest lake, can be as dramatic. It was such a storm in 1816 that produced one of the greatest Gothic novels in English literature, although the main character is a local boy.

The poet Lord Byron spent that summer beside the lake at Cologny, near Geneva, with Percy Bysshe Shelley and Mary Wollstonecraft Godwin, Shelley's soon-to-be wife. On a dark and stormy night (and for once that tired cliché actually applies), they scared each other with ghost stories. Shelley ran screaming from the room and the 18-year-old Mary had nightmares, although maybe that was the wine – or the opium. Whatever the trigger, her bad dream became a great novel, published in 1818 with the sub-title *The Modern Prometheus*. Its hero is one Victor Frankenstein, who introduces himself with "I am by birth a Genevese, and my family is one the most distinguished in that republic." Cue Boris Karloff and endless Halloween costumes.

Getting up at 4am in the rain – that was how Miss Jemima & Co. made up for lost time and finished their city tour before leaving town. I can sense that my mother would prefer her first visit to Geneva not to be coloured by memories of pre-dawn expeditions and, given the price of our hotel room, I'm keen to milk every possible hour of sleep from it. So after breakfast at a normal hour, we trot off under a cloudless sky to see something very few of today's tourists visit and indeed few modern guidebooks to Switzerland even mention.

From the point where the lake meets the river, we skirt around the old town to the base of the ramparts, then it's a leisurely half-hour walk through a part of Geneva that barely existed in 1863. Boulevard de Saint-Georges isn't as pretty as the old town, but it's more lived in, with traffic and trams, pan-Asian restaurants and modest cafés. Above the street-level *tabacs* and *coiffures*, almost every building is an apartment block, few taller than six storeys but most with curly iron balconies stacked up across the façade. The further west we go, the earthier the area becomes, and the more prolific the graffiti: this is definitely no longer the Geneva of private banks and luxury shops. There's no sign of the lake or the mountains, just people and their daily lives.

As we pass the walls of Plainpalais cemetery, I can't resist popping in to see its most famous resident. After 23 years of being a curmudgeonly killjoy, Calvin died in 1564, aged 55, although he still managed to control things after he'd gone. Geneva was forbidden from building any monument to him, which probably suited a fair few of the locals, and could only mark his grave with nothing more than "J.C." – instead of being super-modest, that smacks of him having delusions of grandeur. Perhaps that's why Grave No. 707 now has simple iron railings and a small plaque saying that Jean Calvin "wanted to make this town a model city and established a religious discipline here". Nevertheless, his legacy isn't this unadorned grave or the Calvinist churches across the world, it's something far more important to Switzerland today. In his quest for puritan perfection he banned jewellery, prompting Geneva's craftsmen to turn to a new, acceptable product. Almost 500 years later, and the Swiss watch industry he kick-started now creates adornments far more ostentatious, indulgent and expensive than anything to which Calvin objected.

We walk on, past the bus depot and run-down warehouses where once meadows and country houses stood, then down to "the blue waters of the arrowy Rhone", as Byron described it. The canoe clubhouse can barely be seen beneath the weight of multicolour graffiti, but the wooden platforms punctuating the riverbank are pristine, waiting for a hot summer day and locals seeking a cool dip in the river. Urban swimming is a popular pastime in every Swiss city, with Geneva, like Zurich, having both river and lake options. The lake-less Bernese like nothing better than to jump in the fast-flowing Aare after a long day at work; it beats a pint in the pub, that's for sure. Some are even crazy enough to do it in winter.

Finally we reach our goal, the tip of a tongue of land between two rivers. You may be wondering why on earth anyone ever visited here, but it all becomes clear once you arrive; or actually half-clear, half-cloudy. On the right is the Rhone, a deep turquoise stream of crystal water gently flowing ever onward; on the left is the Arve, a swirling mass of murky grey that tries to invade its neighbour's purity. Whereas the Rhone dumps its sediment as it flows through Lake Geneva, the Arve carries tons of it straight from the Alpine glaciers. It's a struggle for supremacy that both refuse to lose. For a long time after they meet the two don't merge, so a wiggly battle line stretches far beyond the high-arched railway bridge, and on downstream from where we are standing.

It's a strangely mesmerising sight and one you rarely see in a city, one where the sole visitors are locals – or people who have read a 150-year-old diary. I'm only here because of Miss Jemima, and I'm rather glad that she came all this way at 5am in the rain. Maybe the past can show us things we'd otherwise overlook, although she does admit that some of her group were more sat-isfied "from the feeling of having 'done it' than in the wonder of the sight thereof" – seeing sights merely to tick them off really is nothing new at all.

These days the meeting of watery ways fails to compete with Geneva's museums, shops and 140m fountain for attention. No tour buses stop here and no clicking cameras can be heard, although that may well soon change. The bus depot will close in 2016 and this whole neighbourhood should get a new lease of life as a trendy urban space. That's the plan, anyway. Whatever happens the rivers will carry on their battle, one the Arve eventually wins in terms of water clarity, although it's the Rhone whose name flows all the way down to the Mediterranean.

That was pretty much it for the first Cook's Tour to Geneva. The visitors arrived at midnight on Saturday and left at 8am on Monday: 32 hours in Switzerland's largest city, almost like the kind of trip at which the Japanese now excel. That first Cook's Tour was noticeable for its pre-dawn starts, 18-hour days and the place-a-day itinerary. It would exhaust most modern British tourists, who wouldn't pay to go home more tired than when they left; unless they're on a party holiday to Ibiza or a camping trip to Scotland.

To be fair, the group did see the main sights Geneva had to offer in those days, particularly as no Red Cross meant no Red Cross Museum, one of my favourite museums in Switzerland. It could be hard to get an idea of how the city looked back then, how compact it really was without the international quarter, modern shopping districts and airport. Luckily, there is a way of looking into the past, thanks to a very committed model maker.

Before leaving Geneva, we pop back to the old town to visit Maison Tavel, a fortified mansion that is the oldest private dwelling in Geneva and home to the city history museum. Filling the top floor is an intricate scale model built by Auguste Magnin between 1880 and 1896. It shows the whole of Geneva in miniature, although the model is definitely not small: its oval base is 7.2m by 5.65m, with a horizontal scale of 1:250 and a vertical one of 1:200. The mini buildings are fronted with zinc and the roofs with copper, making it startlingly realistic and unbelievably heavy, at 800kg. What is interesting for us is that Magnin built the model to represent the city at the beginning of 1850, only 13 years before Cook & Co. came to visit.

Those were a crucial 13 years, nevertheless. Much of Geneva would have looked exactly as it does in the model, particularly the old town, but with one huge difference. The impressive snowflake-shaped city walls, with their mighty triangular bastions, which surround the city and dominate the model were pulled

The lakefront Pont du Mont-Blanc was only a few months old when Miss Jemima visited Geneva

down in 1850. Their demolition led to rapid urban expansion, with new streets and residential districts and, as we've seen, an English church where the walls used to stand. More importantly, a modern transport system was created: the train station opened to great fanfare in March 1858 and the Pont du Mont-Blanc, the vital road bridge across the mouth of the Rhone, followed in December 1862. Until then, Rousseau's statue had an uninterrupted view of lake and mountains from its island in the stream; today its view is still blocked by the bridge, itself spoiled by the volume of traffic flowing over it. Those few years witnessed the birth of modern Geneva, so it's fascinating to see the city frozen at the moment before it all started.

With the help of the museum guide, Madame Hexel (who seemingly knows everything about Geneva), we locate one particular building in the model: the Hotel de la Couronne, where Miss Jemima stayed, a fairly imposing affair on the lakefront. I can't resist walking back that way to our own hotel so we can see what now stands on that site, rather aptly across the road from the Jardin Anglais, which itself dates from 1854 (although the famous

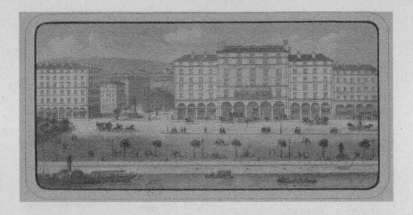

Hotel de la Couronne, Geneva: Miss Jemima's bed for the night and "Mr Cook's principal house in Switzerland"

floral clock didn't start ticking until 101 years later). The building is still there and still looks the part, with iron balconies and chunky pediments, but glittering trinkets now fill the windows and the door is opened for us as we enter. Miss Jemima's hotel succumbed to the same fate as many posh buildings in Geneva – it became an exclusive watch shop, the kind that has countless Swiss timepieces with the four-figure price tags discreetly hidden. While the hotel came and went just like its guests, plenty more were built. Geneva has over 10,000 hotel beds, including the hundreds in Switzerland's biggest hotel, the Starling, with its 496 rooms.

Given that we can't sleep in a watch shop, we've been staying in a hotel that from the name alone is the epitome of Swissness: the Edelweiss. From the outside it could be any other modern building, but stepping inside is like going through the looking glass. As the hotel's website puts it: "Discover the Alps in the heart of Geneva. Come to the Hotel Edelweiss and delight in the warmth of an authentic Swiss chalet." It's touristy but tasteful, with acres of bare wood in every room, stencilled flowers on the bedheads, log fires, and red-and-white checks in the fondue restaurant. The only thing missing is some yodelling, but apparently that makes a live appearance every evening – it is Disney Switzerland. Tourism today isn't always about authenticity, but it is always about making money. I blame Thomas Cook. It's his fault I've been sleeping in a fake chalet, avoiding the restaurant for fear of being yodelled at and wondering how long the smell of cooked cheese lingers in the air. It's time to go.

Leaving Geneva is not as easy as it looks – if you're heading south to the Alps, that is. It's all a matter of finding the right train station. The obvious place to start is the main one, Gare Cornavin (sadly no longer the original building, which burnt down in 1909), which has both Swiss and French platforms. Since Switzerland signed up to the Schengen agreement in 2004 for border-free travel, there is little difference except for destinations. There is no passport control, as we realised on arrival from Paris, and no customs. However, having French platforms does not mean that all French trains from Geneva start here; that would be too Swiss in its logical simplicity. It's perfect if you want to go to Lyon, Paris or even Barcelona, but we soon discover that Chamonix is not included. Actually nowhere in Savoy is on the departure board, possibly in revenge for the Escalade. For those destinations you must take the tram to Gare Eaux-Vives on the other side of town, and on the other side of the tracks in terms of appearance.

Whereas Cornavin is an impressive stone edifice that seems to be in a state of constant improvement, Eaux-Vives looks like it was last used in about 1947. Its half-timbered façade is covered in graffiti and peeling paint, windows boarded up and ticket office closed. More Eaux-Mortes than Eaux-Vives, and rather like the set for a *film noir* featuring an abandoned railway station and two unsuspecting tourists. To make matters even weirder, the only other people on the platform are seven Swiss border police, all looking down the tracks for the train. It must be full of football hooligans or drug dealers to warrant such an official welcome.

The two-carriage train duly arrives, on time, prompting the police to edge forward, but there are no rampaging hordes, no dodgy characters, in fact no excitement at all. Only six people get off and none of them is stopped, so the officers wander away, leaving us none the wiser. Perhaps it was an office outing. They do at least smile and nod as they pass us. Friendly but superfluous, which is probably many visitors' view of Swiss police in general.

We have the train to ourselves as we trundle through the suburban sprawl of Geneva, a continuous procession of housing estates, allotments and factories. It's a bit like being on a giant tram, albeit one with curtains at the windows: close enough to buildings to be able to see fleetingly into people's flats, but abnormally high off the ground. Car parks host a mix of Swiss and French number plates, so it's never clear where and when we cross the border, but it can't be that far from the station. Geneva is one of the smallest Swiss cantons – Voltaire, a local resident, memorably said, "When I shake my wig, I powder the whole republic" – and is almost entirely surrounded by France; its sole internal Swiss border, with Canton Vaud, is only 4.5km long. A change of trains in Annemasse, most definitely in France, and we set off to the Alps, following the Arve upstream towards Mont Blanc.

It's only later I discover that Eaux-Vives station closed down not long after we visited, although there's no connection between the two events. We were there in the twilight of its life, our clattering train a part of its death rattle. It is due to be revived in 2016 in a redevelopment scheme that includes a new train line connecting Annemasse directly with Gare Cornavin. Well, it's not exactly new, as the line was first proposed in 1881, approved in a referendum of 1884 and ratified in 1912. That's slow even for Swiss bureaucracy, but more than 100 years later it looks like it will finally happen. In the meantime, the train journey to Chamonix has become substantially more convoluted and time consuming. Most people prefer to go by road, which is exactly what the Junior United Alpine Club had to do.

This is a route that has barely changed in centuries. Nature did all the hard work, with the Arve cutting a valley from the foot of Mont Blanc down to the shores of Lake Geneva. Today's motorway and railway merely follow in the footsteps and carriage ruts of travellers past. The Cook group, reduced to 30 people in three

A diligence: a convenient mode of transport,
if not too comfortable, especially for those sitting outside

separate parties, covered the 52 miles by diligence, a horse-drawn stage-coach that held up to 18 people and was the forerunner of the public bus system. *Cook's Tourist's Handbook* described it as a "strange machine. Imagine a covered cart, a carriage, an omnibus, a hansom cab, an open fly, a coach, and a dickey, all jammed up together and drawn by six stout horses, with jingling bells." It was the only option other than walking or riding, but it was not particularly comfortable. Forget sea-sickness, this was carriage-sickness from all that swaying around, bumping over mountain roads and enduring the smells emerging from your fellow passengers and their food.

The carriages couldn't always cope with the hills, as Miss Jemima writes: "soon we come to steep ascents, where we alight to walk and have additional mules yoked to the carriages". However, there was no shortage of diligences or mules on this route – in *The Excursionist*, Thomas Cook reports that "by a little pre-arrangement, from sixty to one hundred passengers may be provided for in a day by diligence and post conveyances, and of mules any number may be had up to 200". The logistics of transporting 100 customers in a fleet of carriages seem mind-boggling. Travel in our time has become much more individual: we might be in a train or plane with countless others, but we're not actually travelling with them.

The route along the river may not have changed, but the time it takes certainly has. Our train trip, with a second change in St Gervais, feels slow at 2½ hours considering the short distance involved, but that's super-speedy compared to 11 hours by coach, with one change in St Martin. Murray gives us a clear idea of the speed – "from St Martin to Chamouni [sic] 5 hrs. Pedestrians will find it as pleasant to walk, and will traverse that distance as fast as the chars, ie in about 4 to 5 hours" – and comfort – "the roads to Chamouni are practicable only for light and narrow chars; in some places they are very steep, rough and stony". Eleven hours of bone-shaking torture are possibly why Napoleon III ordered a new road to be built to Chamonix. Its completion in 1866 reduced journey times by a third and doubtlessly increased comfort levels by far more. Train travellers had to wait much longer; the railway didn't reach Chamonix until 1901.

Whatever the mode of transport, it's a pleasant enough journey, not the most spectacular but offering a taste of things to come. At first the valley is broad and shallow, its river banks dotted with light industry and modern houses: a cheese factory here, a vast campsite there, inflatable pools adorning many gardens and the first chalets shyly appearing. Going round the bend at Cluses everything changes, with both the valley sides and the house roofs becoming ever steeper. Main road, motorway, river and railway must all squeeze through the same narrow band, criss-crossing over and under each other like an unruly four-stranded French plait. The Autoroute Blanche balances on massive concrete stilts, only to be down at ground level a bit further on, while the train steadily climbs until it runs high above the milky river. It has to if it is to reach Chamonix, 660m higher than Geneva.

"Every roll of the carriage wheel brought us in sight of a new view, or an old one in a new aspect", noted Miss Jemima. The same

The view of the Alps from St Martin was celebrated by British visitors

is true from a train carriage, except that it's not exactly the best weather for scenic trips. Clouds shroud every cliff and mountain top, so low that in places they seem to reach down and stroke the roof of our train. Sadly, that means we miss "one of the noblest views in the Alps", that of Mont Blanc from a bridge over the Arve.

For us, there's no vast white peak crowning a horizon of jagged mountains. All we see is endless grey, and reading the weather reports from 1863 only makes our day seem even duller:

> "Such heat! A still, white glistening heat that strikes with reflected strength upon you from those stuccœd white-washed houses, a heat that produces silence and must send the inhabitants to sleep, for where are they?"

At least Miss Jemima and Miss Sarah stayed upright. Cook writes of "a burning sun, beneath the rays of which one or two ladies fainted". I blame the tight corsets and heavy skirts, not a winning combination for hot weather.

Heat means thirst and whereas we have bottles of water with

us, Miss Jemima had to go in search of liquid satisfaction:

> "Wishing to see an interior, we enter a chalet under the pretext of thirst, but that desire vanishes when a little dirty child points to an old broken cask of turbid Arve water, in which apparently rests the only drinking vessel in the chalet, viz. the remains of an old cankered pan; of furniture there was none to bear the name, only a keg or two, a stool and a propped-up table, all denoting the extreme poverty of the peasantry."

Undeterred by local conditions, she asks at the next chalet, where "a smart little woman smilingly hands us with a professional air a round waiter bearing two glass tumblers of sparkling water".

By the time we deboard (I'm beginning to warm to this word) in Chamonix, the grey is thickening into black. Having missed us in Geneva, Miss Jemima's storm is threatening to wreak its revenge on us now. That's bad timing, as Chamonix, like many Alpine resorts, is not a great place for dismal days. Its life is anchored to outdoor activities of varying degrees of sanity, so that when you can't even see the peaks let alone go up them, you're reduced to sitting in cafés or walking in the rain. Hence the pedestrianised town centre is full this afternoon, with pavement diners and window shoppers out in force, at least until the rain begins falling in earnest.

The storm advances, so rather than get completely drenched we retreat to our hotel. It's a lovely old stone building, dating from 1903, and the receptionist cheerily tells us there's a perfect view of Mont Blanc from the balcony – never mind that it's too grey and grim to see over the road. Still, after three days on the go it's actually pleasant to have an enforced moment of rest. Keeping up with the Junior United Alpine Club is hard work and I'm beginning to think the Victorians were superhuman.

The weather forecast for tomorrow is just as bad, so we'll be lucky to see anything other than cloud and rain. As for the Mer de Glace, the famous glacier that was the main draw for Victorian visitors, I fear it will not be a sea of ice but a sea of fog. Miss Jemima is little help on these matters, as their weather was good enough for the hike up the mountain, although I get the feeling she would have gone up in a blizzard. Murray is a little more forthcoming:

> *When cloudy weather forbids your thinking of excursions in which a distant view is the chief object, a visit to the Cascade du Dard may be made. It will well repay a visit on an "off" day.*

Said Cascade is marked on our town map, seemingly not too far from the centre. So Plan A for the next day is essentially splashes of culture, dashes of window shopping, a waterfall and getting wet one way or another. Plan B is to hope for divine intervention.

L ying in bed that night, listening to the rain, I start thinking about toilets. It's a subject that has been troubling me since we left England. What did Miss Jemima & Co. do when they needed the loo? We have the comparative luxury of being able to go while on the go, be that on a train or in a city. For Victorian travellers such conveniences were a relatively new idea, even in Britain. In 1851 George Jennings built the first public flushing toilets for the Great Exhibition inside the Crystal Palace, charging customers a penny to use them. Even today, some people still use "spend a penny" as a polite euphemism for doing the necessary. The first municipal toilets followed in 1855 in London, which along with loos in private houses and new sewers helped improve the crappy conditions in the ever-growing cities. Given what Miss Jemima thought of Dieppe's streets, I fear the Continent was not so advanced in the matter of public toilets.

The same was indeed true of loos in hotels, which rarely had private bathrooms, with most having shared facilities on each floor. If they were very lucky, guests might have had the chance to use a new American invention, toilet paper, which first appeared in 1857. Here's Murray on the subject of Swiss hotels:

> *In many instances, even in first-class inns, the houses are deficient in proper drainage and ventilation, and the passages and staircases are unwholesome and offensive*

from bad smells. Care should be taken to impress on
the landlords how disgusting and intolerable to English
ideas such a nuisance is.

He even goes so far as to report on individual inns along the touring routes. For example in Arth, near Lake Zug, he lists the "Schwarzer Adler (Black Eagle), good but bad smells". Not exactly a glowing recommendation.

The aptly named book *The Smell of the Continent* takes an entertaining look at British travel in Europe after the fall of Napoleon and devotes a whole section to matters lavatorial. It reveals that many hotels had a Room 00 or 000, which was the one communal, and therefore rather disgusting, toilet. Other hoteliers started installing water closets (or WC, a term that is still used all across Europe, particularly in Switzerland where it overcomes the language barriers) after being "impelled by the continual ... complaining of their English visitors", although they don't sound too nice, as a travel pamphlet from 1863 made clear: "In a hotel with, say, sixty rooms it was not unusual to have only four WCs and in some cases these simply did not work or were just filthy." Plus it gave this handy tip for couples travelling together:

Men should always inspect the toilets before allowing
ladies to enter, to check for graffiti and to make sure that
"moustachioed" foreigners were not using the neigh-
bouring closets without closing the doors.

Chamber pots were still very much in use, but weren't that portable for travelling, so quite what Miss Jemima did while on the move I have no idea. In those days train carriages were simply boxed seats on wheels, with no room for a loo; even if there had been one, you couldn't move between carriages to reach it. So it must have been a case of cross your legs until the next stop, which luckily were frequent and long, so that water and coal could be taken on board, giving passengers time to do the opposite. And if there were no facilities, then presumably you found the nearest bush – which was the only option when hiking in the mountains all day. For a society preoccupied with respectability and decorum, it's a very odd state of affairs, not to mention the practicalities of it all when encased in layers of petticoats. Of course, Miss Jemima makes no mention of such things in her journal; that would have been most unseemly.

Train toilets finally arrived in the 1880s, when carriages got bigger and trains longer, though even then they were separated by class. Third-class pee was not allowed to sully a first-class loo.

Not wanting to dwell on a subject that isn't conducive to a restful night, I contemplate instead how much Geneva has changed since Miss Jemima's time. For one thing, time itself has changed. In the heart of the city, on a small island in the Rhone, there's a chunky stone clock tower – the Tour de l'Ile (shown in the picture on page 45) – that used to have three clocks side by side on the front. The largest one showed Geneva time, the others Paris and Bern time, none of them the same. Geneva was five minutes behind Bern but 15 minutes ahead of Paris, which in turn was 9½ minutes ahead of Greenwich Mean Time. By 1894 Switzerland had adopted a single time zone, Central European Time. Today the clock tower has been reduced to only one clock face and has been integrated into the private bank next door. Time and money are sometimes the same thing in Geneva.

As for the city itself, back then it was relatively small (though still the largest in Switzerland), but with a reputation far larger than one of similar size in Britain. It had recently burst out from its city walls and was growing in both size and stature. Today, Geneva remains a small city, with a population about the same as Portsmouth. Having grown up a few miles from the latter, I can say without hesitation which I prefer. Portsmouth might have the sea and HMS *Victory*, but it also had the Second World War and the 1950s, neither of which brought aesthetic improvements. On the other hand, I have yet to find good fish and chips in Geneva, although the heavenly macaroons are almost compensation enough.

Geneva might today be half the size of Zurich but, by both accident and design, this city by the lake has found a global role in the past century and a half. It is feted no longer as the Protestant

Rome but now as the Capital of Peace, which for once is more than tourist-board hype. The Red Cross, the United Nations, the World Health Organization and so on and so on – the list of worthy organisations is almost endless, right down to the headquarters of the Scout Movement.

How different would Geneva be today without the events of 1863? Very, though that's not particularly thanks to tourism or Thomas Cook. Foreign visitors were nothing new – it was merely the numbers that changed – whereas becoming the centre for international diplomacy gave the city a role on the world stage that it has not yet lost.

THREE

UNWRAPPING THE ALPS

Within the last few years the character of Chamouny has much changed; it was quite a secluded spot and now, in the busy season, it is full of business and bustle.
—Cook's Tourist's Handbook to Switzerland, *1874*

*The aptly named mauvais pas, or false step, was a treacherous
way to reach Chamonix*

Mont Blanc might be the highest point in France, and indeed in western Europe, but so far it is proving to be elusive, with all 4810m permanently swathed in cloud. It is Mont Invisible. As I stand on our balcony the next morning, looking at where the mountain is supposed to be, I begin to think that the postcards have all been Photoshopped and there is actually no mountain at all. Every so often the clouds swirl around enough for a tantalising glimpse of rock through a fleeting gap, rather like a dance of the seven veils where the mist never reveals its secrets. It's hard to tell which particular lump of rock it is, but it's certainly not white. The good news is that it's stopped raining. The weather is still grey, cold, damp and miserable, but at least no water is falling from the sky, so we venture out in relatively good spirits. Only the British could be so wildly optimistic about the weather.

The first item on the day's agenda is breakfast. Our hotel is depressingly one of those that thinks this is an optional extra, to be charged at the maximum possible rate. That makes three hotels in a row now, including Paris and Geneva. Charging extra for breakfast was quite normal in Thomas Cook's day, too. *The Excursionist* states that breakfasts without meat or eggs were cheaper than ones with them, so hotel and tour prices were labelled "with meat breakfast" to make it clear what the customer was getting for his money. That's little wonder, as of course the meat involved wasn't merely a couple of rashers of bacon, but steak, chops, cold cuts and the like. As for other oddities on the table, there was this warning in the *Guide to Cook's Tours*:

> We desire to put our friends on their guard against excess in the novelties of continental tables. Honey, which is always set on Swiss breakfast and tea tables, should be taken with great caution by those disposed to relaxation of the system; we have seen many suffer from its too free use.

Clearly Swiss bees were collecting pollen from far too many dandelions and cowslips, but I can't say that I've noticed any untoward effects from eating Swiss honey.

Miss Jemima rarely makes more than a passing mention of breakfast, probably because they set off before dawn most days. In Paris she does note, however:

> "at our five-o'clock breakfast how that little ubiquitous waiter tantalised us by his constant reiterations that coffee was 'coming, coming'! And when at last that beverage appeared it was conveyed in minikin coffee pots only copious in a supply to Lilliputians."

Our first stop of the day is the Tourist Information Centre, where the forecast printed out and posted up on the board shows a distinct lack of significant improvement, and a webcam confirms that the clouds are deep enough to cover the mountains. I'd hoped it might be a case of *unten grau, oben blau*, as the German-speaking Swiss say; in other words, down in the valley it's grey and dismal, but up in the mountains it's blue sky and sunshine. In the Alps, you can glide up in a cable car and emerge from the gloom into glorious weather. Better yet, you can look down on a sea of fog and feel superior in every sense. The weather forecast even details the upper limits of the fog so you know how high you have to go to reach the sun. We have no such luck today, nevertheless.

Instead of going up to see the glaciers, we look at the information panels about them; or more specifically, about how much they are shrinking. The before and after photos are like a record of some extreme diet regime, with the glaciers wasting away every year. In the earliest picture, from 1865, the Mer de Glace is truly a wonder, a frozen torrent filling its valley and surging forwards towards Chamonix. Today, it has lost both its majesty and 1.2km in length, plus over half its depth. The neighbouring Argentière and Bossons glaciers have suffered the same fate, retreating by a kilometre or more since the end of the nineteenth century. Computer simulations predict a further 800m of shrinkage by 2030. And some people say that climate change is a myth.

Two factors determine our next move, given that we are unable to follow the Junior United Alpine Club. The Alpine Museum is open only in the afternoons and, even more unbelievably, the weather has improved so much that we're in danger of seeing a spot of blue sky. So we decide to follow the "off" day advice and walk to the Cascade du Dade, without umbrellas. What could possibly go wrong?

There are no prizes for guessing the outcome. Far from being "about ¾ of an hour from the village" as stated, the waterfalls seem to get further away the longer we walk. And naturally, the drizzle starts before we can even leave "the village", although Chamonix has long since outgrown that label. With hoods up against the rain, we enter the woods where the path becomes ever steeper and slipperier, so much so that we fashion a walking stick from a fallen branch for my mother. Combined with her all-encompassing raincoat-and-hood, the stout staff makes her look like Gandalf from behind; I begin to feel like a hobbit on a quest.

It's not the peacefully bucolic outing we had expected. Sadly, the constant hum of traffic is never far away, and is sometimes too close for comfort, thanks to the Autoroute Blanche climbing up the same hill towards the mouth of the Mont Blanc tunnel. At last, we leave it behind and turn the final corner – and we're rather underwhelmed. The cascade is nice enough, but it's not exactly huge as waterfalls go, more of a watertrickle.

"Perhaps it was better when the glacier was bigger," my mother says, looking higher up the hill, "when all the meltwater would have been coming down?"

I follow her gaze up to the distant pinnacles of ice poking out above the dark pine trees. In the 1860s, the ice used to reach right down into the valley, not far from where we're standing; Miss Jemima talks of the "acres, nay, miles of ice, spreading and penetrating into the vale". We bid farewell to the disappointing spectacle and head back to the hotel, in need of dry clothes and a hot drink.

Miss Jemima's excursion that day to the Mer de Glace also ended in everyone getting soaked through, despite seeking shelter in a mountain hut. Dressing for dinner that evening was an unusual challenge:

"mighty amusement had we in trying to make a presentable appearance ... out of the remnants of the wet clothing that had weathered the drench. Miss Mary took the monkish character, arrayed in cloak and girdle. Miss Eliza personated the decayed gentlewoman in limp garments, another, our artist, ignored crinoline for the graceful folds of drapery, while Miss Sarah, who had been befriended by her mackintosh, had to make presence for the whole party in modern attire."

Standards of decorum could obviously lapse while abroad, something that has not changed at all. But the lack of dry clothing does raise one interesting point: luggage. What did Miss Jemima pack in her suitcase? And indeed, how much baggage did she take with her? The answers are not so easy to uncover, except in general terms.

In *The Excursionist*, Thomas Cook is clear on the question of luggage: "Baggage is one of the greatest nuisances in travelling on the Continent", not least because it had to be "weighed, registered, ticketed and paid for at every station where the journey is broken". Luggage limits are listed as 60lb per person in any class of travel; that's about 27kg, so marginally more than a normal check-in allowance on flights today. But did Miss Jemima really take that much with her? This was not a coach tour, with cavernous luggage compartments under the seats, and she rarely mentions carrying any bags. Before departing from London, she notes that "the baggage of the members was then, after much effort, considerably reduced in bulk", confirming that holiday packing was as much a dilemma then as it is now. She boasts of her prowess in this matter:

"the Misses Jemima, Sarah, Eliza and Mary have settled the universally important baggage questions and claim to have travelled in the Alps with less luggage than any previous tourists, the porters of the Hotels unconsciously pouring delicious flattery in their ears by the enquiry 'Where are your boxes?'"

In contrast to her reticence on the subject, the *Guide to Cook's Tours* devotes two whole pages to luggage; imagine any modern guidebook doing that. Its main advice is still just as valid:

> Every traveller should study the most rigid economy
> in the amount of luggage and means by which it is to
> be conveyed ... It would be preposterous to attempt to
> take trunks and heavy packages over passes and other
> mountain roads.

More interesting are the details it gives: luggage over the weight limit is charged at a penny a pound, while registering baggage from London to Paris cost one shilling and needed a minimum of half an hour extra at the station for processing. The simple suggestion was to take less: "For those who intend to 'foot it', a small light knapsack made of American cloth or mackintosh is recommended; for others a good-sized carpet bag or small portmanteau is most suitable."

Murray agrees:

> It saves a world of trouble to have no other baggage than
> a knapsack; one containing 3 or 4 shirts, socks, drawers,
> slippers, alpaca coat, thin waistcoat and trowsers [sic],
> dressing materials, &c., need not exceed 12 or 14lbs.

The advantage of travelling light is also made clear: "a portmanteau requires a luggage-mule or porter, whilst a carpet-bag will go behind the saddle".

What is apparent is that Miss Jemima's group took all that advice and travelled very light on a daily basis, while sending large luggage on ahead. Halfway through the tour the party arrived in Interlaken, where "the ladies, having got possession of the long-absent trunks, dazzled our eyes with almost forgotten splendour". The next day, before setting off on a walking tour, the trunks were dispatched again: "Once more we trust our baggage to the care of the Post Office to be forwarded to Neuchâtel." Miss Jemima would not arrive in Neuchâtel for another five days, so how did she cope in the meantime?

Essentially they sent their Sunday best on ahead and survived on whatever they could carry in a knapsack, which was not a lot. An appendix at the back of my edition of the journal contains suggested items to pack for both genders, quoted here in full:

"Gentleman's outfit for a tour of fourteen days in Switzerland with portmanteau, from which to refit at the close:
Small bag containing:
        One clean shirt
        Pocket handkerchiefs
        Two clean collars
        One pair of stockings
        Toothbrush
        Writing materials
        Pocket comb
        with
Umbrella and Greatcoat
The above outfit obtained the prize medal of the Junior United Alpine Club.

Ladies' outfit for seven days
    Mackintosh in case
    Umbrella
    Small deal box ten inches long by eight (one used by the grocers for supplying Borwick's German Baking Powder answers admirably). The outside label can be taken off or not at discretion. This contained the minimum of articles for a lady's toilet.
N.B. Dirty linen can be washed at the hotels."

I know what you're thinking: they effectively wore the same clothes every day, all the while walking for hours in the heat and without a daily bath. By day three or so the smell must have been overpowering. But we should remember that our nostrils are used to a modern regime of daily showering, deodorising and changing clothes; if everyone smells, you probably no longer notice it after a while. Personal hygiene wasn't totally ignored, however. Murray gave explicit advice on what to do after walking all day:

> *Immediately on your arrival, after a day's walk, wash extensively with cold water and change your linen before sitting down to rest or eat. When you have only a knapsack you should keep one set of linen for the evening exclusively.*

From now on I will always carry a pair of evening underwear with me. It gives dressing for dinner a whole new meaning.

But what did they wear in those days? The short answer is quite a lot, especially the women. Think of *The King and I* or *Gone with the Wind* and you'll get a picture of how voluminous the dresses were, although travelling outfits were slightly less bulky than ball gowns. This was the era of the crinoline, a cage-like device of light steel hoops linked by cotton bands that sat under the dress to give it that typical bell or beehive shape. By the mid-1860s it was fashionable to have a flatter front with the back sloping out at 45 degrees; within 20 years that would shrink down to a straight skirt and a bustle at the back. Then there were several petticoats and the yards of fabric of the dress itself, plus long drawers underneath to save any blushes when the wind caught the dress. In contrast to this billowing mass, the upper body was tightly fitted with a chemise, corset, blouse and jacket, plus a shawl or overcoat; not forgetting all the accessories, such as hat, muff, gloves, parasol and boots. It would be hard enough to walk down the street in all that, let alone hike over glaciers. No wonder some women had ties attached to the bottom of the dress so they could hitch up the hem when walking. Incidentally, women generally made their own dresses (paper patterns were available by then) or had them made; ready-made clothing would not become popular for another two decades or so.

Menswear was less cumbersome, though just as formal. Jackets (single breasted) and trousers were typically of contrasting colours and different fabrics, but the "tourist's suit" was popular when travelling abroad. In *The Smell of the Continent*, the suit is described as a checked shooting jacket with matching knickerbockers, which makes it sound truly hideous. Suffice to say that a gentleman who wouldn't be seen dead in such an outfit in Britain was quite happy to sport this leisure wear while on holiday; the Victorian equivalent of rolled-up trousers and a knotted hanky.

As for what extras to pack, *The Excursionist* warns its readers to "Take care and not go without soap", while Murray advises that "No pedestrian should travel without a pocket-compass, nor without a leather drinking-cup", but decides that "a telescope is not of much use, as the view is seldom minute". The *Guide to Cook's Tours* has a helpful list for ladies: needles, thread and buttons, strong but light umbrella, writing materials, opera glasses, alpenstock, sticking plaster and salve, and a "little medicine chest for disordered interiors" – presumably not referring to untidy hotel rooms.

There was also the need for a phrasebook, such as *A Handbook of Travel-Talk*, published in 1858 for the English abroad. It's full of useful phrases for travelling – "May I not be allowed to carry ashore my carpet-bag?" or "Sit still! The train is moving" – eating out – "I do not like garlic or oil" or "Which is the strongest wine?" – and everyday situations – "What do you charge for the hire of a grand piano per month?" or "You must have some leeches put on. I must bleed you". All were translated into French, German and Italian.

After a change of clothes, we are warm and dry again, but the weather is neither. We've learnt our lesson from the morning's adventure, so indoor cultural pursuits are top of the afternoon's agenda and we make a beeline for the Alpine Museum, not for the old skis but for a picture of how Chamonix used to be. First we stop to admire the building itself, easily one of the largest in town.

Seven storeys high, with the last two tucked into the near-vertical grey roof giving it a very French look, the façade stretches across a whole block. Black iron balconies and shuttered windows punctuate the bright white walls at precisely regular intervals. It looks remarkably like a grand hotel, the kind that was built for well-heeled tourists of a bygone era. And that's exactly what it was: the Chamonix Palace Hotel. It opened 50 years after Miss Jemima's time, in 1914, but it was merely the latest in a long line of big hotels in Chamonix. From the 1770s onwards, what had been a quiet mountain village was transformed over the decades into the tourist capital of the Alps:

> [Chamonix] is now a large and important community, which displays almost the bustle of an English watering-place in what was once the most retired of Alpine valleys. With the exception, however, of the enormous hotels which appear to have been dropped there, the village, as most other Swiss and Savoy villages, retains its pristine appearance.

Perhaps appreciation is only a matter of time. What was then seen as too new and too large, spoiling the character of a village, is now almost treasured as part of local history; maybe in 150 years, our glass-and-concrete constructions will also be regarded with affection. Nevertheless, inside the museum the old prints and engravings from the 1860s make it abundantly clear how much those "new" hotels stuck out like sore thumbs or, more correctly, eyesores. They were huge and often detached from the rest of village life. No wonder they had grandiose names invoking images of size and superiority.

The Palace wasn't the only hotel that didn't survive in its intended form (it was converted into apartments above the museum). The Hotel Royal once hosted princes and emperors, as befits its name, as well as Thomas Cook himself during that first tour. It is now a casino. And the imposing Hôtel de Ville, or town hall, actually once was a real hotel. Others simply disappeared, replaced by one of the countless modern creations, although Chamonix seems to have avoided the worst excesses of development in architectural terms, at least, with many fine examples of old buildings still around. They might be disfigured by the tourist trappings that dominate the town – the pedestrianised centre feels like one endless shop-bar-restaurant-café, with little sign of real life or business that isn't tourist related – but it could be much worse. This isn't Benidorm in the Alps, despite (or perhaps because of) a long history of tourism.

The Hotel Royal, where Thomas Cook stayed, is now a casino, but Mont Blanc and the dark pinnacles of Aiguille de Midi have stayed the same

Chamonix was discovered in 1741 by two young Englishmen on a jaunt around the Alps. Of course it had long been there, thanks to a Benedictine convent, so its "discovery" was in a similar vein to that of America by Columbus. The two gentlemen in question were William Wyndham and Richard Pocock, and it was their reports to the Royal Society of mighty glaciers and mountains that made this Alpine valley the must-see of any Grand Tour.

Shelley, who seemed to get around an awful lot, waxed lyrical about the place, and by 1865 the village was welcoming 12,000 visitors a year, a huge number considering the time and effort involved in reaching Chamonix. The turn of the century saw winter sports blossom, fuelling the construction of more hotels and attractions, culminating in the first ever Winter Olympic Games in 1924. And in all that time, one thing hasn't changed much: the headache of accommodation in high season. Look at these two guidebook entries:

*In August and September the inns are frequently so full
that travellers arriving late at night have the greatest difficulty in obtaining accommodation.*

*One of the biggest headaches in Chamonix is finding
a bed, especially if, as a walker or climber, you're having to sit out bad weather while waiting to get into the
hills. All hotels need booking in advance and tend to be
expensive.*

The first is from my trusty Murray Handbook, but isn't so different
from the second, taken from the *Rough Guide to France,* published
150 years later. What has changed is that there are now two high
seasons, as in any Alpine resort: summer for walkers and winter
for skiers.

Our visit to the Alpine Museum makes me appreciate two
things. The first is how comfortable tourism has become.
Looking at what yesterday's travellers had to put up with in the
way of heavy clothes and rickety carriages, uncomfortable shoes
and simple skies makes me thankful to be a twenty-first-century
tourist. A train tour of the Alps may no longer be the cutting edge
of travel, but at least you won't get blisters or heatstroke along the
way. You only have to see black-and-white photos of ladies clam-
bering over glaciers and up ladders in full-length skirts and heavy
coats to understand that we take a lot for granted. Perhaps that's
why those pictures are popular postcards in every Chamonix souvenir shop.

Secondly, I realise how shockingly ignorant I am about Savoy,
the French province that encompasses Chamonix and Mont Blanc.
To me it means green cabbages and posh hotels, neither of which
brings snowy mountains to mind. But the lovely old maps, with their
sepia tones and ragged edges, make it look so much more intriguing, somewhere worth exploring historically if not geographically.

Savoy was one of those royal states that inhabited the European
map for centuries and then simply disappeared, swallowed up by

larger, stronger neighbours. It wasn't the only duchy or kingdom to vanish, but it had one of the more ignominious exits: traded away in a secret deal. At its height Savoy stretched from Lake Geneva down to the Mediterranean and its rulers married their way into other royal houses. The reason there's a Savoy Hotel in central London is because when Eleanor of Provence married Henry III, she brought her pack of Savoyards with her – including her uncle Peter. In 1263 he built the Savoy Palace (which later burned down during the Peasants' Revolt) before heading back to Savoy to become its Count. However, being sandwiched between France and the Austrian Empire wasn't so great, and repeated French invasions meant that Savoy's independence was fairly fluid. It was one such defeat by France in 1536 that led to the Bernese annexing Vaud and Geneva gaining independence. Realising that their capital, Chambéry, was far too close to the enemy, the Savoyards made Turin their new capital, and that changed everything.

With an HQ behind the protective wall of mountains, Savoy could survive continued French attacks, but with the centre of gravity now in Piedmont, the French-speaking parts of the realm lost their importance. Life became more Italian, which didn't just mean a healthier diet but also a new outlook. In 1720, Savoy-Piedmont gained the island of Sardinia, which meant that the Duke of Savoy was now also King of Sardinia. Napoleon tried to spoil the party by conquering everything except the island itself, but after his defeat the House of Savoy (and Sardinia) was stronger than ever and had its eyes on a bigger prize.

Italy in the 1850s was even more chaotic than it is today, not least because there was no country to speak of. The King of Sardinia, Victor Emmanuel II, realised that to unite Italy under Savoy/Sardinian rule he would need help kicking out the Austrians. So he made a secret pact with Napoleon III of France: he would get Savoy and Nice in return for giving them troops to fight Austria. No one thought to ask the people. The war didn't last long and in the peace treaty (signed in Zurich in November 1859) Austria ceded Lombardy to the French, who then gave it to Sardinia in exchange for Nice and Savoy. To make things look legal, the Treaty of Turin (24 March 1860) made the French annexation formal and a referendum a month later added the seal of popular approval. An astonishing 99.8 per cent of Savoy said yes to joining France, possibly because the vote was rigged or maybe because there were no alternatives: staying part of Sardinia, independence or joining Switzerland (as some in northern Savoy wanted) were not on offer.

And that was the end of Savoy. Its fate was to instigate the unification of Italy (the hero of that campaign, Garibaldi, was born in Nice), only to end up being swallowed by France. But at least it survived in one form, two French *départements*, which is more than can be said for its royal house. The former duke, Victor Emmanuel II, duly became the first king of Italy in March 1861, with a capital in Turin, but then it was pretty much all downhill. After centuries of ruling Savoy, the royal family lasted only 85 years in Italy and the fourth king, Umberto II, abdicated in 1946. They might have been better off staying where they were; who knows, Savoy could have survived as a small independent duchy, a mountainous Luxembourg, if you will.

Thankfully, one good thing came out of this tale of cabbages and kings. During the short Austro-Sardinian War, the two sides clashed on 24 June 1859 at Solferino in Lombardy, and Henry Dunant was there to witness the horrific aftermath. He went back to Geneva a changed man. Perhaps, in a roundabout way, the Red Cross is Savoy's legacy to the world. In the giant game of political chess that was nineteenth-century Europe, Savoy was a pawn sacrificed by its owner for bigger gains. Without that move, there might have been no war, no Solferino and no Damascene moment for Monsieur Dunant.

That potted history finally makes it clear to me why the Murray guidebook has the long-winded title of *A Handbook for Travellers in Switzerland, and the Alps of Savoy and Piedmont*. When the book was written, Savoy and Piedmont were not part of France and Italy respectively, but were (together with Sardinia) a separate country – one that was a natural extension to a Swiss tour. By the time the guide was published the borders had changed, so that Thomas Cook's first tourists actually visited only two countries: France (including Chamonix) and Switzerland.

f it had carried on raining for another day, we would have said an early goodbye to France and headed for the hills of Switzerland, in the hope that the weather would improve. Another wet day in Chamonix was too much to contemplate. Instead, we wake up to sunshine and now have the problem of deciding what to see in our one fine day. There isn't enough time for everything (we have to be over the border by this evening), so we plump for the two main sights, the two reasons Thomas Cook brought his group here: Mont Blanc and the Mer de Glace. Snow and ice here we come!

It turns out that the rumours were true: you can see Mont Blanc from the centre of Chamonix. It really was there all along, behind the banks of cloud and sheets of rain. And it is white, sparklingly white against a deep blue sky. However, it's also very round, more dome than peak, so it doesn't look like it could be western Europe's highest mountain at all. It's just a lump that's marginally higher than its neighbours, and most probably would have been ignored if it hadn't been the tallest one around. That accident of nature meant that Mont Blanc was top of the list of Mountains To Be Conquered, which it duly was on 8 August 1786 by two Frenchmen, Jacques Balmat and Michel Gabriel Paccard. The closest we will get today is Aiguille du Midi, an eagle's nest of a pinnacle reached by cable car – on a very long cable.

Of course, we aren't the only ones desperate to get out and up now the sun has graced us with its presence. After days of being cooped up, everyone else has exactly the same idea, so although we arrive at the cable-car station in good time, there's already a lengthy queue. It's probably like that every day in fine weather, with a steady flood of tourists desperate to experience the ride up. And it's quite a ride, an ear-popping, jaw-dropping 20 minutes inside a giant glass box that holds 72 people at a time.

Our cable car has half of Japan in it, including a giggly clutch of ladies swaddled in layers of fleeces and hats. Each time the car lurches over a pylon, they all fling their arms in the air and whoop with delight, as if we're on a theme-park ride. Not everyone finds it amusing. At the halfway point we deboard one car and reboard another that's waiting to take us up to 3842m above sea level (and more than 2700m above Chamonix). The second section has no pylons, just one long cable, so the whoopers are temporarily silenced. Instead, we all concentrate on the ever more dramatic views, up to Mont Blanc, across to the glacier and down to Chamonix, which already looks like a model village on the valley floor.

The cable car glides into its upper station and we are disgorged, light-headed with excitement and altitude, only to find that there's still one stage before we get to the top. The Aiguille (which means "needle" in French) is divided into two columns of rock linked by a metal bridge, with the cable-car station, plus the café and shop, on the lower North Column, looking down on Chamonix. To reach the very top, and so the panorama terrace, it's necessary to cross the bridge and take a lift up the last 65m. No one is rushing to step out onto the icy metal. After such a quick ascent, the change in the air is a shock – not so much raspingly thin but achingly crisp. Every breath seems to reach the farthest corners of my lungs, so my alveoli all crackle with the cold. They've never known anything like it.

My mother isn't enjoying the altitude so instead opts to take in the view from the café over a hot chocolate, but I slither across the bridge, glad to have a warm coat and thick gloves. The metal handrails would probably freeze a layer of skin off if you touched them with bare hands. Long stiletto icicles hang from every ledge and form a dramatic pelmet across the doorway to the Central Column. Inside it isn't much warmer, but at least there's no wind. I squeeze into the lift for the final spurt, feeling like a giant as I'm the only passenger over about 1.6m tall. I begin to wish that my Japanese extended beyond *konichiwa* and *arigato*.

The 360-degree views from the top can for once be truthfully described as breathtaking. It's a winter wonderland on a summer's day: peak after peak after peak in every direction, all snow clad in the squintingly bright sunshine (even with sunglasses). From this angle and (shorter) distance, Mont Blanc looks more imposing, though still not as majestic as the Matterhorn, which is visible to the southeast. But both are overwhelmed by the vast proportions of the landscape as a whole. Standing on top of a pillar of granite, which is actually nothing more than a rocky needle in a mountainous haystack, I feel very insignificant.

Immediately beneath us the snowy slopes are dotted with tiny black figures in groups of three and four, following thin grey lines in the pristine white expanse. This hardy few are using the good weather to achieve their dreams of scaling Mont Blanc. Rather like Mark Twain, who "climbed" the mountain from Chamonix via a telescope, I'm content to admire it from afar, albeit closer than Miss Jemima ever got. Modern technology (this cable car opened in 1955) means that visitors are now able to do and see things of which the Victorians could only dream: sailing up into the sky to look down on the world below, all without breaking into a sweat. The splendour of being on top of the Aiguille will stay with me for ages, but it felt a bit too easy, as if we were not respecting the mountains themselves. Then again, I was never going to climb up, so it was either this or the telescope. And, following Murray's advice, I hadn't packed mine.

After Balmat and Paccard, there have been many others brave, or foolish, enough to tackle Mont Blanc. The first woman to stand on the summit was a local servant, Marie Paradis, in 1808, although some say she was carried part of the way by the men in her group, including Jacques Balmat. A rival claim for being the first woman on top came 30 years later, in the shape of Henriette d'Angeville, a 44-year-old French aristocrat who lived in Geneva but whose grandfather had been guillotined during the French Revolution. She most definitely was not carried up, as her guides already had their hands full. Her 1838 ascent is famous for its excess: six guides and six porters had to carry two legs of mutton, two loins of veal, 24 chickens (cooked not live), 18 bottles of fine wine (plus one small barrel of plonk for the porters), a bottle of cognac and 3kg of chocolate. Henrietta wore a special outfit of pantaloons and petticoats to overcome the disadvantages of climbing in heavy dresses with long hems, but even that weighed over 7kg (including the black-feather boa). She became known as "la fiancée de Mont Blanc" and was still trotting up mountains at the age of 69.

It took another 17 years for anyone to reach the summit without a guide, let alone six, but in August 1855 Charles Hudson, a village vicar from Yorkshire, did exactly that. And that was barely two weeks after he had been one of the party to conquer Switzerland's highest mountain for the first time. At 4634m high, Dufourspitze (or Monte Rosa in Italian) was obviously used as a practice run for the main event; quite some warm-up. Hudson was one of the stars of the Golden Age of Alpinism, when British mountaineers were climbing peaks almost as fast as their compatriots were conquering countries. It all came to a tragic end on the Matterhorn ten years later.

Switzerland's most famous mountain had been one of the last great Alpine peaks to be tamed when, on 14 July 1865, Reverend Hudson and six other men stood on the pointy peak for the first time. Four of them would die during the descent from the summit when a safety rope snapped, dragging the helpless men over a cliff. The calamity was front-page news in Britain, where the continuing exploits of the nation's fearless mountaineers had long been celebrated. Hudson fell to his death along with Chamonix-born guide Michel Croz, fellow climber Douglas Hadow and Lord Frederick Douglas, brother of the Marquess of Queensberry and uncle to Lord Alfred (Oscar Wilde's boyfriend). One of the survivors, renowned mountaineer Edward Whymper, endured the inquests and rumours and went on to write a bestseller about his feats, *Scrambles amongst the Alps*. One of the mountains he scaled in the Canadian Rockies is named after him, as is a street in Chamonix, the town where he died (in 1911) and is buried. Hudson's remains lie beneath the communion table in Zermatt's English church, which opened five years after the tragedy; a suitably fitting last resting place for an Anglican vicar.

As for the fastest ascent of Mont Blanc, that was achieved in July 1990 by a Swiss climber, Pierre-André Gobet, who recorded an amazing time of 5 hours, 10 minutes and 14 seconds – and that's for the round trip from Chamonix. He ran up to the top in 3 hours 38 minutes and then sprinted back down in 1 hour 32 minutes. The extra 14 seconds was probably how long he spent on the summit.

These days about 20,000 people a year follow in the footsteps of those past climbers, though most take a little more time than M. Gobet. You can book five- or six-day guided packages, which include three days of acclimatisation and practice on nearby peaks. Apparently, the climb itself isn't technically one of the hardest. The Mountain Spirit Guide website summarises it thus: "If you ask the 'climber' – the ascent is a walk, but if you ask the 'walker' – the ascent is a climb." And if you ask a normal person, it's a step too far.

We shouldn't forget that the real height of Mont Blanc changes, depending on the depth of the snow-and-ice cap that crowns the peak. Officially the mountain is always 4810m above sea level, but the actual summit (that is, the highest point of rock) is only 4792m. Those extra few metres probably make all the difference when you're climbing up.

Our descent into the valley feels faster than the upward journey, although of course it isn't. The two cable cars operate in tandem, one going up as the other comes down. Watching the other car glide past as if hanging by a thread, albeit a reassuringly stout metal one, I'm sure I'm not the only one thinking that our little box is travelling just as precariously. And I'm not at all certain Miss Jemima would even have set foot in such a terrifying contraption. Usually I love cable-car rides – Switzerland has plenty of them – but on this one my mouth is dry, my palms wet. I take my mind off the fact that we're dangling hundreds of metres above the ground and tune into the English voices among the background chatter: a party of male climbers comparing achievements, the mountain equivalent of a pissing contest. It's a relief to get back on *terra firma*.

After a couple of hours up above, the air feels oddly heavier and the sun so much warmer down in the valley, and we aren't the only ones stripping off outer layers as we walk beside the muddy Arve. What was very necessary up there now feels like it's cooking us alive, baking us in our jackets. By the time we reach the train station, I'm down to a T-shirt. It couldn't be more different from yesterday.

No wet walk in the woods for us today; we're going to see a glacier. Since we're having to compress our whole Chamonix experience into one day, we no longer have time to walk up, as Miss Jemima did. Luckily, there's a rack railway to take us up to Montenvers (or Montanvert, as English visitors wrote it in the nineteenth century), at 1913m above sea level and overlooking France's largest glacier. Next stop Mer de Glace, the Sea of Ice.

For the Junior United Alpine Club, the hike up to see the glacier was not only their first Alpine ascent, but also the first real natural highlight of their tour. In their excitement they were up very early, "cheerfully" paid well over the odds for their alpenstocks (large walking sticks) and engaged a guide

> "from among the groups that stood around the hotels, each man awaiting his turn, a rule which is rigorously enforced by the authorities. Our guide bore the celebrated name of Balmat, and probably owed his position to the name rather than for any shining merits of his own."

The Chamonix Guides' Company was founded in 1821, making it the oldest company of mountain guides in the world. It is still going strong with 240 members, two of whom bear the surname Balmat.

The guidebooks of the day had very clear advice on footwear for hiking: "The shoes or half-boots ought to be double-soled, provided with hobnails ... and without iron heels, which are dangerous, and liable to slip in walking over rocks; three rows of nails are better, and Swiss nails are better than English, which are often too hard and slippery." They don't sound too comfy to me, but they helped our hikers toil up the zigzag paths, though Miss Jemima got a little distracted by the views, and also by the unexpected profusion of Alpine flowers:

> "If, like us, you had the impression that those Alpine mountains were sterile and bare, you will find it erroneous. For there, extending to a height of 6,000 feet, through a partial forest of firs, rise storey after storey of verdure, their banks blossomed over with deep rose Alpine rhododendrons. We gather its abundance, deck our hats with its branching sprays, and pluck bouquets from

Hiking over the Mer de Glace was a must for every Victorian visitor

either side of our path which here and there is literally ribboned
with a border of variegated flowers."

The local fauna was as delightful to the visitors as the flora, with
one of the group chasing after and catching a goat so he could milk
it for all of them to taste. That's not exactly a normal habit for tourists, either then or now. And then there were the other travellers:
"A German gentleman of comfortable dimensions, with his Frau of
ditto, passed us on mules." It certainly wasn't a dull hike up.

Our own journey up is much shorter thanks to Swiss engineers.
They came and built the rack railway in 1907, and there's still one
of the old steam trains on display, built in Winterthur and in use
until the line was electrified in 1953. Our modern one is a sweet
little train, painted bright red and with wooden seats that must
win an award for their lack of comfort. At least the windows open,
unlike so many trains these days where passengers are sealed
into carriages. Chugging up the hill and curling round through

pine-scented forests, we get fleeting glimpses of the valley below, receding further and further with every bend. From up here it's easy to see how developed Chamonix has become: a wide ribbon of semi-urbanisation all along the banks of the Arve, with chalets creeping up almost every slope.

The trip only takes 25 minutes (half the time of the inaugural journey in 1908) and is not nearly as busy as the Aiguille du Midi, but it's much, much louder. A raucous gaggle of Italians fills most of the carriage, all of them talking at the same time, none of them listening. It reminds me of my childhood meals in Italian restaurants. Two voices rise above the others, those of two older men who are doing what older Italian men love to do: holding court and loudly declaring their views on anything and everything, except the passing countryside, which is ignored completely. Little do they know that my mother understands every word.

At Montenvers it's immediately clear that the journey time isn't the only thing that has changed dramatically in 150 years. We all pile out of the train and head straight for the edge, eager to be amazed by nature at its most spectacular. According to Murray:

> The view of this enormous sea of ice is one of the most striking scenes of wonder, but its great extent, from the vast size of every object about it, is not appreciated at first.

Not any more. The grandeur of the setting is still there, with its towering backdrop of spiky mountains, but the ice is missing. What was once a sea of ice is now a river of rubble. A wide, S-shaped swathe of grey grinds its way between the sheer slopes carved out by the glacier, with a tide mark showing how high the ice once was. Towards the head of the deep gorge, the grey slowly gives way to white, with more ice than rock making up the surface of the glacier, but it's a distant taste of past glory. Even so, the scale of the whole scene is still impressive, particularly once you spot the tiny black dots moving across the ridges in the ice: people, small enough to make Lilliputians look like giants.

The reduction in drama feels like discovering that the Grand Canyon is the size of Cheddar Gorge. This was once a giant glacier that filled the whole U-shaped scene, with a tongue that stuck out so far beyond the mouth of the valley that it could easily be seen from Chamonix. The surface used to be almost level with the train station, its glacial tendrils lapping against the rocks beneath our feet. No wonder people came from Britain and beyond just to see the pinnacles of ice, a frozen forest that has long since melted away.

Luckily, Miss Jemima's words still conjure up something of its unique beauty, with her glacial version of finding figures in wispy clouds or flickering flames:

> "One writer compares it to a stream of ice-witches, hob-goblins and their children, and bag and baggage on their journey to the lowest pit, and to monks without heads, and giants. We traced the serrated spine of some antediluvian monster urging a kilted Highlander to charge on some enemy below. There, too, sat Sir Cresswell Cresswell, with wigged counsellors in a crowded court of blanched plaintiff and defendants. There were also hooded friars, a Madonna and Child, and ghostly figures such as would pass through Bunyan's brain when he peopled the Valley of the Shadow of Death. Spires, pyramids, sphinxes, obelisks and every design in monumental marble might find a model in that sea of rugged ice."

I leave my mother to inspect the photos on display in the old stone hotel and jump into a tiny cable car that starts this next journey.

The red gondola lift was originally built in 1960 to take people directly to the Mer de Glace. Now it's merely a quicker way to begin a much deeper descent, as the glacier has long since retreated from its position in the 1960s, let alone the 1860s. The rest of the way is on foot, and walking down the zigzagging staircases towards the wall of ice is a sombre experience. Small wooden plaques nailed into the cliff at various intervals mark the spot where the glacier was in that year: a procession of gravestones charting the slow

In the 1860s the Mer de Glace still had its famous
forest of pinnacles

death of a mighty beast. The first marker, some way below the gondola station, is dated 1980, and it's hard to believe that in a few
decades the glacier has shrunk so much.

The more I descend, the greater the distance between the
plaques: the 1990 level is another 53 steps lower, then 103 more
stairs down to 2003, and still 155 more to today. How long until
nothing remains? The staircases can barely keep up with the
shrinkage. What started as wide concrete steps cemented into the
rock become narrow metal ones that can more easily be extended
and moved as the ice retreats.

At the final platform is a hut beside a gate, which leads out to
the rocks and then up onto the glacier. A notice says that it is only
for experienced and properly equipped walkers, and I am neither.
As tempting as it is to follow in Miss Jemima's footsteps (albeit at
a few hundred metres lower down), I know it wouldn't be long
before someone came after me, either to stop me going any further
or to rescue me after going too far.

Instead, I walk across a long gangplank connecting the last step with a hole in the grubby ice, gateway to the latest cave inside the glacier wall (the first was carved out in 1946). A few metres to the left is the previous one, now disused and out of reach. Even as it shrinks as a whole, the glacier is still edging ever onwards as it always has done. Today it moves at 1cm per hour, or half the rate of 1890. The loss of ice has reduced the pressure from behind and above, and so also the speed (it was partly that speed that produced the eerie pinnacles when the ice was forced up and over rocky obstructions). I try not to think about it moving at all as I step onto the ice. As for the three people crushed to death in 1797 while in one of the glacier's natural ice caves, they are not on my mind in the slightest.

Outside, the ice is grey, covered in dirt and moraine carved off and carried along by the glacier. Inside, it's another world. Glistening walls of bluish white, polished smooth by hundreds of passing hands but still with intriguing undulations and depressions. Just beneath the surface thousands of tiny bubbles lie trapped inside the ice. It really is like standing inside a river that froze instantly, its powerful motion trapped for ever. Even more incredible is its age: this ice I am caressing was formed at roughly the same time as Napoleon was fighting his wars. It's over 200 years old but as pristine as ever. It is a magical moment – or at least would be if I were somewhere else. As it is, I'm trapped inside a nightmare of new-age music, polar-bear carvings, official photo ops and coloured lighting, not forgetting the cacophony of voices: this is the Tunnel of Babel. There are also constant drips, most of which seem to know exactly when I'm passing beneath them so that every few metres is marked by an icy dribble down my neck. The ones that do manage to miss me splat onto the soggy carpet, there to stop us slipping, so we all squelch rather than slide our way round. I can't wait to get outside again.

In the mid-nineteenth century it was all very different. Most tourists came not to admire the glacier from above or below, but to walk across it. They had no training and no equipment, but no problem. Never mind that there were countless bottomless crevasses waiting to swallow anyone who missed their step, or that the sartorial rigours of the nineteenth century weren't exactly suited to scrambling across ladders and over boulders of ice (at least as far as the ladies were concerned). They put on their hats, picked up their sticks and went for a jolly hike across to the other side, Miss Jemima included:

> "We were continually surprised to find that the proverbial dangers of Alpine travel to be, when in the beaten track, mere creatures of fancy, yet the descent into the bed of the glacier from the Montanvert at first tried somewhat the nerves of some of the lady members as yet unaccustomed to dizzy heights, when the strong arm of our new member was most acceptable! How strange, how intensely incongruous it felt on that hot summer's day, to be crunching ice under our feet, and to be looking down yawning crevasses that showed eighty or a hundred feet of their blue and crystal-lined jaws. We step carefully in the track chipped out by the guide as we intersect the numerous pitfalls at our feet, spending about half an hour on its slippery surface."

Slippery indeed. Even with hobnail boots on, it must have been a daunting hike across the frozen ridges between the ravines, knowing that at any moment you could slip on the ice and disappear into a void. While your crinoline cage might have broken your fall, the sheer weight of clothing might equally have propelled you ever downwards. The Cook group did at least hire a guide, whose strong arm proved useful, but possibly only because there were ladies present. The Murray Handbook advises women about undertaking the trip, which "in ordinary seasons presents no danger. Ladies now very frequently cross, and the expedition is well worth taking, though those who are timid and nervous ought not to be urged to it. Each lady will require a guide to assist, and the guides generally make an extra demand for so doing."

As if crossing the glacier wasn't enough, the group then had to negotiate the mauvais pas (literally "bad step") in the rain:

"We crawled along its slippery ledge, our only safeguard from slipping down 400 feet and alighting on the rocky moraine below being a hand-rail formed of a rope, fastened to the rock by iron holdfasts."

This precipitous route wasn't exactly a relaxing stroll in the park, but it was the most direct back to Chamonix. It was either that or return across the ice, though sliding along the top of deep crevasses seems preferable to slipping down the wet rock of a cliff face. I was happy just to clamber back up from the glacier without letting the altitude go to my head. Miss Jemima was certainly a gutsy lady.

A few hours later we're on board another train, a little larger and a lot whiter than the one to Montenvers. As we clatter up the narrowing Arve valley towards the Swiss border, we are treated to views of more rivers of ice spilling out from between sheer-sided cliffs. Streams tumble down from the tips of the ice fields, as if the glaciers are crying themselves to death. Come back in a few decades and even these distant peeks of ice may have become a memory.

Perhaps it's no surprise that Chamonix is now officially called Chamonix-Mont-Blanc. It's as if the town realised it needed to remind everyone why to keep on coming. The Victorians flocked in their thousands for the Mer de Glace, a sight that is melting away as quickly as an ice cream in Baghdad. So Chamonix has reinvented itself as an adventure playground, in summer and winter alike, using the mountains as its trump card.

Chamonix was already a prime destination when Thomas Cook brought his first customers here that summer. For them, it was one of the undoubted highlights; for the villagers they were most likely nothing new, another bunch of Brits eager to do mad things like walk across glaciers for fun. But it was a taste of things to come. Whereas previous visitors had arrived in ones and twos, groups were the new way to travel. And groups needed more hotels, bigger restaurants, better connections – even in somewhere that was already quite advanced in terms of tourist development. And Chamonix just carried on developing.

Going down via the mauvais pas was a hair-raising hike

Today there are 82,000 tourist beds (compared to a resident population of 10,000 people), although only about 5000 of those are in hotels; the rest are in chalets, holiday apartments and second homes. In contrast to the 1860s, the winter season is now busier than summer: of the 4.5 million overnight stays in Chamonix every year, well over half are in the winter months. Skiing is more popular than hiking. Foreigners make up around half of the guests, with the UK still dominating the annual invasion; in summer 35 per cent of foreign guests are British, whereas second-placed Japan manages only 9 per cent.

Sightseeing in the mountains has become both more and less impressive at the same time: we can experience so much more but with much less effort. We expect to be able to go higher, faster, further than ever before and we no longer take the time to appreciate the simpler things. Why just admire the beauty of a mountain when you can heli-ski off the summit? Maybe that's what yesterday's travellers can teach us. Miss Jemima's delight at the abundance of

Alpine flowers is almost as great as her wonder at seeing the profusion of icy stalagmites.

In our collective rush to see the sights, we often overlook what is in front of our noses; or by trying too hard to avoid the crowds, we miss something truly worth seeing. Of course, I am sometimes as guilty of that as anyone.

My mother and I wanted to do as much as possible on one day, giving in to that subconscious fear of missing out. We could have walked up to Montenvers, appreciating the flowers in situ (Alpine flora is not for picking these days) and missed out on the Aiguille de Midi. But there's always that niggle at the back of your mind, the dread that most travellers face: a snide comment on your return, complete with raised eyebrows and pursed lips. Not forgetting that some people go out of their way to avoid the mustsees in the mistaken belief that it makes them "real" travellers. Peer pressure and snobbery are as prevalent in travel as in any other part of life.

The funny thing is that Miss Jemima was actually doing exactly the same, just at a slower speed. That first tour crammed in as much as humanly possible, with early starts and long days, so that its participants could go home with their heads held as high as the mountains they had seen. For Miss Jemima and her companions this was all completely new and impossibly exciting, so of course they wanted to see everything, particularly what were then called the "lions", the must-see list. At one point, as the group walked up out of the Arve valley, she commented on exactly that. The travellers couldn't resist constantly looking back at the view, as if they regretted having had so little time in Chamonix:

> "When the labour of reaching this celebrated valley is taken into account it is much better to devote a longer time to its wonders. Indeed, to gain the fullest and most permanent satisfaction from the magnificence of national scenery, time is an essential element in order that every impression may be deepened, and rendered permanent possessions for life."

This is one of the few moments when she acknowledges the speed of their tour, which although slow by our standards was practically breakneck for that period. It was these package pioneers who set the agenda for every tour that came afterwards, even when the pace got faster and faster, a bit like the factory conveyor belt scene in *Modern Times*. The improvements in transport didn't necessarily mean you spent more time in each place, it meant you saw more places in the same time. It wouldn't be long before Cook's customers were being loudly disparaged by other travellers, who moaned that they were rushing around and ruining the very things they had come to see. The same could be said today of Lonely Planet readers or TripAdvisor followers.

Whether it's seen from a passing tour bus or admired for days up close, Mont Blanc is the same as it has always been – big and white – but our relationship with it is not. We have climbed up it (and that "we" does not include me) and skied down it, tunnelled under it and flown over it. We've even moved our borders around it: the peak used to be totally within the Kingdom of Savoy-Piedmont-Sardinia, but since 1860 it's been shared by France and Italy, where it is known rather unsurprisingly as Monte Bianco.

Thomas Cook unwrapped the Alps with his package tours, making them reachable for people with limited time and money. In doing so, he changed the way we interact with the mountains. For many, they are now just another holiday stop, another photo for the digital album, another tick off the wish list. But even if their romantic mystique has diminished, their natural splendour has not. The Alps remain as thrilling and dazzling as ever, no matter why or how people come to admire them.

Patients would sit for up to ten hours a day in Leukerbad's hot baths

FOUR

IN HOT WATER

There are many mineral springs in Switzerland, much resorted to by the Swiss themselves and by foreigners, but treated with utter neglect by the English, not one in a thousand of whom ever goes through a course of one of these baths.

—*Murray Handbook*

Almost any route into Switzerland is a scenic one. Well, perhaps not the motorway from Germany into Basel, although that has been improved in the last few years. But enter the country from most other directions and you are spoiled by an unparalleled view of lakes and/or mountains that makes you want to see more. Some routes have become famous in their own right, such as the Great St Bernard Pass, with its barrel-toting dogs and hospitable monks. Others have slowly become less significant, bypassed by shorter, faster ways around (or under) the mountains; for example the one between Chamonix and Martigny. Here there's no motorway or huge tunnel, just an ordinary road and a rack railway. It's a journey that still takes time, one that encourages you to enjoy the views at a slower pace, and for that the Mont-Blanc Express is perfect. Although it does indeed go to the foot of that mountain, it's express in name only; and as we are travelling in the opposite direction, for us this really is the slow train to Switzerland.

By the time we set off it's late afternoon, a full 12 hours behind Miss Jemima. She had been "aroused at four a.m. by the tinkling of bells of a herd of cattle as they passed through the village", with a long day ahead. No train or carriage for her, as neither road nor railway had been built. Instead there were four mules for nine people, so each could ride and walk alternately, along with the same guide as the day before. A 5am start for the 25-mile journey over the Forclaz Pass was an impressive achievement. The walk up to Montenvers had been but an appetiser for the hike over the border into Switzerland, a hike that she liked:

> "More than one sawmill, the only sign of machinery by the way, was worked by an active stream that flowed from the cascade and which, as we advanced, dashed over precipices and giant boulders that have been hurled from the mountain heights above. The margin of the path edges over a ravine, and passes under a rock-hewn tunnel overhanging a dark gorge, many many hundreds of feet below."

This is a wild part of the Alps, one where you half expect to come across a witch's cottage tucked away in the "dark mountain forests",

Crossing over the Alps: on horse or on foot were the only options in Miss Jemima's time

or feel the gaze of a wolf's eyes on your neck. Even on the sunniest day, these dense tracts of pine trees are filled with foreboding as they crowd right down to the path's edge. But, despite the sporadic deep shadows, walking up was hard work on a hot day. After toiling up past the forbidding Tête Noire, the travellers could at least rest in the shade at the top of the pass. And Miss Jemima's first comment about Switzerland? "These refreshments, laid out in tempting array at every little chalet we pass, form quite a considerable item in Swiss expenses." No change there, then.

It was downhill all the way after that, but seemingly just as bad, if not worse, for their feet:

"Each short turn but reveals a path of multiplied length instead of a direct incline, which path is rugged with loose stones which threaten to make mincemeat of our shoe soles. Even the mules are again discarded, for the fatigue of a descent on a mule exceeds the same taken on foot. In fact, one mule discarded its rider, though, to give the animal his due, there was some display of oriental grace in the camel-like kneel with which he preceded his non-chalant roll across the path."

No wonder that by the time they reached Martigny that evening, she noted that "with our hunger we felt our fatigue". Thomas Cook wrote that "none but the strong and agile should attempt many of the celebrated Passes", and the Junior United Alpine Club had passed that test. The ladies had on average walked 17 miles, the rest being on mule-back, while Mr James walked the entire 25 miles. Now I understand completely why they didn't carry any-thing more than a knapsack.

Their route across the Forclaz Pass is today taken by the mod-ern road as it switchbacks its way up and over the hills to Martigny. Many walkers prefer the path down the neighbouring valley, a deep gorge carved by the River Trient. That's also the way the train goes, diverging from the road shortly after the Swiss border at Le Châtelard. The line threads its way along the top of the ravine, past acres of untouched forest and through villages balanced precari-ously along the cliff edge. An untamed landscape of waterfalls and precipices is quite a contrast to the lights and crowds of Chamonix. This is surely one of Switzerland's great train rides, and I'm left wondering why it isn't better known.

Is it simply a case of being overshadowed by lines that are older, higher or steeper? This cog railway, between Martigny and Chamonix, opened on 20 August 1906, making it one of the later ones. By then the Swiss had long since conquered the likes of Pilatus, with the world's steepest rack railway, and were halfway up inside the Eiger to Jungfraujoch, Europe's highest train station. The high point of the Mont-Blanc Express is only 1224m, an alti-tude that leaves many other trains looking down on it. Or maybe it's the name. Until 1990, it was the plain old Martigny-Châtelard Line, which makes it sound like a suburban commuter train. The Swiss don't like to oversell things, but thank goodness someone somewhere sexed up the name of this train.

It was a 25-mile hike over the Tête Noire pass from France into Switzerland

A few months after passing through on the train, I can't resist coming back by car to drive over the Forclaz Pass. Naturally, it isn't so different. The valley's a bit wider, the slopes shallower than the Trient gorge, but there's the same abundance of greenery and feeling of being away from the real world. That is, until you reach the top and find a café full of bikers where Miss Jemima once sat in the shade eating wild strawberries. And I mustn't forget the souvenir shop: it might be a little off the tourist track, but you can buy a cow-shaped mug or a Swiss-flag tea cosy; made in China, sold all across Switzerland.

Far more interesting than a pink Swiss army knife (really, it was pink) are the information boards showing the local fortifications installed as part of Fortress Switzerland during the Second World War. From Forclaz down to Le Châtelard, a network of 15 concrete bunkers was built, complete with anti-tank guns and underground quarters. The road and railway were both mined, anti-aircraft guns sat on the hilltops and anti-tank barriers sprang up – all in case the Nazis decided to invade from the west through France. Rather surprisingly, the board says that the fortifications stayed until 1989, "in case of conflict between NATO and the Soviet Union".

Both routes, either over the Forclaz or down the Trient, lead to the same place: the Rhone valley. After trundling through rugged hills and steep-sided valleys, the wide expanse of cultivated fields and horizontal streets comes as quite a surprise, and a reminder of civilisation. Miss Jemima declares seeing the Rhone valley for the first time thus:

> "one of the views of the Alps ... like a mirage, unrolled before us. The furrowed mountain ridges are draped with pines and mantled with craggy stones, while in the background, crested with snow against a sky of azure blue, rise the Diablerets, the Strubel and the naked Gemini, presenting a scene of vast and solitary grandeur."

The view from the Forclaz road is maybe not as majestic as it once was, with Martigny sprawling out along the valley and the motorway leaving a scar as far as the eye can see. But the succession of fir-clad hills and jagged peaks still frames the picture perfectly, and the ruler-straight road has a certain Roman charm.

Martigny marked a crucial turning point on the original tour, and not just because it's where the River Rhone makes a near 90-degree turn and heads north to Lake Geneva. Up until now, this had been a Conducted Tour under the guidance of Thomas Cook himself. After almost a week of shepherding the ever-decreasing group around, he was leaving the last participants to their own devices and returning to London, via Lausanne and Neuchâtel. As he travelled back round Lake Geneva, he must have been contemplating what he'd achieved. The tour had been a leap into the unknown, almost a leap of faith given his dire need for success if he were to survive financially. After the losses incurred in Paris and Germany, and the loss of Scotland as a destination, Switzerland had to succeed.

I think he would have had cause to be rather satisfied with how the trip had gone, given he had originally stated he did "not intend to take more than 25–50 in the first Swiss party". Without much planning or preparation, he had succeeded in taking 130 or so tourists by boat and train to Paris, around 60 of whom carried on with him to Geneva by train; of those, half travelled on in carriages to Chamonix and then the final eight were hardy enough to walk to Martigny and were now ready and willing to venture off without him. Cook had certainly come a long way, in every sense, since taking teetotallers to Loughborough 22 years earlier, particularly given how many setbacks he had overcome in the process.

However, he wasn't the only one with tours to Switzerland. His arch rival was Henry Gaze, who offered a very similar service: in 1863 he was selling "Switzerland for 10 Guineas" tours, although Cook was disparaging about them. Comparing his tours with Gaze's, he wrote: "the provision is really luxurious in contrast with his third class travelling, hard walking and low hotel charges". In his book *Switzerland: How to See it for Ten Guineas*, Gaze is clear about how to save money – overnight train trips, staying on the top floors of hotels – and as he put it, "if you would enjoy it to the utmost, and would appreciate health and strength, economy and independence, ROUGH IT. I say emphatically ROUGH IT!" (his caps, not mine). Gaze was serious competition for many years, but after he retired the business went rapidly down into bankruptcy. Cook was left to rule the world.

However, when he left his first Swiss tour Cook probably had no idea of what it would lead to. He should have had some inkling, given the immediate and enthusiastic response to that first announcement, but after his previous calamities he might well have been cautiously pessimistic at best. His goal was clear: to bring Europe within reach of the masses: "My constant aim has been to render excursion and tourist travelling as cheap, as easy, as safe and as pleasant as circumstances would allow." That was a noble aim, but would it pay off? The answer lay not only with him but with seven others. With Cook gone, the Junior United Alpine Club was now all that remained of the original Conducted Tour.

This group were going to set off across Switzerland together, but first they stopped in Martigny for two hours of rest and rejuvenation. For our part, my mother and I decide to carry on towards our final destination that day, Sion. The sun, which we were so overjoyed to see that morning, is beginning to desert us once again. After a day zooming up and down mountains, I can think of nothing better than finding a bed for the night and something to eat, preferably in that order, given that it's already late enough for the shops to be closing.

The train ride from Martigny along the Rhone to Sion only lasts 14 minutes, but is significant as it was the first train wholly within Switzerland taken by our original tourists. And it would be the last for some time. Back in 1863, when the line to Sion was itself only three years old, the Swiss train network did not yet extend into the mountains, so for the next ten days the visitors walked, rode, took carriages and boarded boats around the country. That's very different from how today's tourists experience Switzerland, most of whom travel by train, helping to make the Swiss network one of the most used in the world. It's a remarkable turnaround for a country that arrived very late to the idea of a national railway system.

In 1850 Switzerland was still recovering from the Sonderbund War and, despite the new federal constitution, the cantons were often at loggerheads over a whole range of issues. Building the railways with any sense of national coordination was particularly problematic, as nearly every line had to cross one or more cantonal borders, and getting everyone to agree on the route and costs was no easy feat. The Murray Handbook explained:

The real difficulty consisted in the extraordinary and incredible jealousies between not only the different cantons, but the different communities or parishes, and the legal difficulties in obtaining the land.

There was also no national rail company – the Swiss Federal Railways, or SBB, was not created until 1902 – and the federal government was only two years old, so it was not yet that strong.

The government did make one crucial decision, however, and commissioned an independent report on the future of the transport system in Switzerland, not simply as a practical solution to a political problem but also as a means of achieving economic progress through national unification. It called in the experts, and that meant English engineers. It's hard to believe these days, but in 1850 the British train network was the envy of the world, already 25 years old and 10,000km long. Britain had invented the railway, or more precisely George Stephenson (with his son Robert) did when his passenger train line between Stockton and Darlington in northeast England opened in September 1825. In doing so, he helped standardise the distance between the rails at 1435mm, which became the normal gauge for many railways around the world.

In 1850, Switzerland had 25km of railways. That was it: a single line from Zurich to Baden. It had opened in 1847 and was known as the Spanisch-Brötli-Bahn (Spanish roll railway), not because any Spaniards or bread rolls were involved in its construction but because of a pastry speciality baked only in Baden. This was much sought after in Zurich, so servants were sent to Baden by train to buy the rolls and bring them back for their masters to enjoy; the 90-minute round trip was far better than walking there and back, as they had to do before the train. While the Brötli-Bahn was the first Swiss line, there was already one other station in Switzerland, in Basel, where the French terminus for the Alsace line had been located since 1845. There were various ideas and plans for a larger network, but nothing concrete. Whereas Britain had sound economic reasons for building train lines, such as to connect factories and ports or coal mines and the main cities, Switzerland had no mines, small cities and few big factories. It also had squabbling cantons. What caused the problems in Switzerland wasn't the geography but the politics. An outsider was needed to come and show them the way – enter Robert Stephenson.

Along with Henry Swinburne, Stephenson proposed a cruciform network north of the Alps, with one line running north–south from Basel to Lucerne and the other west–east on a Thun–Bern–Zurich–Lake Constance axis. The latter had to run along the south bank of the River Aare, which was the first line of defence against any potential invasion from the north, so the railway would be defensible and usable in wartime. Steamboats on the main lakes and short train lines between them would indirectly link Geneva and Chur to the network. Those parts south of the Alps, such as Ticino, were deemed beyond reach. Central to the plan was the small town of Olten, near Basel, which lay at the heart of the giant X.

In the end, the Swiss government favoured a cantonal solution rather than a national one, with private money financing the lines. The final result would turn out to be something very similar to the British plan but with vital improvements, such as direct lines to Geneva and Chur rather than leapfrogging over the lakes. A new railway law was passed in 1852 and then it was full steam ahead for the various train companies, with "many of the lines being executed by English engineers and with English capital", as the Murray Handbook notes.

The first project was to link Basel (and so the French network) with the rest of Switzerland, a scheme that involved building the first Swiss rail tunnel. Again English engineering expertise was needed, this time in the shape of Thomas Brassey, the mastermind behind the 2.5km-long Hauenstein Tunnel. It wasn't an easy job. A fire in the tunnel killed 63 men and delayed the project by two years. When it finally opened in 1858, however, it prompted a railway rush across Switzerland. By the late 1860s, over 650km of lines were already built, far beyond the Stephenson plan, from Lake Geneva to Lake Constance, from Basel to Chur, and from Neuchâtel up to the watchmaking town of La Chaux-de-Fonds.

And it wouldn't be long before the greatest Swiss rail project of the century – the Gotthard line – got underway, this time with a Swiss engineer in charge. Sadly, Louis Favre didn't live to see the grand opening of his masterpiece, the Gotthard Tunnel, on 22 May 1882; he had died of a heart attack inside the tunnel three years earlier. In 30 years the Swiss had catapulted their network from one short railway to a masterpiece of rail engineering that astounded the world.

It was British know-how that helped the Swiss railway network in its infancy, from planning the lines to building the tunnels, and even building the locomotives; Charles Brown co-founded the SLM train works in Winterthur, which produced many Swiss trains. So it is deliciously ironic that when a line to the top of Mt Snowdon, the highest peak in Wales, was announced in 1894, the technology and expertise came from Switzerland (just as it had at Montenvers). A few years ago I took a steam train to the top of Snowdon and the locomotive was one of the original ones, bought in Switzerland. From their slow beginnings, the Swiss had quickly learnt how to send trains up, under or round the mountains, something they have been doing very well ever since.

In December 2016 the new Gotthard Base Tunnel, flatter and deeper than the original, is scheduled to open. At 57.1km, it will be world's longest rail tunnel. Switzerland no longer needs Britain for its railways, except for providing customers, but there is one lasting link to the past that has yet to be broken. Swiss trains run on the left, just as British ones do, whereas on Swiss roads you have to drive on the right. I only hope the train drivers don't get confused when they switch to a car.

None of that was important to the now-Cookless group. They were more than content to enjoy a train ride after all that walking, even if the line only ran for 18 miles, ending at Sion, although it was planned to go further. As Miss Jemima said, it was a line "that is to be, when completed, the wonder of Northern Italy and the triumph of modern engineering". That was true enough once the tunnel under the Simplon Pass to Italy opened in 1906. At almost 20km long, it was for many years the longest rail tunnel

*In the mid-1860s Switzerland only had 650km of railways
compared to 5000km today*

in the world, a record the Swiss will soon reclaim under the
Gotthard.

At this point in its lengthy journey towards the Mediterranean,
the River Rhone meanders through a broad valley running
east to west and framed on either side by steep, stark mountains.
The Swiss part of the Rhone is 264km long, making it Switzerland's
third-longest river after the Rhine and the Aare. Upstream, to the
east, the river has not long stopped being a fast-flowing torrent;
a few miles downstream, its muddy waters disperse into the blue
expanse of Lake Geneva, only to re-emerge in Geneva itself. To the
north lie the peaks of the Bernese Oberland, to the south are the
4000m summits that line the border with Italy. In effect, the Rhone
is one long cleft in an endless parade of mountains, and one giant
funnel for all the water coming down.

That funnel sometimes fills to overflowing. Disastrous floods once
used to devastate the Rhone valley, twice almost washing Martigny
away in 1595 and 1818, leaving the Swiss no choice but to try to

control the river. While two attempts at correcting its course and flow have already been made, they haven't been enough. More floods in October 2000 prompted the approval of a third 30-year programme, at a cost of 1.6 billion francs. That's expensive but essential, not only to protect the population but to make more land usable and productive.

This is how the valley around Martigny was described before the first correction, which started in 1863:

> a flat swamp, rendered desolate and unwholesome by the overflowings of the Rhone and its tributaries, which, not being carried off by a sufficient declivity in their beds, stagnate, and exhale an injurious malaria under the rays of a burning sun, and generate gnats not much inferior to mosquitoes.

Things have improved somewhat since then and there's no sign of much swampiness in the fields and farms. Valais, Switzerland's third-largest canton, is the nation's fruit basket, with orchards full of apples and pears but also cherries, plums, quince and, most famously, apricots. When they come into season, supermarkets across the country are piled high with the plump little furry fruit from Valais, always more expensive than imported ones and always more popular. They even achieve immortality in the form of Abricotine liqueur, an AOC-protected apricot brandy (minimum 40 per cent proof) that is only made here. Valais also produces over a third of all Swiss wine, more than any other canton. All in all, it's quite a fruity place to be, and it makes for rather a pleasant train ride past gravity-defying vineyards on the south-facing slopes and fruit trees marshalled in rows along the valley floor.

In the centre of it all are the twin peaks of Sion, the cantonal capital and the sunniest town in Switzerland (though there are a few other claimants to that title). Sion is one of those towns that should really only exist in fairytales or fantasy films. Bang in the middle of a valley that is otherwise as flat as the proverbial pancake stand two mini-mountains right beside the river. They can be seen from

*Sion's twin peaks crowned with castles dominate the flat
Rhone valley*

miles away because, although much smaller than nearby peaks,
these two pointy hills are stranded almost midstream, surrounded
by the flood plain of the Rhone. One is slightly higher but both
are crowned with fortifications, and together they overshadow the
town clustered around the base. In the fading light they even start
to seem faintly menacing and more than a little spooky the closer
we get. I half expect to hear of a dragon living under one hill or for
the castles to be inhabited by warring brothers, who periodically
lob missiles and fireballs across the gap.

Let's hope the hotels are more welcoming, although Miss Jemima
described hers (Lion d'Or) as "a grimmish, granite, prison-looking
building", and Murray notes that at the Hotel Poste, "landlord very
civil and attentive; head-waiter much the contrary".

As it turns out, neither hotel exists any more, so we end up at
the modern Hotel Elite. It's not the town's most beautiful building
by any stretch, but it's not a prison, and the staff are far friend-
lier than most Swiss hotel workers (or jailers). That seems true of
Sion itself. On this warm Friday evening the town centre is buzzing

and pavement cafés are packed, everyone indulging in some thank-goodness-it's-the-weekend merry-making. It's a splendid welcome back to Switzerland, so we join the crowds for a while, but certainly don't have the stamina of our predecessors: even after their 25-mile hike, they still had the energy for a "short stroll" at 10pm to see the castles. Our stroll through the old town can wait until the morning.

We have a small moment of celebration the following day: breakfast is finally included in the room price. Not only that, but it's not a bad spread. Swiss hotel breakfasts are generally a buffet offering bread, croissants, cereals, yoghurt, cold meats, cheese and boiled eggs. Cooked food – sausages, scrambled eggs and what the Swiss think of as bacon – rarely makes an appearance except in posher places. But *Birchermüesli*, essentially cold porridge with yoghurt, fruit and nuts (far nicer than it sounds), is usually offered.

Although the rest of the world dismisses muesli as something for birds and hippies, in Switzerland it's a popular dish at any time of day (partly because the Swiss know how to make it properly). Sadly, whoever made ours today needs to go to muesli school, although I have a sneaking suspicion that it's closer to the original recipe from Dr Bircher-Benner of Aarau. Back in 1900, he created a healthy meal for his patients by mixing oats with water, condensed milk, lemon juice and grated apple, so the result was sweet yet watery at the same time. Muesli is one of the few Swiss German words to have crept into English, although Miss Jemima wouldn't have had a clue what it meant: she was here 37 years before the dish was invented.

No breakfast buffet in Valais would be complete without the local sourdough rye bread. Cunningly disguised as a rock, the hard dark-brown round could probably kill someone from 30 paces if thrown the right way. It carries the AOC seal of approval, but did not get one from Miss Jemima:

> "the bread in this district was of a character highly calculated to embitter a dyspeptic, and any who hold to the anxious ... 'Waste not, want not' would see a prospective hungry pauper in every tourist as he excavates a four inch cube of bread from an unbeatable thick wall of crust. Query – are the dentists in league with the bakers?"

SION

reparing for their days work we saw, from our casemen, the women of Sion, sitting on the Rerl stones and offering cherries for sale - wearing the peculiar costume, hat of the district. Its narrow brim is neither a -

Miss Jemima's Swiss Journal is full of her pen-and-ink illustrations

With a population of 30,000 Sion isn't huge, but it's been around for quite some time. It claims to be Switzerland's oldest town (7000 years and counting) and at its heart is a compact warren of cobbled streets and handsome stone buildings radiating out from the cathedral. The chunky square belfry would dominate any other town, but in Sion it doesn't stand a chance against the two hill-top castles, one or other of which seems to pop up at the end of every street and around every corner.

The one closer to town, Château de Valère, is actually an eleventh-century church, albeit a very robust, fortified one surrounded by curtain walls. It is suitably medieval inside – that is, minimalist with delicate faded murals – and is home to the world's oldest playable organ (dating from 1431). On the opposite, higher hill, Château de Tourbillon is most definitely a castle, though it was partially ruined by a disastrous fire in 1788 that destroyed most of Sion. The steep climb up to either summit is rewarded with extensive views of the whole valley.

With the long, wide exception of the Rhone valley, most of Valais is mountainous, with many peaks breaking the 4000m mark, including the Matterhorn and Switzerland's highest point, Dufourspitze. Its rugged landscape is also home to the Aletsch Glacier, Europe's longest, and this challenging topography meant that for centuries the canton was isolated from the rest of Switzerland, accessible only via the Rhone or one of the high passes. So in winter many parts were largely cut off from the outside world, and even in summer some of the more remote valleys and villages could only be reached by mule. It is that very remoteness and the unspoilt scenery that have made Valais so attractive. Once it was mountaineers who came to conquer its peaks; now skiers, hikers, bathers, bird- and trainspotters also arrive, together with millionaires.

It wasn't always like that. Murray is less than complimentary about the canton of Valais, calling it "One of the most miserable and melancholy districts in northern Europe", a description that is hard to relate to when looking out of a train window at vineyards basking in the sun. But the book continues in the same vein:

> At present, with the exception of the hotels, nothing appears prosperous in the Valais itself or in the numerous lateral valleys, and the race of man seems to have deteriorated.

In its semi-isolated state, Valais was indeed a poor rural corner of the country, where the people still scraped a living off the land. In the 1880s, 76 per cent of the local population were still farmers, almost twice the national average, and Valais was bottom of the cantonal school rankings. The terrible transport links (the train did not reach Zermatt until 1891) meant that the crops were grown not for selling but for survival. Throw in periodic floods, fires and failed harvests, and it's no surprise to learn that even the rest of the country looked down on Valais, or the "Kashmir of Europe", as one Swiss magazine called it in 1800. However, it wasn't only the poverty that Victorian visitors found alarming, it was the prevalence of goitres and cretinism, two medical afflictions that were once very common in this part of Switzerland.

A goitre is a swelling of the thyroid gland, which in some cases takes the form of a huge mass of tissue that all but obscures the person's neck. Cretinism results from a severe deficiency of thyroid hormones during pregnancy, and manifests itself from birth through stunted mental and physical growth. The sufferer can be severely handicapped, or as Murray put it, "The cretin is an idiot – a melancholy spectacle – a creature who may almost be said to rank a step below a human being."

The book devotes two pages to the ailments, detailing the latest scientific knowledge. In the mid-nineteenth century both conditions were thought to be caused by something in the water, genetic defects from inbreeding, low-lying fog, carrying heavy weights on the head, or a mixture of every sin known to man. "Superstition, ignorance, poverty and the dirty habits of the people, combined with the unhealthiness of a close low valley, are said to be the causes of this visible wretchedness" is how Miss Jemima put it.

However, it is now known that it was the absence of iodine in the soil, and therefore in the food, that was the root cause, and Valais was badly affected, not least because the local people could not afford to import food. A Napoleonic census in 1800 found 4000 cretins in the canton (out of a population of 70,000), with "scarcely a woman free from [goitre], and it is said that those who have no swelling are laughed at and called goose-necked". Miss Jemima contrasts the "luxuriant" vegetation and "exquisite" views with the "many poor miserable cretins and goitres".

Once it was realised that iodine, or a lack thereof, was the problem, it was a matter of finding the most effective way of administering it. In the end it was the Swiss themselves who instituted the simplest of ideas: adding iodine to salt. The village of Grächen, near Zermatt, was the site of the first mass trial in 1918, partly because it was so isolated and also because most of the children had goitres. The idea worked, and in 1922 the federal government recommended the iodisation of Swiss salt. This being Switzerland, where each canton is responsible for its own affairs, the take-up was initially patchy. Appenzell Ausserrhoden was the first canton to introduce iodised salt, but it did eventually happen nationwide. Today over 90 per cent of Swiss table salt, and around three-quarters of industrial cooking salt, is iodised, although legally non-iodised salt must still be available. Ironically, one of Switzerland's largest salt mines is at Bex (pronounced with a typically silent French x, just like Chamonix) in neighbouring Vaud. The solution was on its doorstep the whole time.

Valais today is a different world, home to some of the ritziest ski resorts, such as Verbier and Saas-Fee, and no longer the poor man of Switzerland. Its transformation came about thanks to trains and tourists, which travelled hand in hand. Visitors had always found their way into the valleys of Valais, mostly mad Englishmen climbing the mountains, but the advent of the railway made it less of an adventure to see the Matterhorn. The train lines opened up both the countryside and the minds of the locals, who were renowned for their mistrust of strangers. One book on the history of Valais quotes a man from Solothurn (in northern Switzerland) who visited in 1830, only for an old lady to cross herself and run away at the mere sight of him.

Tourism meant money coming in and hotels going up. Zermatt once had a single hotel with three beds; by 1881, there were 490 beds (not all in one hotel) and in 1914 there were 2235. On the eve of the First World War, the 321 hotels in Valais employed over 5000 people. Living off the land(scape) had taken on a whole new meaning. However, the railways also brought industry in their wake, as cement, paper and hat factories could at last be built in the Rhone valley, whereas before it had been too distant and thus not economically viable to do so. The industrial revolution arrived in Valais about half a century late, but it made up for lost time: the cantonal total of only 9 factories (with 374 workers) in 1884 rose to 80 (with 2700 workers) in 1910. All those apricots and bottles of wine could finally reach a national market.

From Sion eastwards to Leuk is only a matter of a few miles, and a few minutes in the train, but it passes over a significant boundary: the watershed between French and German. Looking at a map, you might think it logical if, for example, French was spoken on the south bank of the Rhone and German on the north. But this imaginary line runs north–south, dividing the canton between the French-speaking Lower Valais to the west and the German-speaking Upper Valais to the east. And it is immediate: Miège and Venthône couldn't look more French as names and yet they are almost next door to Salgesch and Pfyn.

This division is the last section of what is known as the *Röstigraben*, the invisible linguistic barrier that cuts across Switzerland. Its name (literally "fried-potato trench") refers to the fact that the German-speaking Swiss eat Rösti at any time of day or night, while the French speakers stick to fondue. Of course that's a huge oversimplification – both sides eat both dishes – but the term has become Swiss shorthand for the separation of the French-speaking part (20.4 per cent of the population) from the German (63.7 per cent). Switzerland is in fact quadrilingual, with Italian (6.5 per cent) and Romansh (0.5 per cent) the other two national languages, but it is the French–German divide that figures most strongly in the national psyche. It isn't merely linguistic but political and cultural as well; both sides see the other as something different, as if they aren't really members of the same clan. In essence, though, both sides are Swiss.

In bilingual Valais, the different languages are immediately apparent in the place names. As is often the case in Switzerland, many places have two names, so the canton itself is Wallis in

German, while the French Sion, Loèche and Cervin are the German Sitten, Leuk and Matterhorn respectively. It doesn't matter that Sion is 82 per cent French speaking and Leuk 92 per cent German speaking, they both have two names. While this could have been confusing for visitors, English tourists pragmatically used whatever they heard in the place itself. So Miss Jemima only ever refers to Sion and Leuk, although the spelling of such foreign names often caused problems, as we have seen with Montenvers/ Montanvert and Chamonix/Chamouni. Naturally it's not always that simple, so Valais is the usual "English" name for the canton, rather than Wallis, while it's Lucerne in English as in French, not Luzern. Things do change, nevertheless: using French names for German-speaking areas is a tad old-fashioned, almost on a par with still talking of Ceylon or Peking. So Bâle, Argovia and Grisons have long since given way in English to Basel, Aargau and Graubünden.

On the train it's usually easy to tell when you've crossed the border, and not only because the station names change. The bilingual announcements reverse their order: *Prochain arrêt* before *Nächster Halt* in the French-speaking part and vice versa once over the *Röstigraben*. On long-distance trains, English is often thrown in as well, while trains heading towards Italy obviously include Italian. Travellers can pick whichever suits them from this multilingual buffet. At least the German bits are in High German, the official formal language, rather than one of the many Swiss German dialects. In Valais that would flummox even some Swiss visitors, as the canton is renowned for its strong accent and *Walliserdeutsch* dialect, where, for example, the Rhone becomes the Rotten.

Once off the train – reaching the spas of Leukerbad requires an uphill bus journey – bilingualism gets left behind. No doubt the driver speaks French, but he greets everyone with a Swiss German *Grüezi miteinand* as he boards the bus and we (or at least the Swiss on board) respond with the same. It's all very polite.

For all their reputation for being a bit cold and distant, the Swiss really can be a friendly bunch sometimes. Of course, with the bus drivers it might be seen as courteous formality, although without the superficiality you might find in other cultures. They're not about to show you photos of their grandson or ask about your holidays, but they will be welcoming up to a point, and usually bid you goodbye as you leave their vehicle. It's one of the things I love about riding in the yellow Postbuses that criss-cross the country. That and the three-tone horn, which gets a lot of use on twisty mountain roads. The notes, taken from Rossini's "William Tell Overture", were first used in 1923 but quickly became a Swiss institution.

On our bus ride up from Leuk to Leukerbad (*Bad* means "bath" in German), I begin to think we won't hear the horn at all. The problem isn't the road, which is suitably winding and steep, but that the driver can see round almost every bend, so doesn't need to give a burst of Tell as a warning. Instead we have two little girls counting the corners as we swing round them, and this long bus really does swing round the bends, making me glad to be sitting down at the front and not throwing up at the back. The first few corners are no problem for the girls, as they can quite easily manage *drü, vier, füüf* (three, four, five in their Bernese dialect), but when they reach the thirties they get a little lost. The old lady sitting across the aisle from us gives me a knowing smile when they jump from *sächsedriissg* straight to *nüünedriissg* (36 to 39). By the time they get to the sixties, I don't think anyone's sure what number they're really at, particularly not them.

Their melodic chanting fades into the background as I enjoy the view. This must be one of the most scenic bus rides in Switzerland. We leave the valley behind, watching the hills of Sion and braided riverbed retreat into the hazy distance, and climb up through dark forests and over crashing water. The road hugs the side of the Dala gorge, zigzagging its way up so that we have rock on one side of the bus and a precipice on the other, only to switch round at the next hairpin. A graceful arched bridge to the other side of the gorge isn't wide enough for a bus and anything else, so an oncoming car wisely decides to reverse slowly off it to let us pass, though only after our driver blasts his horn (at last!). Wisps of mist and cloud drift across the road, offering fleeting glimpses of stone way above our heads. A few locals get on and off the packed bus (so full that a second bus had to be organised and is somewhere behind us), but most people stay on for Leukerbad. And our first sight of it duly appears through a cleft in the cliffs, a flash of grassy meadows and wooden chalets that disappears again almost immediately behind a protruding flank of rock.

Miss Jemima was equally amazed by the (then still relatively new) road – or, as she described it, "another example of Swiss engineering prowess" in "one of the finest gorges in Switzerland", where at some points "the rocks on either side of the ravine seem almost to embrace". It must have been quite a hair-raising experience to travel this switchback road in a horse and carriage, swinging out close to the edge at every turn. Perhaps that's one reason an electric railway was built up the gorge in 1915. By the mid-1960s Leukerbad had become so popular that the slow train could no longer cope with the numbers – almost 134,000 passengers in 1966 – and the road couldn't be upgraded with the train line in the way. So the railway was dismantled in 1967 and a bigger, better road created to deal with the annual influx.

As we round the final bend (number 134, according the two girls who have counted themselves to a standstill), Leukerbad appears in its entirety. The village itself is attractive enough, with the usual Swiss mix of wood and concrete dotted across the slopes, but the setting makes it spectacular. The gorge ends in a cul-de-sac, a towering semi-circular wall of rock that almost encircles Leukerbad and casts a long shadow over it morning and evening. But the sheer mountain wall of the Gemmi is not actually a dead end: there is a cable car and, almost unbelievably, a hiking path up to the top. It isn't for mountain goats and Spiderman, but a regular path, albeit a seriously vertiginous one.

This was once the quickest and shortest route from Valais into Canton Bern – it was either walk up over here or go the long way round via Lake Geneva, a 200-mile diversion. That, and not the famous hot springs, was the principal reason our first tourists came this way. There was no real alternative until 1913, when the Lötschberg rail tunnel opened further up the Rhone valley.

It takes 40 years for the rain that falls on the surrounding mountains to percolate through the rock and bubble up in Leukerbad.

Leukerbad has been a popular spa resort for over 500 years

During its long journey it doesn't gather any speed but ends up piping hot: 51 °C, to be precise. Too much for even a hot bath, so the water is used to heat normal shower water (and keep the car park snow free in winter via underfloor pipes) before flowing into the 30 spa pools in the village. There it's a relaxing 36 to 40 °C, perfect for therapy of one kind or another. Visitors have been coming up here to soak since Roman times, but it was really only in 1501 that spa tourism took off, thanks to Cardinal Schiner from Sion. He transformed Leukerbad into an international hot spot, with proper baths and hostelries for guests from across Europe. He went on almost to become Pope and died of the plague in Rome; perhaps he should have stayed at home.

For centuries, Leukerbad was essentially a summertime resort. Reaching it in winter was no mean feat and avalanches periodically swept through the village. The one on 17 January 1719, when 53 people died and barely a building remained standing, is still commemorated on that date every year. Nevertheless, avalanche-protection ditches were built, as was the precarious path up the cliff to Gemmi; oddly enough it was constructed by Austrian workers from the Tyrol, not the Swiss. And still the bathers kept on coming in their thousands. Long before Zermatt was really on the tourist map, Leukerbad had large hotels to cater for its visitors, most of whom stayed for three weeks.

With so many wanting to take the waters, in 1825 it was necessary to introduce strict bathing regulations. For example, those entering the baths not wearing the right apparel (a long, loose shirt of suitable material) were fined two francs, as was anyone who entered a changing cabin when someone else was in there. Men and women sat in separate baths, and it was forbidden "to splash others, to spit in the water, to whistle or smoke, to sing, to have religious discussions, to conduct immodest activities or argue". In other words, people had to sit still, be silent and soak – for hours, day after day. The usual "cure" was an hour on the first day, two hours on the second, three on the third, until the patient was sitting in hot water for eight to ten hours a day for three weeks, along with up to 20 other people. They must all have looked like giant prunes.

By the time Miss Jemima came along, things had changed. Modesty still applied to the apparel, but mixed bathing had become the norm. Not that she would have gone into the baths even if they had been segregated by sex. That was something for heathens and foreigners, although she couldn't resist going to take a peek:

> "There are two bath-houses, each containing four large tanks and a gallery where the friends of the bathers can pass through and converse with them whilst in this amphibious state. The patient is often doomed to sit four hours in the morning and four hours in the afternoon. Further to relieve the monotony of such an existence the ladies and gentlemen bathe in common and may be seen sitting around the bath, engaged in the various pursuits compatible with their adopted element."

Her fascination got the better of her again the next day:

SLOW TRAIN TO SWITZERLAND

"Accordingly in the morning we rose at five o'clock and already saw the bathers, in semi-toilette, crossing to the baths, to commence their day's soak. We followed them, not as bathers but as observers. It was difficult to shake off the feeling that we were indulging in an excess of curiosity, and still more difficult to maintain a sobriety consistent with good manners."

Manners went out the steamy window, probably at the same time Miss Jemima was pressing her nose up against it, and the whole group went inside to stare at the unnatural goings-on. For them it was a human zoo:

"She was taking her next meal up to her shoulders in water; on a wooden tray was placed a tiny coffee-pot, a pat of butter and slices of bread. We could discern the seat or benches running round the bath on which were seated persons in dark blue or dark red gowns. A moustached gentleman, who would consider himself in the prime of life, was cutting leather work on his floating table, other bathers were preparing for a game at draughts, whilst one portly round-shouldered party of sixty summers was executing a roving commission across the water to salute some ladies in the opposite corner. Not being very careful of others, in his transit he received as fair a share of splashing from various mischievous maids en route. Judging from the array of work-baskets on the ledge of the bath, the ladies dry their hands for knitting and crochet, though we saw nothing accomplished in this line."

Mr William was more succinct, simply writing, "It is a most ridiculous sight." It couldn't be more different today. For one thing, although there is a large rehabilitation clinic, most people are there to relax rather than recuperate. Now it's all about wellness not illness, indulgence not endurance. The two principal public baths are pleasure palaces where skiers and walkers come to soothe aching limbs and the rest of us simply slide into the hot water and forget about the world. We only have time for one session of hedonism, so we have to choose our bath. The larger Bürgerbad (recently rechristened Leukerbad Therme to try to add some style) puts the emphasis on family fun, with giant water slides alongside the outdoor pools and bubble baths. Its style is so 1980s that I'd feel underdressed in swimming shorts instead of a leotard and leggings. So we plump for the smaller, newer and slightly more elegant Alpentherme, where the average age is older than the water we are stewing in – apart from one toddler who's quietly enjoying his inflatable armchair-cum-lifejacket. One of the indoor pools is so hot I feel like a lobster being slowly cooked to death without noticing and my glasses keep steaming up. So I paddle outside and instantly promote the Alpentherme into my Top Ten of public spas.

Lying neck deep in hot water on a bed of bubbles and looking up at the mighty cliffs, I realise why people travelled across Europe for centuries to do exactly this. It's not necessarily the water, which can be found in many natural spas, but the location, 1411m above sea level and surrounded by natural splendour. It helps as well that every bather is clad in swimwear, unlike one spa I visited in Stuttgart where everyone had to be naked. No choice and no segregation. That was revealing, to say the least. I'm not advocating a return to Victorian prudery and long shirts, but there's only so much sagging, wobbling, unwrapped flesh I can sit beside.

This spa does indeed have a section where swimsuits are swapped for birthday suits, but I decide that today isn't the day for saunas and steam rooms. Instead, we opt for the full-on wellness experience and book a massage each. Wellness is one of those "English" words the Swiss love to use even though it's not exactly in common use by most English speakers. Where they say wellness hotel or wellness weekend, we would say "spa", although in America wellness can take on a medical sense. Oddly enough, it encompasses both meanings for me today: after the pleasure of the pools, the pain of the massage. It isn't the candles-and-incense experience I was expecting but something much more medicinal. To make things worse, the masseur is wearing what appears to be hospital scrubs and we're in a large, echoey room divided into long cubicles, rather like a hospital ward. Perhaps these solid beds were once mortuary slabs in a former life.

Miss Jemima and her companions stayed at the Hôtel des Frères Brunner, but alas, the Brunner Brothers are no longer around. Maybe it was their food that killed the business, although hopefully not the customers. Here is our heroine's description of their "repast of seven courses":

> "The soup was decidedly watery – the slices of beef with its border of fried potatoes – starved – the mountain trout had exchanged its natural element for one of oil. The fowl and rice were passée. Slices of chamois, alias chèvre, were served in a vinegared gravy and were evidently an important and popular course. But we never loved the dish, and here we rejected it to the contemptuous astonishment of the waiter, who with a pity for our ignorance of its superior merits, entreatingly asked 'N'aimez vous pas le chamois?' ... Other novelties were peas in the pod and an ice that exactly resembled half-pounds of butter."

As hard as we try, we cannot find vinegared chamois on any menu. The disappointment is crushing, so we comfort ourselves with a plate of Rösti; it seems only fitting now we have crossed the *Graben*. But we do at least uncover the modern incarnation of the Frères Brunners. Their hotel was knocked down in 1982 and re-emerged as the Hotel Grichting & Badnerhof, run by Angela and Klaus Bauer-Grichting. She comes from a family of hoteliers (three sisters who married three chefs and run a hotel each) and for the anniversary of that night once served a modern version of that infamous dinner, with lamb instead of chamois. It was a feast to remember.

Chatting to the owner, it's clear that in the grand scheme of things Cook wasn't important to Leukerbad. Admittedly the man himself didn't come here on that first tour, which by then was Self-Conducted (only without an audioguide), but it's more that a group of eight British travellers who stayed one night was a mere drop in the ocean. Not even that, given that the springs pump out the water at the rate of 1400 litres a minute. Leukerbad was a resort long before Cook was born and the British have never been its

The A-framed building in the centre of Leukerbad
is the Hôtel des Frères Brunner, where the
Junior United Alpine Club stayed

main market. Today, 75 per cent of visitors are Swiss and the new five-star hotel being planned by Kempinski, with a thermal jacuzzi on every balcony, is most likely aimed at them, or at Russians in Versace swimsuits.

Any British visitors who do come might be tempted to stay in the most English-sounding hotel in town: the Derby. It is, however, English in name only and very Swiss in nature, with bedrooms completely decked out in wood and menus that include half the butcher's shop. The strange thing is that there are Hotel Derbys dotted all over Switzerland and no one can agree why. One manager told me it was because the original owners were Anglophiles and loved visiting Derby; another because when the Earl of Derby was on his Grand Tour, every place he stayed renamed the hotel after him (it beats a blue plaque with "Derby slept here", I suppose); in this case, the owner explained that his predecessor was a football fan and in Switzerland, as in Britain, a match between two local teams is a Derby (with a capital D and pronounced the American way, with an -er not an -ar). As for the numerous Hotel Bristols (including one in Leukerbad), I won't go into any theories at all.

Leukerbad has never been a typical Valais town. It exists purely for one reason, tourism, albeit a very specific, water-based sort. Without the hot springs, visitors would simply have passed through on their way to or from the Gemmi Pass; once the rail tunnel was built, even that passing trade would have vanished. This town of 1500 people survives (and thrives) now thanks to the regular influx of tourists; without them the only jobs left would be the few farmers who make a living from the fields. Speaking to David Kestens, the marketing manager of the tourist office, it's clear that the locals know how much depends on keeping the tourists happy. He says:

> We go into the schools and talk to the kids about the economy in the town and the role that tourists play. When some children say, "But my father works in a shop, or is a doctor, or a bus driver," we explain that without tourism to pay the bills none of those jobs would exist. The town would die.

The irony is that Leukerbad did almost die in the 1990s. An excess of optimism in the 1980s resulted in the new public baths along with a sports hall, bus station and many other tourist projects, all financed on credit. The cards eventually came tumbling down and in 1998 Leukerbad was declared bankrupt, with 340 million francs of debt, and the receivers were called in; until 2004, the town was under the direct financial control of the canton. This wasn't all down to overexcitement – the town president went to jail for fraud – but it was a lesson in not counting your chickens, or your tourists. And that in a place with 500 years' experience of tourism. Even the naturally cautious Swiss can make mistakes with money – and with architecture. As David Kestens points out, "The boom years in Leukerbad were great as long as you don't look at some of the things they built, such as the clinic. At least we now build things in keeping with the town, in chalet-style." It's never too late to look to the future by learning from the past.

Perhaps just as ironic is the fact that after being so dismissive of it, the British soon got used to the idea of wellness, even if they have never used the word. Far from being "treated with utter neglect", in the late nineteenth century Alpine cures became the trendy way to treat all manner of ailments. This didn't necessarily incorporate bathing, which still involved an uncomfortable degree of nudity and familiarity between the sexes, or even some of the weirder cures Miss Jemima described:

> "We heard too, of other 'cures' adopted by the Swiss. There is the 'grape cure' near Vevey, where a patient eats six pounds of white grapes in the forenoon, and near Neuchâtel there is the 'curd whey' establishment where the prescribed diet is one of milk, left after the cheese has been made."

Instead of taking the waters, or anything more exotic, the British started taking the air. It was clean, fresh mountain air that was dry and smog free, perfect for those suffering from tuberculosis, emphysema, bronchitis and all manner of lung disorders. For late Victorian Britons, whose air was increasingly thick and dirty, being able to escape to the sunny Alps for weeks or months of treatment must have been a godsend, if not a lifeline. High Alpine villages reinvented themselves as health resorts and quickly expanded thanks to all the fresh-air visitors and patients from the industrial cities of Britain, Germany, France and beyond.

A prime example is Davos, which was a retreat for the sick and ailing long before it was an escape for the rich and powerful. In the 1880s, British author Robert Louis Stevenson finished *Treasure Island* while convalescing in a Davos sanatorium. How apt that a tale of pirates and hidden treasure was written in the town that is now famous as the home of the annual World Economic Forum.

While the clinics and sanatoria remain, most of today's guests come to rejuvenate, not recuperate. Deep breathing is still on the agenda but with a new purpose: de-stressing the mind rather than de-clogging the lungs. Different ailments, same cure. Cool air, warm sun and hot water are the perfect ingredients for relaxing the body and soul. Miss Jemima and all those other early tourists didn't know what they were missing out on.

FIVE

OVER THE HILLS

The Gemmi is one of the most remarkable passes across the Alps. Its scenery is, perhaps, extraordinary rather than grand, and to be seen to advantage it ought to be approached from the Valais.

—Murray Handbook

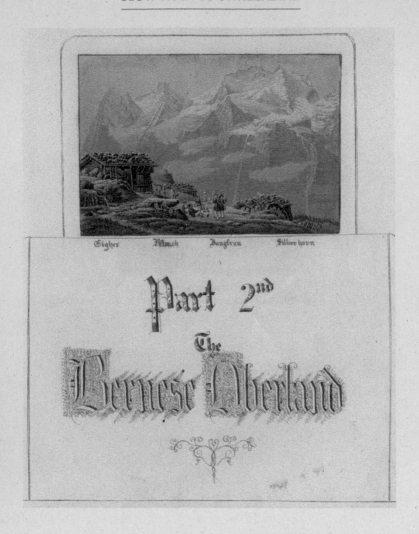

Miss Jemima illustrated her journal with postcards pasted in
as well as her own drawings

S heep – hundreds of them wherever we look, bounding down the slopes, bleating all the way to the lake. The first hint of their arrival had been the bells, a distant tinkling that prompted everyone to turn away from the water and focus eyes (and cameras) on the rocky horizon. Then a single pointed face appeared on the crest of the hill and stopped a moment to survey the scene, before plunging headlong towards us. The deluge had begun. Soon a few of us were stranded on a tufty mound halfway down the slope, an island in a stream of off-white, and the odd brown, clouds on legs that poured downhill, leaping over gullies, following their leaders, ignoring the strange humans taking photos. Welcome to the annual Gemmi sheep festival!

A casual comment over breakfast had turned our plans for the day upside down. At the table next to ours sat an elderly German couple, who had been married long enough that they no longer made conversation over their cornflakes (or muesli). The man was part of the way through his boiled egg when he leaned across and spoke to my mother. *"Gehen Sie heute zum Schäferfest?"*

Now that I live in Switzerland, my mother is trying to learn German, from scratch with *Der-Die-Das*. She's fluent in French and Italian, but is making the effort with Swiss national language number 3. Still, I'm sure that her vocabulary doesn't yet stretch to "sheep festival"; it's not exactly the normal thing to learn in a conversation class in deepest Hampshire. So I reply for both of us. *"Was für ein Schäferfest?"*

And that's how we learn that the 54th annual sheep festival is taking place today beside the Daubensee, the lake that sits up on the Gemmi Pass. Every July, farmers and herders from Cantons Bern and Valais assemble, with their sheep, for a day of grilling sausages, throwing flags and catching up with old friends. Plus a spot of yodelling and alphorn blowing to liven things up. It's an excuse for the locals to get together for one day when very often they spend the other 364 hardly seeing each other. Their farms and herds may be quite close as the crow flies, but little inconveniences like cliffs and mountains get in the way. However, like many a festival in Switzerland – and there are many – what started as a local affair has become a minor tourist attraction, not just for the folklore but also the 900 or so sheep.

So instead of taking the cable car to the top of the cliff with a view to walking across the whole Gemmi Pass to Kandersteg, I decide we'll go up purely for the sheep party, then come back down and travel round the long way by train. I'm rather relieved I don't have to literally follow in Miss Jemima's footsteps. The logistics of the day had meant I was going to have to walk for four hours, only to arrive in Kandersteg and leave straight away in order to come back by train, fetch our bags and return the same way. No wonder Miss Jemima travelled without a suitcase. This way we can enjoy an unexpected burst of local life and I can come back another time to walk across the Gemmi Pass, without luggage and without a mother who needs a more restful day.

Dangling from a cable is possibly the best place to get a perfect view of the Tyrolean handiwork on the Gemmi wall – assuming you are safely inside a cable car, of course. From this bird's-eye perspective, you can't help but be astounded at the impossibility of the path carved into the cliff face. Every bend looks sharper than the last, every overhang more unnerving, and every metre of path a triumph of mind over matter. It's a two-hour hike up to the top, or a seven-minute ride in a cable car, and today either route takes you through the thick mist still clinging to the cliff face. The thought of walking that path without clearly being able to see where you're going leaves me with sweaty palms.

The Junior United Alpine Club tackled the perpendicular path partly on foot, partly on a mule:

> "on looking up its bare vertical surface we were hard put to discover a path, or to understand how we should reach its summit. In some parts the path was a mere groove, cut in the face of this huge cliff, just wide enough for a mule to pass and at the turn of the zigzag we constantly overhung a depth of 500 or more feet. It is classed as one of the most extraordinary of all Alpine roads. ... Its zigzags have been ingeniously contrived, for in many places the rocks overhang the path and an upper

A mountain path on horseback was not for the faint-hearted

terrace of rocks projects further out than the one immediately below it."

Those are almost exactly the words used in Murray, although that adds a reassuring "There is no danger in it, and the terrors have vanished of late before improvements in the path and balustrades at the side." The group dismounted from the mules once they decided that two feet were surer than six, and they might have been right to do so.

> *A young American girl came along on a mule, and in making the turn the mule's hind foot caved all the loose masonry and one of the fence posts over board; the mule gave a violent lurch inboard to save himself, and succeeded in the effort, but that girl turned as white as the snows of Mont Blanc for a moment.*

That comes from *A Tramp Abroad*, Mark Twain's wonderful account of his walk through Europe in 1878, including a descent along "this dreadful path". He also relates the story of a newly married countess on "her bridal tour" who fell from her saddle over the precipice; she made the mistake of going down on horseback. With that in mind, I am decidedly happy to be gliding up in a gondola rather than riding up on a mule. The tiny figures hiking way beneath us appear very weary as they toil upwards, but it's probably a walk worth doing for the path itself if nothing else. I might need a couple of valium beforehand, though. Incidentally, 1863 was the year when Samuel L. Clemens first used Twain as his pseudonym.

At 2348m up, this is the highest point the Junior United Alpine Club reached on their tour and the view from the top is truly memorable. Over 900m beneath our feet is the model village of Leukerbad, or "a bed of mushrooms" as Miss Jemima described it. Some of the mushrooms have grown quite a bit since then, but from this height even the ugly fungus of the clinic is almost appealing. The azure of the Alpentherme baths is a clear blue, inviting patch of calm amid the brown and grey. Then come the velvety green fields and tree-covered slopes, topped by a hazy strip of dark-blue ridges, all of it crowned with a jagged white horizon. The procession of snowy peaks has Weisshorn as its tallest, though the Matterhorn is the best known – except that from this angle you wouldn't recognise it at all. The iconic crooked pyramid has transformed into something much wider and flatter, as if a duck-billed platypus is sticking its bill up into the air. It's rather disconcerting.

A deep-throated blast of an alphorn wafting up from the valley behind us acts as a timely reminder of why we are really here, so we reluctantly turn around and pick our way down the rocky slope. As we clamber down, we are serenaded the whole way by alphorns echoing off the mountains surrounding this deep bowl of a valley. It really is one of the sounds of Switzerland, designed to carry across the hills and send tingles down your spine. Miss Jemima was equally enchanted:

> "It is a wooden tube from five to six feet long bound round with split withies of willow. This he rested on a wedge-shaped

hollow trough, and blew as we approached. He must have prac-
tised long to emit such a flow of mellow, sonorous notes from so
unmusical-looking an instrument. The notes died away in softest
cadence, which notes were taken up by the mountains and rever-
berated by them again and again. We had scarcely a moment's
interval to remark on their sweetness, when the rocks echœd the
same notes in fainter strains, another pause and we heard their
vibrations still lingering among the cliffs till they expired in but
a musical sigh."

The festival is taking place on the shores of the Daubensee, a
murky grey-blue lake that lurks in the shadow of the surrounding
mountains. It is fed entirely by melting ice and snow, which carry
all manner of deposits with them, giving the water a hue that is
less than enticing. In winter the lake pretty much disappears, with
whatever water that is left frozen to the bottom. Come the spring
and it returns, filling the valley with meltwater – and mud. At the
near end, a huge fan of sludge spreads out like a mini-Mississippi
delta, with little rivulets wiggling their way through the flat expanse
on the way to dumping more material into the water.

However, what makes the Daubensee interesting is not its source
but its outlet: it has none. No stream flows out of the lake. In fact
there is a small hole at the bottom, and for ages everyone presumed
that the water eventually found its way down to Leukerbad. One
year the authorities decided to test that theory and added some
harmless red dye to the water. It went down the hole and never
came out, at least not in Leukerbad. But in Salgesch, on the way to
Sion, the sudden appearance of red water caused a few raised eyebrows. The mystery of the Daubensee's plughole had been solved.

The water doesn't appear any more appealing close up, but
there's plenty else to look at. Long before the sheep make their
grand entrance, the flag throwers, alphorn players and yodellers
are out in force, entertaining the crowd. Yes, it's a little kitschy,
but it doesn't feel contrived and most of the onlookers are Swiss
rather than tourists. It's just one of the many festivals that pop
up all over Switzerland, so you're never far from an embroidered

Tracht (traditional dress) or sizzling sausage, especially in summer. Or, come to think of it, from flaming carriages, fighting cows, burning snowmen and wailing women. All of those feature in one Swiss festival or another, as does a lot of food, whether it's onions, chestnuts, carrots or (of course) cheese – and a lot of cervelat, the Swiss national sausage.

Miss Jemima had no such festivities laid on, but instead made her own entertainment: a snowball fight. It was 3 July and baking hot, but the group found their first snowfield at the top of the cliff. They ran around like children, pelting each other with hastily made snowballs and sheltering from the blows under umbrellas, three of which were left "shattered wrecks". These were some snowballs! There was human damage as well, when one ball "unfortunately struck the eye of our gallant Professor, with a blow that made him motionless. His glass eye rolled to his feet!" Clearly the sun and the altitude had gone to their heads; either that or the holiday spirit was finally triumphing over Victorian propriety.

The only snow we can see today is the odd patch on the mountains that ring the lake. While this is not an unimpressive stretch of countryside, with a sense of space and size, it's not particularly beautiful. The "ghastly desolation of the place" was Twain's description and it certainly is rather austere, with no trees or flowers, no birds or bees, just endless rock and scrubby grass. This is not the normal picture-postcard view of Switzerland, although being a little less manicured makes it all the more interesting. What a pity the rugged scene is spoiled by a long line of giant, skeletal pylons straddling the hills on the far side of the lake. They're a necessary evil, though, as it's the most efficient way to transport one of Valais's main exports, electricity.

The topography that once isolated half the canton is perfectly suited to hydroelectric power (HEP), thanks to the combination of narrow valleys and plentiful water. Giant concrete dams, such as Grande Dixence (the world's tallest gravity dam), were built in the remote valleys of Valais and help Switzerland produce 56 per cent of its electricity from renewable sources, nearly all of it from HEP. That percentage will only increase in the next decade or so, as the

Swiss government has announced that it will not replace the country's five nuclear power stations when they are decommissioned. By 2034, nuclear power, which currently accounts for about 40 per cent of Switzerland's electricity production, will have been phased out. That's quite a challenge for a small country with no coal or gas of its own. The sad thing will be if Switzerland gets rid of its nuclear stations and then simply imports atomic-powered electricity from abroad.

No one seems to mind the metal arms and looping cables in the background, least of all the sheep. After their mass helter-skelter down the hill, driven on by men with sticks but very few dogs, they're happily munching away on tufts of grass. It's what sheep do best. I've never seen so many sheep in one place in Switzerland (this is cow-land, after all) and that, along with the scenery and singing in the background, makes me think of Wales. There's something about hills and music that belong together. I wonder how the Swiss would react to a full-volume rendition of "Bread of Heaven" from a Welsh male voice choir. It might scare the sheep. In terms of area, Wales is half the size of Switzerland, but whereas the principality has 3 million people and 9 million sheep, the republic has 8 million people and not even half a million sheep. No wonder you rarely see them (the sheep that is, not the Swiss) or get Swiss lamb on a menu, but Valais is the place to come for some Swiss sheep-spotting: with over 62,000 of the bleaters, it's the ovine capital of Switzerland.

Funnily enough, Swiss German speakers refer to the whole French-speaking part of the country as *Welschland* or *Welschschweiz*, and use the adjective *welsch* to describe anything from there; even the people become *Die Welschen*. You might think that Valais (Wallis in German) has some direct connection to Wales, like the Welsh immigrants in Patagonia, but the only link is terminological: Wales, Wallis, Valais, welsh and *welsch* all come from the same stem. This also isn't anything about being the most westerly part of the country, as Wallonia also has the same root and that's in southern Belgium. Originally it was a term used by the Romans for those areas of Celtic origin and goes back to the Volcae tribe; then it graduated into a German word for people who were not Germanic, particularly those who spoke a Romance language. In both cases it was a way of casting them as outsiders, people "not like us", whether they spoke a Celtic language or a French one. And it certainly has nothing to do with leeks, although our friend the Savoy cabbage is also known as *Welschkraut* in German, revealing its French roots.

After a couple of hours, I decide I'm not cut out to be a Swiss shepherd, even on a feast day like today. I've had my fill of baas and bells, and if anyone else yodels at me or blows his horn in my direction, I might scream. What was delightful at first has become frightfully repetitive. Perhaps you need to be Swiss to appreciate yodelling for more than ten minutes; after that it all begins to sound the same to me. Swiss television regularly has programmes (sometimes whole evenings) with traditional music, not just yodellers but *Hudigäggeler* bands as well. That's usually an accordion or two, a bass and a violin, sometimes a clarinet as well. Maybe once I've been here 30 years, I'll be watching it and tapping along with the polka-esque beat.

Our journey round to Kandersteg takes almost as long as walking across the pass: hike back up to the top, cable car down to Leukerbad, bus to Leuk, local train to Brig and regional train through the tunnel to Kandersteg. That's three hours or so, and that's with modern transport. It's no surprise that everyone used to walk over the Gemmi, which is exactly what I plan to do on my next visit.

Two months later, I return to Leukerbad without valium but with the intention of walking up and over the Gemmi. Once again my plans are thwarted by a local event, this one far more exhausting than a sheep festival: the Gemmi triathlon. The victims, sorry athletes, must first swim 900m in the Gerundensee (down in the Rhone valley), then cycle 23km up to Leukerbad before running to the top of the Gemmi – madness. The winning time is usually around two hours, in other words the same as it takes for many people to walk up the last leg of the race. Even if the path were open to the public today, which it isn't, I've been put off by all those super-sporty people jogging up. Luckily I can go by cable car, something that was not possible until 1957.

This is one of the few privately owned cable cars in Switzerland; it belongs to the Loretan family, who have been running it for three generations, along with the hotel-cum-restaurant that is at the top. Sitting on the panorama terrace eating a plate of Rösti and fried eggs is the perfect way to start any hike, so that's precisely what I do. Incidentally, the rather antiquated, cramped old cable car was replaced in 2012 by a sparkling new one with giant windows and more space. Not only is the journey a whole minute faster, but the new car doesn't need an operator inside it, merely at the station. That means it can run without a lunch break. Such is the nature of progress in rural Switzerland.

Duly fed, I set off, tacking round the far side of the lake. The hills are still as bare and bleak as before, with severe grey cliffs and coarse grass, but the pylons are soon behind me and the lake is trying hard to sparkle in the September sunshine. That's not easy when you're as much mud as water, but it gets an A for effort. At the halfway point is the Schwarenbach, a solitary but sturdy stone inn that has been quenching travellers' thirsts since 1742. Murray warned that "Complaints of extortion have been made", but apart from the lake itself it's the only watering hole along the route, so everyone calls in – including Pablo Picasso, Alexandre Dumas, Miss Jemima and, in 1904 while in exile in Switzerland, Vladimir Lenin. Twain stopped for a "nooning" (or midday break) and memorably described the exposed location:

> It sits in a lonely spot among the peaks, where it is swept by the trailing fringes of the cloud-rack, and is rained on, snowed on, and pelted and persecuted by the storms, nearly every day of its life.

It would be the perfect setting for a Gothic horror story and a shiver skitters down my spine.

The Schwarenbach inn also once served as a customs house, as it's the closest building to the border between Cantons Bern

The Schwarenbach inn on the Gemmi Pass was once a customs post between Switzerland and France

and Valais. For many centuries the Swiss cantons were in effect independent states tied together in a loose confederation; they had their own money, taxes and tolls, and there was no national internal market to speak of, so customs houses were needed at the borders. This one was there to impose taxes on goods like salt and wine, as well as to search for mineral water being smuggled out of Leukerbad. For a while this cantonal boundary was also the Swiss national border: after Napoleon conquered Switzerland in 1798, Valais was briefly a separate republic and was then annexed by France as the *département* of Simplon. The canton of Valais finally re-entered the Swiss Confederation in 1815, and the internal customs borders disappeared with the single market under the new federal constitution of 1848.

The second part of the walk is decidedly less bleak, with a softer edge to the landscape. Dark pines and lumpy meadows replace the relentless acres of scree slopes and bare rock, but it's still no picnic ground. Death can come in an instant. What appears to be a large gravestone beside the path is actually a memorial to six people killed by a glacial avalanche, though the 158 cows that also died don't get a mention. On 11 September 1895, 4.5 million cubic metres of ice calved away from the Altels glacier and came crashing down, covering two square kilometres of land with ice up to 7m thick. The spookiest thing is that Miss Jemima had commented on that very glacier three decades earlier:

> "[it] accumulates into a prodigious mass that once in a century loses its balance to come thundering over to the base. It is now sixty-seven years since the last crash."

The ice collapsed almost exactly 33 years later, and less than 24 hours after a large Thomas Cook group had passed beneath it. Luckily, there's no danger of a new crash now that the ice has retreated so much; one of the few advantages of climate change in the Alps.

Aside from the pylons and cable cars (and disappearing ice), this part of Switzerland has changed little since Miss Jemima walked this way, and probably for quite a while before that. The Gemmi was an important route between the south and north of the country, but only while there were no alternatives; as soon as the train arrived, its well-trodden path was off the beaten track. Its relative inaccessibility and challenging scenery (which isn't pretty enough for tourists who want chocolate-box Switzerland) have meant that it has remained undeveloped, although a road from Kandersteg to Leukerbad was briefly planned in 1948. It is a place to escape the crowds and trappings of modern tourism, which is probably why it's a popular hike with the Swiss themselves. Nevertheless, it is now back on the tourist trail, although a very specific one created by Via Storia, an organisation that researches and protects historical traffic routes in Switzerland. It offers guided walking tours along those routes and one is along what they call the Via Cook, in stages from Geneva to Kandersteg. With the hotels, luggage and transport (in between the walks) all organised, it's a natural successor to Cook's pioneering conducted tour. The guides even quote Miss Jemima along the way. When she wrote her daily travel journal back in 1863, she could never have guessed that it would become a historical source for twenty-first-century hiking tours. Would she be proud or embarrassed? Maybe a bit of both.

After three and half hours (and a second cable car, at the end of the path) I'm down in Kandersteg station, where we deboarded our train two months before. This village resort (more village than resort; it is not Chamonix) sits astride the tumbling Kander river and in the shadow of the majestic Blüemlisalp, one of the many Swiss peaks first conquered by an Englishman, in this case Sir Leslie Stephen, a Victorian man of words and deeds. In August 1860 he arrived in Kandersteg with his favourite Swiss guide, Melchior Anderegg, and asked if there was any local man willing to guide them to the top. There was only one volunteer, Fritz Ogi-Brügger.

For most Swiss people the mountains were the backdrop to their lives; they weren't there to be climbed, they were simply there. The English had a different idea: plant a Union Jack on top, just as that same flag had been planted on every continent of the globe. They had even founded the world's first Alpine Club (in London in 1857); Stephen would later become president of the club and carried on bagging Swiss summits, including Schreckhorn, the conical mountain that is the most northerly Alpine peak over 4000m. Not content with that, he used his pen as well as his pickaxe, writing the bestselling book *The Playground of Europe* and editing the first *Dictionary of National Biography*. Oh, and he found time to become a father of four, including a certain Virginia Woolf.

Melchior Anderegg went on to guide another Brit, Lucy Walker, when she became the first woman to climb the Matterhorn in 1871. By then the Swiss had long caught the climbing-for-fun bug, and in April 1863 had founded their own Alpine Club, the third oldest in the world after the Austrians, one of the few times in history that Switzerland lost out to Austria. Theirs is a rivalry resembling that of English and French, stretching all the way back to the creation of Switzerland in 1291 and the legend of William Tell. From then on, almost every battle has the Swiss on one side, the Austrians on the other (and usually losing). These days the contests are played out on the ski slopes every winter, and especially every Winter Olympics, where there's nothing more humiliating for a Swiss skier than being beaten by an Austrian.

As for the brave Fritz, without whom Sir Leslie might never have triumphed, his name lives on inside the village church, and in Kandersteg's most famous son, Adolf Ogi, former Swiss president and currently the wise old man of Swiss politics. Ex-presidents are ten a penny in Switzerland as the holder of the position changes every year; at any one time there are probably 13 or 14 ex-presidents floating around. Herr Ogi is one of the few who is still asked his opinion, and he's fondly remembered by most Swiss for his infamous television appearance in which he taught the nation how to boil an egg economically. Who said Swiss politics was dull?

Egg-boiling politicians aside, Kandersteg doesn't often make the national news. It's a gentle place with few cars (the road doesn't go much further) and a smattering of handsome wooden buildings. In tourist-brochure-speak it's probably "a sleepy village nestled between the mountains that boast a wealth of outdoor activities for all ages". But Kandersteg simply doesn't feel like the kind of place that would brag about anything. One main street, a pretty church, a great cheese shop, mountains all around and a river running through it; I can see why the Scouts come here. The International Scout Centre is near the village, offering plenty of opportunities to earn badges in camping or climbing, though I'm not sure it's quite right for crime prevention or traffic safety (both real badges for American Boy Scouts).

The Murray Handbook barely mentions the village, most likely because in those days there wasn't a lot there, but it does give us a picture of rural life in those parts where the villagers and farmers were self-sufficient:

> An Englishman accustomed to buy everything, can hardly realise the domestic economy of a Swiss peasant. He has patches of wheat, of potatoes, of barley, of hemp, of flax, and, if possible, of vines; his own cows, his own goats, his own sheep. On the produce of his own land and flocks

> *he feeds; his clothes are of homespun, from the wool of
> his sheep; his linen and the dresses of the women of his
> family are made from his own flax or hemp, frequently
> woven by the women of his own family. The timber he
> requires for his house or for firing is supplied from the
> land of commune or parish, either for nothing or a very
> small sum. What little money he requires is derived from
> the sale of cheese. The interior economy of a Swiss vil-
> lage is very interesting: it is only by ingenious contriv-
> ances for saving labour and by amazing industry that it
> is possible for the inhabitants to maintain themselves in
> such a climate.*

Miss Jemima doesn't reflect much on such subjects; she seems
happy simply to find food and shelter after another long day's
walk. The group had been on the go since getting up at 5am to
peer into the baths at Leukerbad; no wonder they decided "to
spend the night rather than walk to Frutigen, a few miles far-
ther". That's a slight understatement, as it's actually 17 hilly kilometres between Kandersteg and Frutigen, or about five hours of
walking.

They stopped at the "first habitation gained", the Hôtel de l'Ours
(or Bear Hotel), even though it was still being repaired from having
had the roof blown off the previous winter. Dinner was as ad hoc
as the sleeping quarters:

> "We ordered dinner and awaited its arrival until a dish of fish had
> been caught in the stream for our consumption. The good landlady
> did her best to make a stylish table d'hôte, and to multiply courses
> first served slices cut from the joint and followed that by clean
> plates and the joint itself!"

She adds a sad footnote at the end of the entry.

> "Alas! for the Hôtel de l'Ours – since our sojourn friends have
> passed its charred ruins and tell us of its complete destruction."

*The Hotel de l'Ours, Kandersteg burnt down soon after
Miss Jemima stayed here*

There's no sign of any ursine hotels in Kandersteg today, so instead we are being very British and staying in a B&B. Yes, they do exist in Switzerland. Some of them, it has to be said, are actually hotels that don't serve evening meals, so they technically offer a bed and breakfast but not in the traditional sense. This one, however, is the real deal, a proper B&B with a suitably English name, The Hayloft, which happens to be in a sixteenth-century Swiss chalet. It's the perfect British-Swiss combination, much like the couple who run it: Kerry is from Barking, Peter from the Gasteretal, a deep glacial valley near Kandersteg. With its giant A-frame roof, flowery window boxes, green shutters and dark wooden walls, the rustic house really is a picture-postcard place – and so Swiss that I expect Heidi to come running out the door. It's the closest I'll get to the sort of rural accommodation Cook's early guests would have stayed in, though luckily with modern plumbing and heating. And supper is served *table d'hôte* style, with a set menu (minus a still-gasping fish) and everyone sitting at one table; it could quite easily pass for one of the many evenings recounted in the journal.

While Kerry and my mother trade stories of B&B guests (my parents turned the family home into a B&B once all their children had left), Peter waxes lyrical about growing up in the Gasteretal. It was that, and wanting to be part of a community again, that brought him back – and I can understand why.

The community has a central role in Swiss life. As a political unit, it is the bedrock of the Swiss system of democracy; each is a self-governing entity with its own council, tax rates, schools, roads and rubbish bags. Today many communities are merging as they cannot cope with the financial burden of independence, so there are currently 2,495 communities in Switzerland, or about 500 fewer than 20 years ago. Some are tiny villages (Corippo in Ticino has a population of 12), others huge cities, such as Zurich with 375,000 people. The smallest is little bigger than a farm (Rivaz in Vaud is 31 hectares in area), but the largest (Glarus Süd at 430km²) outranks six of the cantons. No matter what their size, these smallest units of the Swiss political system are all controlled by the people who live in them – direct democracy in its most basic form.

Swiss communities are proud of their heritage, which in most cases stretches back for centuries. This isn't a political attachment, it's an emotional one, as every Swiss person derives his or her nationality (and even identity) from the community. In German this is known as the *Heimatort*, or place of origin, and isn't necessarily where you were born; it's the place your family comes from, perhaps generations ago, and that's what is listed in your passport rather than your place of birth. You might never have even seen it as it could be a little mountain village that your great-grandparents left behind long ago, but it is home, in the Swiss sense. Until 2012 that community was responsible for your welfare, even if you had never lived there, so it had to support you in times of need; that duty has now passed to the community of residence rather than the place of origin. Immigrants who apply to become Swiss must first be accepted by the community in which they live, whether that's by a public vote (a secret ballot is no longer allowed) or by an immigration committee. Their name usually then appears in the local newspaper, so people can object if they wish, and only once all that is done can they become citizens of the canton and the country.

It is no surprise that many communities (particularly those in tourist areas) have a small museum to display their history with pride. These local museums are never that grand or filled with the latest interactive displays, but they are nearly always fascinating places full of lives long gone. The one in Kandersteg is no exception. In two rooms it manages to give a great overview of the village through the ages, from forest traders through to Boy Scouts, and it even has a newer section on Miss Jemima. As in most village museums, there is a knowledgeable, helpful docent sitting in the corner waiting for a chance to tell a passing stranger all about the place.

Today it's the incomparable Frau Agostino, who becomes very animated when I ask a few questions about life before the trains arrived. She shows me old photos, including one of the ill-fated Hôtel de l'Ours before it turned to ashes, and tells me about the earliest visitors, such as Albrecht von Haller who wrote a famous poem about the Alps. I half expect her to encourage me to try the sedan chair sitting in the middle of the room. Luckily for me that is expressly forbidden, which is just as well as it looks exceedingly uncomfortable. This is no posh box with a satin lining, like the ones you see in films; it's a basic wooden chair with a lattice of ropes serving as the seat. It was carried by two, three or four men, depending on the passenger's weight. Going up, the short carriers went at the front, tall at the back, to keep the chair level; going down, the men swapped over. Three hours of sitting on that while being lugged up and down the hills would be enough to induce bot rot.

Best of all, Frau Agostino is a fountain of knowledge about the coming of the railway and what it meant for the village – jobs and development. The first decade or so of the twentieth century was boom time for the Gemmi Pass, as it was for most of the tourist industry in Switzerland. At the peak, in 1913, over 13,000 tourists made their way along the path between Leukerbad and Kandersteg. Bearing in mind that nearly all of them would have travelled in summer, it must have been like the M25 up there some days. Not everyone walked or was carried in chairs; instead, many rode in a Gemmi-cart, a two-wheeled contraption that cleverly kept the passenger level no matter what the gradient, although it still can't have been too comfy on the rocky route. As with so much development in the mountains, it was the train that was responsible for this explosion in tourist numbers; ironically, it would be the train that later reduced the Gemmi route to a sideshow.

In 1901 the railway arrived in Frutigen, a small village in the lower Kander valley near Lake Thun, which meant that tourists were within an easy carriage ride of the mountains. What had been a relatively remote valley (the first post-coach service to Kandersteg had been introduced only 13 years before) was now easily accessible from the rest of Switzerland. Every summer 100 or so carriages, many of them polished and lacquered, plied the route up river from the new train station to the growing resort of Kandersteg. But the Frutigen carriages and the Gemmi-carts disappeared overnight when the railway was extended up the valley and under the hills. In 1913 the last carriage trotted between Frutigen and Kandersteg flying a black flag to mourn the passing of a once lucrative trade. I wonder what happened to all the horses.

The new line, which was electrified from the beginning, included a 14km tunnel under the Lötschberg Pass and linked Bern with Italy via the existing tunnel under the Simplon. It was christened the Bern–Lötschberg–Simplon line (or BLS) and was largely financed by the French rather than the Swiss government; funnily enough, it was France that had built the first ever railway station in Switzerland, in Basel. After losing the Franco-Prussian War in 1871, the French had ceded Alsace-Lorraine to the new German state. In doing so they lost access to their station in Basel and beyond. Both the British and the French were reluctant to travel through Germany to reach Switzerland, so a new route to the Alps was planned, not least to further French strategic and business interests. First came a new French line to the Swiss border at Delle and then, with the help of Canton Bern (which had its own economic gains in mind), this was extended to the town of Porrentruy in northwestern Switzerland; Gustav Eiffel (of Tower fame) built some of the bridges. The opening of the Gotthard Tunnel in central Switzerland in 1882 made it imperative to find an alternative route through the Alps to Italy, and so the BLS was born.

Venture up to Porrentruy (or Pruntrut in German) today and you'll find a station far too grand for the pretty little country town it serves; a handsome relic of a busy international route. This was once the fourth-largest freight station in Switzerland, with a huge customs depot, and was one of the busiest for passenger traffic. At its height in the summer of 1914, Porrentruy saw 11 daily express trains passing through, as this was one of the main routes for British tourists to reach the Bernese Oberland and Italy; not forgetting the original Engadin Express, a direct train from Calais to Chur with first-class-only sleeping cars. Imagine such a service today.

BLS is now the second-largest train company in Switzerland (after the national rail outfit, SBB). With 436km of rail lines, plus the ships on Lakes Thun and Brienz, it carries 56 million passengers and 1.3 million cars annually. The latter are loaded onto special open-sided carriages (which look scarily like mobile Nissen huts with no walls) and transported under the Bernese Alps to Valais in 15 minutes. It's still by far the quickest way to reach Italy.

Building the tunnel, which was opened with great celebrations in July 1913, took 66 months but came at a cost: 52 million francs and 64 lives. Most of those who died were Italian, mainly because 97 per cent of the 3000 manual labourers who dug the tunnel were from Italy. Avalanches, floods, cave-ins and 34°C heat inside the rock, not forgetting working with 961 tons of explosives, made it dangerous work. Nevertheless, it was also a precision job. After years of tunnelling and thousands of accidents, the final result was remarkably close to the original plans: the differences between the drawings and the actual tunnel were 410mm in length, 257mm in width and 102mm in height. And yes, that is millimetres, in a tunnel that is 14.612km long – Swiss (and Italian) precision, even with dynamite and axes.

The Lötschberg tunnel changed Kandersteg completely. At first the effects came simply from the massive influx of workers

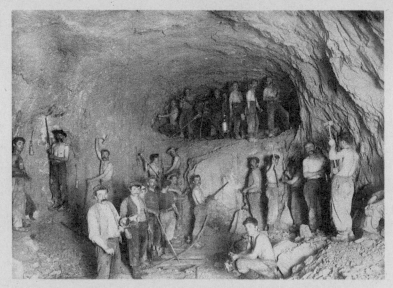

Italian immigrants provided the manpower for building the
Lötschberg line underneath the Alps

and their families. Given that it took seven years of hard labour
to excavate under the Alps, it's no surprise that the men brought
their wives and children with them. The population of the village
mushroomed from 445 people in 1900 to 3554 ten years later, at the
peak of tunnel building. A separate town sprang up with work-
shops and barracks, as well as a school, hospital and a Catholic
church for the immigrants. I'm tempted to ask Frau Agostino if
her name is a result of one of those families staying on after the
work was done; more than likely, but it's rather a personal question
to ask a museum guide, especially in Switzerland. I focus on the
story instead. Once the tunnel was complete, the site was abandoned until Lord Baden-Powell, a regular visitor to the valley, saw
an opportunity and raised money to buy the land, hence the annual
invasion of woggles.

While the Italians were busy constructing the tunnel, the Swiss
were busy building hotels. They foresaw that the new line would
transform the local economy, so they spent the time getting ready

for the onslaught: by 1914 there were 30 hotels and pensions in the village, many with their own ice rinks to cater for the growing winter trade. Confident of the good times ahead, Kandersteg seceded from neighbouring Kandergrund in 1908 and created its own separate community. As we have seen, in Swiss terms that's an important step. Of course, those anticipated good times for Kandersteg didn't last that long. Less than a year after the Lötschberg tunnel opened, an Austrian duke with a big moustache was murdered in Sarajevo. The world collapsed into the disaster that was the first half of the twentieth century, and Kandersteg wouldn't be the only place to see the after-effects. There were no bombs or bullets, but no tourists or trade either. It would be years before the guests returned in force.

The latest chapter of this village history is still playing itself out. In 2007 a new, deeper Lötschberg tunnel opened as part of the national plan for rail transport. At 34.6km long, it is currently the longest land tunnel in the world and has cut the journey time between Bern and Brig by 40 per cent. Double-decker trains, and more importantly a lot more cargo (two-thirds of heavy goods vehicles in Switzerland travel by train), can now whizz under the mountains in record time. The Swiss celebrate the opening of almost every tunnel, but this one was cause for a bigger party than normal: tickets to be the first to ride through it sold out months in advance, bands played, speeches were made and sausages were grilled. The tracks were blessed by both sides of the religious divide, which in Switzerland means Protestant and Catholic rather than any other religion, and everyone rejoiced in their shopping trips to Italy now taking an hour less each way. Everyone except the citizens of Kandersteg, that is.

The railway once brought the masses to Frutigen, where they climbed into carriages for the journey up the valley. Then it carried them right into Kandersteg itself, fuelling a boom that transformed the village. Today the new line bypasses both completely. Intercity trains no longer stop at either village, but instead dive down into the earth just outside Frutigen, coming up for air about 16 minutes later on the other side of the Bernese Alps. The old line still clatters up to Kandersteg before entering the original tunnel and winding its way down to the Rhone Valley, but it is now only for local trains. As Frau Agostino put it, "It was a big shock. Suddenly people were not stopping here any more." Instead, they were going straight to the peaks and slopes of Valais; direct services from Basel and Zurich to Brig now only take two hours, making day trips for walkers and skiers a reality. The Kander valley was in danger of going the same way as the Gemmi Pass, but it has fought back.

Kandersteg has some spectacular scenery on its doorstep, most notably the deep turquoise waters of Lake Oeschinen, but there's quite a lot of that in Switzerland. A beautiful lake and snowy mountains just aren't enough to draw in the crowds. So the village decided to focus on its heritage instead and created a Belle Époque week at the end of January. Every year villagers don period costume and go about their daily lives as if it were 1913: ladies in big dresses with frilly parasols, gentlemen in regimental uniform, "housemaids" pulling sleds loaded with groceries, schoolboys in knickerbockers and woollen socks. People indulge in a spot of curling and carriage riding, or partake in afternoon tea and dinner by candlelight. The post office and the Coop supermarket are dressed in hoardings to transform them back to how they once looked, and posters in the station are all changed to be authentic. It's rather like *Downton Abbey* on ice, and it's proved quite a hit. During that last week of January, it's not unusual to see yards of tweed and lace walking through Bern station as people change trains to reach Kandersteg. Not only villagers but visitors are raiding their grandparents' trunks and rootling around antique shops to find the perfect outfit. Top hats and crinoline are back in vogue, at least in one corner of Switzerland for seven days of the year.

Frutigen, on the other hand, has looked to the future. One unexpected byproduct of digging the new deep tunnel was warm water, although with Leukerbad just over the hill perhaps it was to be expected. The 20°C water was too warm to be pumped straight into the river, where it would harm the fish, so instead it has been harnessed to produce two things: tropical fruit and caviar. At the Tropenhaus the water gushes through at 100 litres per second,

The coming of the railway changed the Kander valley for ever

heating the tropical hothouse so that guavas, papayas, bananas and starfruit can grow. Next door, the mineral-rich water makes the perfect breeding ground for sturgeon, as it mirrors the conditions found in a Siberian summer. Even in the depths of winter, the fish are cosy and warm in their underwater world. So, rather unusually for Switzerland, visitors can buy home-grown mangoes and caviar; at 315 francs for 50 grams, the latter is as much a luxury as anywhere else in the world.

The story of the Kander valley over the past 150 years is almost that of tourism in Switzerland over the same period. A steady trickle of visitors always found their way here to admire the "bewildering beauty", as Miss Jemima described it, but services were low-key. The advent of train travel and group tours provided the impetus for change and the income to achieve it. Shepherds became mountain guides, farm workers turned to bar work, hotels were built and jobs created. Everyone could benefit from the influx of tourists, the cash cow that provided far more income than Daisy and Bella in the back field. But, as any farmer knows, putting all your eggs in one basket is not the best idea. While the scenery might stay the same, war and recession, as well as changes in taste and technology, mean that the numbers of those coming to see it are never stable – and never assured. Switzerland has one big natural advantage in the Alps, but it can't rely on that to be enough. Although the country was the birthplace of mass tourism, it must continually adapt to attract the next generation of visitors.

Today is 1 August, or Swiss National Day, and Kerry decides it's the perfect moment to get out the world's most impractical musical instrument and have a blow. The cosy kitchen-diner of the chalet B&B isn't quite the right place to play a 3.5m horn, so we gather in the garden for an impromptu concert. Sunshine, mountains, muesli and the melodious harmonies of the alphorn: I can't think of a more Swiss way to start a day of national celebration.

Public holidays in Switzerland are religiously observed, including the secular ones. Some are national, such as Christmas Day and 1 August; some are only observed in Catholic areas, for example Mary-went-to-Heaven Day (which is 15 August, for those Protestants who have no idea when that is – me included, until I moved to Switzerland); some are only for Protestant cantons, which typically have fewer holidays so created ones on days like 2 January to make up for the shortfall; and some are specific to one canton, for example Ticino celebrates its patron saint's day on 29 June. In all cases holidays are treated as holy days; that is, they become a Sunday, which means that normal life is suspended.

In Switzerland Sundays are still treasured as a day of rest – not necessarily for praying and going to church, but definitely not for car washing, window cleaning, recycling or doing some DIY. None of those is conducive to rest, relaxation and spending time with family and friends. As for shopping on a Sunday, forget it. There are a few shops open in train stations, airports and petrol stations, but otherwise the high streets of Switzerland are shuttered up until 9am on Monday. Having lived in London for 15 years, it took me a while to get used to the idea that shops were closed for 39 hours precisely when most people have time to spare. Now I rather like the idea, not because I'm at all religious, but simply because it makes a pleasant change to have one day in the week where you have to switch off. You can go to the cinema, visit friends, read a book, or be very Swiss and go for a walk. However, a Sunday walk in Switzerland is a hike in any other country: height differences of 400m or more, stony footpaths, boots and sticks required. Yes, the views are wonderful, but as you're a gasping wreck by the end of it all, you barely remember which mountains you saw.

After slowly and musically breaking our fast, we finally set off for the train down to the lake. For Miss Jemima it was no holiday, partly because she was here before Swiss National Day had been invented and partly because she had a long journey in store. She was, as ever, up at the crack of dawn and on her way before the larks even knew which day it was:

> "Up at 4.30 a.m. – breakfast quickly over, and we were soon seated in a rickety old carriage, drawn by a pair of rough-looking horses, in a hurry to catch the steamer at Spiez on Lake Thun. The hills in our descent to Frutigen were very steep. The chalets along the road were of greater pretensions than any we had seen, the gardens tidier, and some enterprise displayed in a new hotel with tastefully planned grounds, but was not all this easily accounted for? We were in a Protestant canton."

The world was sometimes very black and white to Victorian Britons: Protestant equalled hard-working, prosperous and simply better in almost every way; Catholic meant something slightly suspicious with its papal overlord, unnatural celibacy and bells and smells. You can almost hear Miss Jemima's sigh of relief to be back on Reformed ground. These days the main difference in the standard of living between Catholic Valais and Protestant Bern is that the former has fewer cows but more public holidays. Today is a holiday all across Switzerland, so there are Swiss flags fluttering everywhere. It's a modest but very apparent display of patriotism, not quite on the scale of the Fourth of July but enough to stand out.

The Swiss love to fly the flag, although very often it's the cantonal one rather than the national one. Maybe that's because the instantly recognisable red with a white cross isn't actually that old. The square flag (one of only two square national flags in the world, the other being from Vatican City) was first used as an army flag during that short civil war of 1847, but the exact proportions of the central cross were not settled until 1889. Only the Swiss could argue for years over the tiniest detail like the dimensions of the arms on a cross. In the end it took an act of parliament to settle the argument, meaning that a proper Swiss cross has arms that are of equal length but are one sixth longer than they are wide. Miss Jemima was here 26 years before that act, so it must have been most unsettling for her to have to look at a Swiss cross with disproportionate arms. As for the exact shade of scarlet, that took more than another century to decide: in 2007 it was set as Pantone 485. That's red to you and me.

It's quite hard to go anywhere in Switzerland at any time of year without seeing red and white flapping in the breeze. Maybe the inhabitants need to remind themselves sometimes that they are Swiss. It has often been said that a Swiss person only feels truly Swiss when he is abroad; until then his heart beats for his canton rather than his country. Or perhaps it's simply a matter of good marketing. There's nothing like a bit of brand awareness on a national scale to sell a few souvenirs and make those fleeting visitors aware that they're in Switzerland and not Sweden. And 1 August very handily falls in the middle of the prime tourist season, and was declared to be Swiss National Day only in 1891 for the 600th anniversary of the oath of confederation. The trouble is that no one is really sure exactly when that oath took place. The document signed by the first three cantons (Schwyz, Uri and Unterwalden) states: "So done in the year of our Lord 1291 at the beginning of the month of August." That is worryingly imprecise for the Swiss. After 600 years of doubt, they settled on the first as that is very obviously at the beginning of the month.

By the time we arrive in Spiez on the shores of Lake Thun, we've seen Swiss flags on almost every possible protrusion: car aerials, building sites, balconies and lampposts. There are also quite a few flagpoles, and not just official ones. I can't remember ever seeing a flagpole standing in someone's garden in Britain. Perhaps if I'd lived near Major-General Fotheringay (retired) it might seem normal, but for me there's something rather odd about having a flagpole between the barbecue and the potted basil. It seems very American, but it's apparently very Swiss.

We could simply change trains in Spiez and carry on to Interlaken, but the Junior United Alpine Club did not have that option. The railway would not arrive here for another 30 years, so they took the boat, although even that was not as simple as it sounds. From the dock beside the impressive Schloss, they were rowed out in a barge to meet the steamer coming from Thun, the main town at the northern end of the lake. Today we can sit beside the water and wait for our boat to glide in to pick us up. It's making all the stops like this that has lengthened the overall journey time. It once took 1¼ hours to sail from one end of the lake to the other; now it takes a little over two hours. Not everything in today's world is faster.

The first steamer plied its trade on Lake Thun in the mid-1830s and by the time Miss Jemima arrived to step on board, there was lively competition for passengers, mainly because the railway line had reached Thun in 1859 but went no further. After that travellers had no choice but to go by boat or carriage to Interlaken, although Murray casually notes that "The steamer does not take carriages", presumably a warning for those rich enough to have travelled from Britain with their own wheels. Those were the days, assuming you had the money. Our paddle steamer, the *Blümlisalp*, was launched in 1906 at the height of Lake Thun's popularity, when half of Europe came to enjoy the views from the wooden decks sailing over the calm blue-green water. Then came the wars, severe coal shortages and a switch to motor boats. Elegance was out. In 1971 the *Blümlisalp* was decommissioned, an unwanted reminder of past glory. Nevertheless, she survived the next two decades and came back into service, restored, repainted and more popular than ever – a huge white swan paddling gracefully across the water.

As stylish as she is, the *Blümlisalp* is not petite. Over 63m long and 13m wide, she can hold 750 passengers and travel at 25km/h. She is a dowager duchess at her most formidable, stately, aloof and unstoppable once she really gets going. Today she'll need every bit of oomph to reach Interlaken, as it seems that total maximum capacity is on board. You can barely see any deck at all in second class, with people sitting on every available inch of space, including each other.

Normally I stay down on the lower deck until we're underway to admire the technology of a paddle steamer in action: the heavy pistons pumping back and forth, the huge red paddle wheels spraying water in every direction, the cloying aroma of hot oil, the slight lurching motion until the boat finds a rhythm. It's wonderful, but today we can't get near the brass banister that surrounds the thumping heart of the boat. There are too many people, and the warm stickiness of steam and sweat combined is less than appealing. It's time to travel in style, so we climb upstairs to the relative tranquillity of first class. It's the Swiss boat equivalent of turning left when you board a big plane. From here we have a perfect view of what Miss Jemima called the "panorama of great beauty": the Eiger, Mönch and Jungfrau mountains. And we can breathe.

As the paddle steamer surges forward, cutting a swathe through the water, a welcome breeze tickles our faces and laps at the edges of the giant Swiss flag dangling from the flagpole. This is Swiss bliss. It would be hard to find a more inherently relaxing hour than sitting in one of these Belle Époque beauties, surrounded by polished wood and brass, in turn surrounded by shimmering water and mountains. This is slow travelling at its finest. We can sit back and relax until we reach the tourist capital of Switzerland, also known as Interlaken.

SIX

PARIS OF THE ALPS

*[Interlacken] was once a truly Swiss town; it is gradually
becoming a little Paris or Brussels. Fashion and gaiety
find their homes here, and the pleasure-seeker will vote
the town to be one of the most charming in Switzerland.*
—Cook's Tourist's Handbook to Switzerland, *1874*

*The white peak of the Jungfrau has always dominated the
Interlaken skyline*

Contrary to popular belief, Swiss public transport hasn't always been the epitome of perfect organisation and immaculate timing. Back in 1863 it was very different. The railway was in its infancy, so coaches, boats or horses were the only transport methods for large parts of the country, including Interlaken. This tourist town sits astride the River Aare on a flat plain between Lakes Thun and Brienz, hence its name, although that is a recent creation – the original village was called Aarmühle but was widely known as Interlaken (variously spelt Interlacken or Interlachen) until 1891 when the name was officially changed.

It is this position between the lakes and beneath the mountains that has always made it a must-see on any tour of Switzerland. This isn't because the town is that attractive, but for the setting and as a jumping-off point to explore the heights of the Bernese Oberland. However, before the railway arrived in 1872, reaching Interlaken involved a tranquil steamboat ride across Lake Thun followed by a chaotic coach ride into town. The steamers were too big to sail up the Aare so they docked on the lakeshore at Neuhaus, about 4km from the town centre, and unleashed their passengers into the maelstrom of carriages waiting for fares.

In his book *Die Erste Eisenbahn des Berner Oberlandes* (The First Railway of the Bernese Oberland), F.A. Volmar describes how arriving tourists were pounced on by the carriage drivers, desperate to get some of the action; those who resisted were "showered in curses". Later, when the drivers were forbidden from leaving their carriages, they yelled to attract customers' attention, even taking passengers for free to stop the competition earning anything. In 1870 there were 244 horse-drawn carriages (35 of them omnibuses) running the short route to Interlaken, where the only alternative was walking along the same road. That meant enduring the dust storm created by the carriages and "wading ankle-deep through the horse-shit", as one commentator described it.

Not that taking a carriage was much better. Volmar quotes one visitor, who complains of riding "along the narrow, dangerous route ... for those not sitting in the front carriage of the long procession, it was a trip in a veritable 'Stream of Dust', not forgetting the plague of horseflies, as well as the band of beggars." With thousands of tourists arriving during the summer season, there was good business to be made, even if that meant bitter fighting to win it. And it was big business. In 1863 the six steamers on Lake Thun carried over 160,000 passengers, while in the summer of 1867 a total of 24,684 tourists (a quarter of them British) stayed at least one night in Interlaken. The following year saw the first English winter guests, and by 1870 there were 73 hotels and guesthouses in the town. Today there are 31.

The dusty, dirty bottleneck at Neuhaus might have served the carriage drivers well, but it couldn't cope with the increasing numbers. A railway was the only answer and it wasn't long in coming. The Bödelibahn from Lake Thun to Interlaken (*Bödeli* refers to the flat plain between the lakes) opened its first section in August 1872, running trains with double-decker carriages – the top deck was open – at 25km/h. The loudest opposition came from the carriage drivers, who weren't objecting to the flood of tourists; they merely wanted to maintain their income stream. They all knew what progress entailed: as in Frutigen a generation later, the arrival of railway carriages meant the instant demise of the horse-drawn ones.

Double-decker trains run alongside Lake Thun to Interlaken today, though without open-top decks and with many more than three carriages. The original Bödelibahn disappeared long ago, replaced by more modern tracks, but its presence can still be noticed. Despite only having a population of around 5000, Interlaken has two stations, West and Ost, at opposite ends of the long main street. They are direct descendants of two Bödelibahn stations, relics of long-forgotten planning that survived because of another oddity: a railway that crosses the River Aare twice between the two stations for no geographical reason. The line could easily run along the south bank without any hindrance, but the planners were sneaky; they could envisage a time when the Aare might be widened in order to create a navigable canal between the two lakes. That would put the steamers in direct competition with their trains, and tourists could simply sail past Interlaken altogether. So they purposefully diverted the new line

A fleet of horse-drawn omnibuses once plied the road between
Interlaken and Lake Thun

across the Aare and back again, a double crossing that stopped
any such canal plans in their tracks.

There was once a scheme to have one grand central station in
the middle of town, on the south bank of the Aare behind the line of
posh hotels – convenient for tourists, inconvenient for businesses.
The inhabitants around the West station, the closer to the town
centre, feared "financial ruin" for their shops if that station were to
move. In the end it was the impossibility of getting ships to dock
beside any new central station, thanks to those two rail bridges,
that saved the day. Today's trains continue to make that unnecessary diversion and ships still cannot navigate the Aare, although
canals were built to bring the ships closer to the town centre. And
the two stations carry on serving their respective lakes, West for
Thun and Ost for Brienz, so passengers can transfer directly from
boat to train, or vice versa.

Geographical anomalies aside, the Bödelibahn is an interesting example of how and why many Swiss railways developed: tourism. In Britain and Germany, most lines were primarily built to link cities, factories, mines and ports, transporting coal, goods and workers; the railways were literally the engines of the industrial revolution. In Switzerland that wasn't always the case – it had no coal and small cities. Lines such as the Bödelibahn had one main purpose, to carry tourists to the mountains more efficiently. Interlaken wasn't an important business or population hub and without tourists the line would not have been viable, at least not in the 1870s. Tourism was the blood that gave many train lines life and kept them going. The lakes and mountains of the Bernese Oberland were a prime destination, especially for the British, who came in their thousands. In these mountain regions, away from the factories and money of the cities, tourists became the primary source of income and the main reason for development. No tourism, no trains – but also no trains, no tourism (at least not in massive numbers). It was a symbiotic relationship that suited both sides.

Miss Jemima and her friends knew nothing of all that. They arrived nine years before the train on Platform 1, but cunningly managed to miss out on the unseemly scrum of carriages at the dock. Instead, they took the scenic route to Interlaken via the Lauterbrunnen valley a few miles to the south, although Mr William confessed to his father, "The scenery of the valley of Lauterbrunnen is very famous but we were so tired that we were dozing all the way."

The scenery is indeed justly famous, a deep U-shaped glacial valley that is one of the natural wonders of Switzerland and seems to have leapt straight out of a geography textbook: steep sides of near-vertical rock, green meadows perched on the cliff tops, a wide flat valley floor, a small but lively river and, most memorably, towering waterfalls shooting out into thin air. It's one such waterfall that was the sole reason for Miss Jemima venturing up here: the Staubbach Falls, which Wordsworth called "this sky-born waterfall". Its name literally translates as the "dust-stream-falls", although mist would be equally apt. The Staubbach is a little brook, so there's no raging cataract thundering over the edge of the cliff; this is one long, delicate veil of tiny particles carried by the wind as much as gravity. It's the kind of waterfall that would grace Rivendell, where elves could wash their golden locks in the fine spray.

With a drop of 297m, this is one of the highest free-falling waterfalls in Europe, so definitely warrants a closer look. The path from the station winds through the village, which in winter seems to be almost permanently in the shade: the sheer cliffs are so high that the sun can barely reach the valley floor, even when no fog is lingering along the river. You can see the falls all the way, but can only hear them once you get near the base, so fine is the spray splashing down onto the rock. Lord Byron wrote:

> I have never seen anything like it. It looked just like a rainbow which came down for a visit, and was so near that one could just step into it.

Now you can almost step into it, thanks to a trail that climbs up to the rock face and tunnels through it, coming out behind the veil of water. It's dark and slippery in there, with water dripping from every nook, but worth it for the view of the valley and mountains through "the tail of a white horse streaming in the wind" (Byron again).

What is amazing is not the view but that so few people walk up there to enjoy it. For most tourists, Lauterbrunnen is merely a place to change trains on the way up to Europe's highest railway station at Jungfraujoch, and the Staubbach is photographed from a train window. The valley used to be famous for its lace making, with 450 lace makers (out of 650 families) in business as late as 1917. As with many traditional Swiss handicrafts, such as wood carving or embroidery, it was literally a cottage industry. In the days before mechanised factories, much of the work was outsourced to crafts-men (and women) who worked at home and were paid by the day. For example, a home-worker in the textile industry earned about 1.50 francs (or about 22 francs today) for a 12-hour day, or about half the daily wage of an experienced tailor, but neither amount went very far: a kilo of butter cost over 2 francs, as did a new shirt. In Britain the same workers earned twice as much.

"This sky-born waterfall" was Wordsworth's description of the Staubbach Falls, Lauterbrunnen

Sometimes lace making was the main source of income, but often it supplemented what the villagers could earn from farming, particularly in the winter months. Industrialisation made much of this uneconomic, so production shifted to factories, although traditional handicrafts lived on in the shape of souvenirs. Miss Jemima noted:

> "The road from the Fall to the inn was populated with carved wood stores, and juvenile mendicants [beggars] offering a flower or pebble for sale."

And where that didn't provide enough income, the locals replaced working at home with working in hotels, or as tour guides or porters. They had been used to having more than one job, so all that changed was the nature of the second one.

Lauterbrunnen still has about 20 lace makers, but it's now much better known for something far more thrilling than a doily.

In an attempt to get people to stay longer than seven minutes when changing trains, the village has reinvented itself as a centre for adventure, attracting white-water rafters, climbers and those crazy enough to jump off the cliff tops. They aren't just paragliders but base jumpers, who leap off fixed objects (like a cliff) and fall at up to 190km/h, with only a few seconds to open a small parachute. The resort of Mürren, on top of a cliff 800m above Lauterbrunnen, is a popular jumping-off point. Near the centre of the village is what looks like a metal diving board sticking out over the cliff edge into thin air. It's a nerve-wracking experience to watch someone stand on that platform, take two steps and then jump off with arms and legs in a starburst position. All being well, ten seconds later he (and it is usually a he) will land down on the ground, but sadly all is not always well. Almost every year someone dies, and the Swiss Base Association website has a page called The Dark Side, listing all those who have died in this valley for their sport. Fun can be fatal.

There are 71 other waterfalls in the Lauterbrunnen Valley, although if you come in late summer, when streams are reduced to a steady drip, you'd be hard pushed to count that many. My favourite isn't actually the perpendicular Staubbach but the cork-screw Trümmelbach, a series of ten falls that cascade down inside a mountain and are accessible by a lift inside the rock. The melt-waters of the glaciers high above come crashing down at a rate of 20,000 litres per second, filling the caves with a thunderous roar and soaking onlookers brave enough to go to the edge. It's not Niagara, but you emerge into the glaring sunlight wet, deaf and ready to do it all again, especially when it's 35°C outside. Who needs air-conditioning when you can stand beside an underground waterfall?

Interlaken has no such obvious natural tourist attractions; this place is all about location. While the West station is a tiny two-platform affair, Ost is the Clapham Junction of Canton Bern. The long intercity trains, some from as far away as Hamburg, all end here, as do the normal-gauge tracks. If you want to go into the mountains or over the hills to Lucerne, you must change here to

a narrower-gauge railway. That makes for some fairly busy platforms in summer and winter peak seasons; with Swiss timetables
so finely tuned, you only have a couple of minutes to find your next
train through the crowds. It's not as chaotic as the Neuhaus carriages (with no shouting or begging), but more than a few tourists
lose their way among the waves of passengers streaming up and
down between the platforms.

Having access to all those trains makes Interlaken a convenient
base for a holiday, and as transport hubs go there can be few more
scenically placed, with the ever-white Jungfrau visible from almost
everywhere. The resort has changed in the past 150 years, but that
fact remains the same. As Murray said:

> Interlaken has few sights or lions for the tourist or pass-
> ing traveller, who need not stop here, unless he require
> to rest himself. Its beautiful position, however, on a lit-
> tle plain between the lakes, in full view of the Jungfrau,
> whose snowy summit is seen through a gap in the minor
> chain of Alps, its vicinity to numerous interesting sites,
> and some of the most pleasing excursions in Switzerland
> ... have converted it into a sort of watering-place,
> thronged with English, German, American and other
> foreign visitors.

And that was before the railway arrived, before the real mass invasions started in earnest. The town itself is pleasant enough, though
nothing to write home about. What was once Aarmühle is still
there at the West end, with a few little gems of architectural glory
amid the modern mediocrity. But many tourists don't ever venture
beyond the one long main street stretching all the way to Ost station and lined for the most part with cafés, bars, hotels, souvenir
shops and all the usual trappings of a resort, albeit one with a genteel air; this is no Magaluf. However, it certainly has changed since
the 1860s, when the Murray Handbook said: "The village itself, a
collection of white-washed lodging houses, with trim green blinds,
has nothing Swiss in its character." It still isn't that Swiss, though

*By 1863 Interlaken already had some grand hotels, but the
grandest were yet to come*

there are a few nods to local style (excluding Hooters bar, that is),
but it is no longer a village of white-washed houses; it is a town
of hotels. Some are grand, others are faded, such as the forlorn
empty Schweizerhof right in the middle of town; some have that
faded-grandeur look going on; some have treasured their heritage, others have massacred it. At first glance, the Splendid is anything but, thanks to "the stylistically unfortunate redesign of the
ground and first floors", as the tourist office's historical notice on
the wall diplomatically puts it. An ugly great wart on an otherwise
tasteful façade of Victorian gables and towers would be a better
description.

The queen of Interlaken's hotels is undoubtedly the Victoria-
Jungfrau, one of the grandest Grand Hotels in Switzerland.
When Miss Jemima was here, this was still two separate small

establishments, the Victoria and the Jungfrau, but they were soon transformed by owner Eduard Ruchti and French architect Horace Edouard Davinet into the epitome of luxury on a vast scale: hundreds of bedrooms, stuccoed reading rooms, gilded ballrooms and shady terraces. The hotel had electric lighting eight years before the town's streets, the first lift in Interlaken and Switzerland's largest internal telephone switchboard. The crowning glory was the stylish domed tower, added in 1899 and the town's dominant landmark until it was overshadowed by what would be the runaway winner of Switzerland's Ugliest Hotel award, if that existed. Not only is the concrete tower of the Metropole a hideous building in its own right, it gets extra Brownie points for replacing a grand old hotel, the Ritschard, and destroying an otherwise pleasant urban skyline. Worst of all, it towers over the graceful lines and elegant curves of the Victoria-Jungfrau, a giant bully threatening an old lady. Shame on whoever gave planning permission for that to happen.

Contrast that with an exemplary piece of civic far-sightedness: the large open space that sits in the centre of town opposite the Victoria-Jungfrau. Known as the Höhematte, this was once on the edge of the village and had belonged to Canton Bern since the Reformation, but in 1863–64 the state was selling off its property. With Interlaken expanding, the plan was to parcel it up and sell it to developers cashing in on the hotel boom. That would have meant an end to the unspoilt views of the Jungfrau and made Interlaken a much more urban place, possibly ruining the very reason it was so popular. Luckily, that never happened. Not everyone saw development as the answer and, after much wrangling, the Bernese parliament eventually approved Plan B: the Höhematte was bought by a group of shareholders who vowed never to build on it. And they never have. It remains a green and pleasant patch of land, where it's not unusual to see a farmer out harvesting his hay.

It was the presence of the grand hotels that possibly led Hans Christian Andersen, a frequent guest in Interlaken, to christen the town "the Paris of the Alps". That's a slight overstatement, but then again he was a writer of extraordinary fairytales. Thomas Cook was more prosaic: after his visit to Interlaken in the summer of 1863, he called it "the metropolis of Swiss Tours" and "that Brighton or Scarborough of Switzerland", clearly trying to convey the idea that it was a holiday resort of some note. Nevertheless, the *Guide to Cook's Tours* decided that was a false analogy, given that the sea is 300km away and the lakes cannot even be seen from the centre of town. Two years later, it described Interlaken as the "Leamington or Cheltenham of Switzerland". There is still the slight problem of neither being anywhere near 4000m mountains, but you could put it down to poetic licence. Travel brochures have never been any good at telling the whole truth.

Back in the late nineteenth century Interlaken very probably was like an English country town, not in terms of landscape but society. The English upper-middle classes sometimes stayed for weeks during the "season" and no doubt had the same urge to see and be seen as back home. The local paper even carried details of who had arrived in town so that people knew to call on them – friends for pleasure, local tradesmen for business. As Murray says of Interlaken, "its almost endless walks and rides, its boating parties on the two lakes, its picnics and balls, would, in the society of friends, afford amusement for a season". For Miss Jemima's group, this is where they once again had access to their trunks, sent on from Chamonix a week earlier. Dressing for dinner was now a real option, and most likely expected of guests, so that "the ladies, having got possession of the long-absent trunks, dazzled our eyes with almost forgotten splendour".

And then there were two church services in English every Sunday, which is exactly where the majority of her Alpine Club went at 11am on their full day in town:

> "The sermon was pretty good, although the doctrines were slightly too much in harmony with human nature to arouse the hearers to severe self-scrutiny. It was rather religion presented walking in silver slippers."

The Höhematte in Interlaken has long been protected as an open space since it was bought from the canton in 1863

They were a tough crowd for an English vicar abroad, expecting a bit more fire and brimstone in Protestant Canton Bern. Nevertheless, she does admit that the "English services have a charm of their own", and then expressed what so many English travellers then and since have often thought:

> "How refreshing it is after wandering for days among foreigners to meet again with fellow countrymen and join them in prayer for dear old England, in the familiar language of home."

Substitute going to an English church and praying for England with going to an English pub and praying for England to win, and it's essentially the same experience.

That Sunday for Miss Jemima was most definitely a day of rest, which might sound bizarre given that she was on holiday, but you have to remember two things. First, it didn't matter where you were or what else you were doing, if you were a Victorian

Protestant, you took Sunday very seriously. Secondly, on the seventh day God rested, and he had been only marginally busier than Miss Jemima. The Cook group had had nine days of continual early mornings, long hikes, hot weather, too much excitement and not enough sleep; no wonder Miss Jemima complained of fatigue, even if the moans were good-natured. The longer the trip continues, the more admiration I have for the stamina and dedication of those first tourists. They barely paused for breath most days, and followed a hectic itinerary that would leave modern tourists wilting after a week.

At breakfast my mother makes an announcement. "Today is Sunday."

After being away for so long, every day is beginning to feel the same, but I know that today is definitely not Sunday; it's not even a Swiss Sunday; that is, a holiday disguised as a Sunday. That was yesterday.

I shake my head. "It's Tuesday."

"Not in 1863, it's not."

My mother has been reading Miss Jemima's journal as we go, in order to get a feel for how she saw the world and had to travel. It's easier than dressing up in crinoline and not changing your underwear for a week. And this day in that hectic schedule was a Sunday, which, as we have seen above, was an obligatory day of rest. She opens the diary and shows me the page: "Sunday, 5th July 1863 Interlacken".

"And?" I ask nervously.

My mother smiles. "And I'm making this a day of rest. We are going to go for a walk, indulge in afternoon tea, poke our heads into the church and generally do not a lot. This is the most exhausting holiday I've ever been on. I need a day off."

So we decided that even though in our terms it was a Tuesday, we would have a day off. We take a stroll through town, just as countless thousands have done before us, starting where Miss Jemima finished, over the river in Unterseen. To the unsuspecting visitor Unterseen may appear to be part of Interlaken, but, in true Swiss style, it is actually a separate community, even if its name means the same as its larger neighbour's (*Seen* is German for "lakes"). Unterseen has a distinctly medieval air to it: a cobbled square that used to host cattle markets, the blunt-pencil tower of the bare stone church, the refined townhouses with deep roof overhangs against the snow, the restaurant Bären whose wooden walls were 200 years old when Miss Jemima saw them. It is almost like stepping back in time, especially in the small local tourism museum, which is essentially the community's treasure chest. The undoubted highlights are a model of the Bödelibahn trains (not very comfortable) and the woman in charge sitting behind her desk and knitting all the time we were there (very comforting).

We also discover why Unterseen has that old-world feel going on: the railway bypassed it completely. The horse-drawn carriages from Neuhaus all used to clatter through here, making it the first stop for many visitors, but the railway line was built on the other side of the river, from lakeside Därligen direct to Interlaken. At the time, it was a huge economic setback for Unterseen, with some in the community joining the carriage drivers and canal planners in opposing the railway (though not the tourists and their money). But becoming a half-overlooked sideshow meant that Unterseen held on to its rustic charm while letting Interlaken develop into an international resort.

Round the corner, on the way back to Interlaken, we're confronted with a garish yellow banner touting "Table Dance Night Club" in big red letters. Beneath it is what could pass for a restaurant menu board, but is actually information about the Palace Topless Cabaret and No1 Strip Club, open from 5pm to 5am. It's a startling reminder of the real world, especially as it's located in the Hotel Central & Continental. Its pastel walls and ornamental balconies show that this was once Unterseen's grand hotel, one that advertised having "75 beds, 21 balconies, electric lights in all rooms, foreign newspapers". Now it sits above an "Exotic Night Club", a Bierkeller and a restaurant "Voted #1 for Asian food". That's progress for you.

Unterseen was always far more bucolic than its famous neighbour

Over the Aare again and past the West station, we are back in Interlaken proper. You can tell, because the first two things you see are a souvenir shop and a Best Western hotel (which would be a close runner-up to the Metropole in the Ugliest Hotel awards). Thomas Cook wrote that the shops in Interlaken were "richly furnished with the choicest works of Swiss art and ingenuity". That is still sometimes the case, although you may have to search to find the art, such as hand-carved wooden animals or bags made from old Swiss army blankets. Of course, there are also plenty of badly painted plates, T-shirts with silly slogans and garish fridge magnets, not forgetting the obligatory cow bells. Almost every souvenir shop in Switzerland has a black metal stand outside laden with decorative bells of all sizes; it's tempting to give each one a shake.

Cow bells and mouse mats are simply the latest in a long line of souvenirs that have helped sell Switzerland. Having such iconic products that tourists willingly bought and took home was a

*Hotels advertised their modern comforts, such as
"electric lights in all rooms"*

brilliant early form of guerrilla marketing that did more to advertise the country than the Swiss could ever have afforded. Back in
1863 it was watches, wooden toys and lace, all of which helped
build the Swiss reputation for quality and attention to detail. Then
came milk chocolate, possibly the biggest weapon in the Swiss
souvenir arsenal. Chocolate had been produced in Switzerland for
about 60 years when, in 1875, Daniel Peter of Vevey perfected the
way of making a sweeter milk version. That became so successful, and so readily identified with Switzerland, that even British
chocolate makers like Rowntree of York decorated their wrappers
with bucolic Swiss scenes. Free advertising in every sweet shop in
Britain.

Another success was the little red army knives, which became
famous in America when returning GIs took them home after the
Second World War. This archetypal Swiss souvenir was first created in Schwyz, the town that gave the country its name, by Karl
Elsener, a cutlery maker. In 1897 he transformed the humble penknife into a Swiss officer's knife with screwdrivers, bottle opener,

nail file, toothpick – oh, and a blade or two. These Victorinox knives have suitably rugged names like Champ, Ranger, Huntsman and Mountaineer, as if every tourist who buys one is about to go and descale a fish or defuse a bomb. But it's not only tourists. I'm sure it's in the constitution that every Swiss man has to own one, as part of the national defence system, along with guns under the beds and nuclear bunkers under the houses. And even little Swiss girls seem to be disturbingly drawn to them (which might explain the pink one I saw in Forclaz). Modern-day Heidis are actually all *Pfadis* (or scouts), so they need a penknife for whittling sticks and slicing sausages. By the way, Swiss soldiers are issued with a different knife, big and green rather than small and red, with scarily long blades that are probably illegal in Britain, and no corkscrew.

As for cuckoo clocks, there are plenty of those, but let's get one thing straight: cuckoo clocks are not Swiss. Quite how that myth started is a mystery, although lots of people believe it. Possibly it's down to Orson Welles' (in)famous line in the film *The Third Man*, when he says that 500 years of democracy and peace in Switzerland produced nothing more than the cuckoo clock. That's wrong on two counts: Switzerland had a very bloody peaceless past until it decided to be neutral, and the cuckoo clock comes from over the German border in the Black Forest. While most Swiss people will happily point that out, most Swiss souvenir shops will sell a cuckoo clock to anyone who wants it.

The funny thing about Swiss souvenirs is that they went from advertising the country to being a bit embarrassing, but are now experiencing a resurgence. When I first started visiting Switzerland on a regular basis 12 years ago, you had to go to tourist spots like Interlaken or Gruyères to stand any chance of finding a mug or mouse mat emblazoned with a Swiss flag. I remember seeing my very first cow-that-yodels-when-you-press-its-stomach in Appenzell, the cheesey town in eastern Switzerland that is almost Disneyesque in its prettiness. Now I can buy them in my local Coop supermarket in Bern. While the number of tourists hasn't increased over that time period (it's actually gone down), the Swiss have fallen in love with selling themselves again, or at least the idealised image of themselves. Swiss bashing is out, Swissness is in, whether that's a renewed interest in *Schwingen* (traditional Swiss wrestling); or protecting the quality of goods that are Swiss made; or selling souvenirs with Swiss flags all over them. After the traumas of the Swissair collapse and the Nazi gold affair, not to mention the ongoing soap opera of banking secrecy, perhaps the Swiss want and need to feel good about themselves.

I tempt my mother away from the souvenirs with the promise of tea and cake at Café Schuh. This delightful old building on the edge of the Höhematte, with gables that look like a giant nun's wimple, has been enticing customers with its delectable confections since 1818, so I see no reason to break with that tradition. Sitting on the sunny terrace with a piano being played in the background and the mountains in front of us, it could easily be 1863. And then a tandem paraglider sails over our heads and lands expertly on the Höhematte; that's definitely not 1863.

Our last stop was Miss Jemima's first. The Schlosskirche, where she sang her praises in English, is but one example of the small but significant effects of British visitors arriving in large numbers. It was originally part of the Augustinian monastery that was one of the biggest landowners in the Bernese Oberland. In 1528, when the Reformation was officially accepted in Canton Bern, the monastery was effectively nationalised and taken over by the state. The Oberland didn't react too well to being told to reform, but resistance was futile and the church was converted into a granary, with the rest of the monastery becoming government offices.

It was only in the mid-nineteenth century that the choir of the dilapidated building was used once again for religious services, this time for English tourists. Their arrival en masse, and desire for services in English, led to the parish acquiring the church back from the state and building a new nave. In other resorts the influx of English-speaking Protestants, who didn't want to abandon their strict observance of the Sabbath, led to the building of English churches, some of which still are in use today, for example in Wengen. In addition, as the Murray Handbook notes, "several wealthy innkeepers have even gone so far as to build English

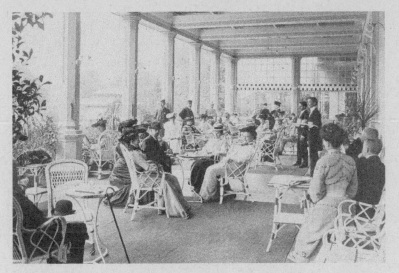

Tea on the terrace of the Hotel Victoria-Jungfrau, Interlaken
was always elegant

chapels for their guests, as an inducement to English travellers to pass the Sunday with them." Today, there are still English Sunday services in high summer, in a small plain chapel near the Schlosskirche. It's something of a local tradition.

After our day of rest, my mother and I are both up early and ready to face the world of travel again. Perhaps those Victorians, and these Swiss, really do have the right idea. "A 24/7 society is convenient but is it healthy? Discuss."

Today's agenda is one of my favourite train journeys in Switzerland, which I have done many times before but am more than happy to repeat: from Interlaken to Wengen, up over Kleine Scheidegg and down to Grindelwald. It has everything a Swiss mountain train journey needs: spectacular views and uncomfortable seats. All we are lacking is some sunshine. Interlaken has the same bad-weather problem that we experienced in Chamonix. When it rains, there aren't too many options for entertainment, so most people end up going to Bern for some shopping. It's

179

pointless taking a train up into the clouds, though I'm sure some tourists do exactly that purely to tick that trip off the list. Our list is slightly different from most: not been-there-done-that, but she-went-there-so-we-must-do-it.

This train seems to go on for ever, stretching the whole length of what is a very long platform. However, the Berner Oberland-Bahn (or BOB to its friends) is a tricksy train because it's actually two linked together, and after a couple of stops they split, one half going to Grindelwald, the other to Lauterbrunnen. That fact is clearly signed and announced, but there's always one poor tourist who is in the wrong half and has to leap out and dash to the other at the splitting station. It wasn't designed to confuse tourists, though I'm sure the locals still find that amusing, but to make more efficient (and so more Swiss) use of the topography. After crossing the Bödeli plain, the Y-shaped line enters the Lütschine river valley at a narrow opening between the hills and then follows it up river. At the point where the Weisse and Schwarze Lütschine rivers meet, the train splits and each half climbs up its respective river: Weisse (or white) to Lauterbrunnen and Schwarze (or black) to Grindelwald. Ironically it's the latter that is popular for white-water rafting, despite the ominous dark grey water, so thick with glacial deposits that it looks like liquid slate. Today we will be taking the route Miss Jemima covered by carriage, following the chalky white arm, although of course in winter both rivers are crystal clear, as there is no meltwater.

Before we can enter the "narrow and savage gorge of the torrent Lütschine", we pass the oddest collection of buildings ever erected in Switzerland: a pyramid, a ziggurat, a golden dome and what appears to be a giant Chupa Chups lolly. That's the Jungfrau Park, Interlaken's answer to the rainy-day problem. It started life as the Mystery Park, although the only mystery is why it ever opened. For a brief moment it was one of the most popular tourist attractions in Switzerland, and then people realised it was actually nothing more than a monument to one man's ego and weird theories. The man in question was Erich von Däniken, a Swiss author famous for his first book, *Chariots of the Gods*. Each pavilion in the park covered a different human mystery, such as the Nazca lines or Stonehenge, and showed a film about it. The answer every time was "Aliens did it!", which is pretty much what von Däniken says in his books. It was a theme park that was all theme and no park. By 2006 it was bankrupt, as dead as the ancient Egyptians. Now it's been reincarnated (presumably without help from ET) as the Jungfrau Park, with daytime fun for kids alongside the Aliens-Did-It pavilions.

Leaving behind that perfect example of how tourism doesn't always equal success, we head on towards the real reason people keep on coming to Interlaken, in rain and shine: the timeless scenery. Whether that was created by God, Mother Nature or Martians, it is truly wonderful.

At Lauterbrunnen it's all change for the ascent to Wengen. The Junior United Alpine Club, having come this far by carriage, now tackled "the usual toilage of zigzags" on foot. First they had to run the gauntlet of the guides awaiting their arrival:

> "We started and set at naught the extortionate demands of a swarm of guides that beset us, who, seeing our independence, came down in their terms. One pursued us who became our guide and porter in one, ingeniously packing all our belongings into a sort of wooden chair, which was fastened to his shoulders."

We have no one hassling us to carry our bags as, in the shadow of the huge cliffs, we swap our BOB for a WAB (or Wengernalpbahn), the yellow and green mountain train that chugs up the steep side of the valley. The higher we climb, the smaller the village of Lauterbrunnen looks, and even the Staubbach Falls become lost in the vastness of the trench-like valley. Every corner brings a better view, but to help you take the perfect photo, at one point beside the track there's a little sign with a pictogram of a camera on it; such attention to detail.

We pass on through the cliff-top resort of Wengen to Wengernalp, which has possibly one of the best views in Switzerland: "in almost military line the pointed Eiger, the cowled Mönch, the glistening

Jungfrau", as Miss Jemima described the trio of grandiose mountains that are the symbol of the Oberland. I always enjoy the fact that the Eiger (ogre in English) is separated from the Jungfrau (virgin) by the Mönch (monk). Henry Wordsworth Longfellow called them "those sublime apostles of Nature, whose sermons are avalanches", and that indeed was what Wengernalp used to be famous for, as an avalanche viewing platform:

> It is from Wengern Alp that avalanches are seen and heard in greatest perfection ... the attention is first arrested by a distant roar, not unlike thunder, and in half a minute, a gush of white powder, resembling a small cataract is perceived issuing out of one of the upper grooves or gullies; it then sinks into a low fissure, and is lost only to reemerge at a lower stage some hundred feet below; soon after another roar, and a fresh gush from a lower gully, till the mass of ice, reaching the lowest step, is precipitated into the gulf below.

The scale of the whole drama is almost lost against the backdrop of such giant mountains, so Murray goes on to remind us that these avalanches are "caused only by the rupture of a portion of the glaciers" and "at each discharge whole tons of ice are hurled down the mountain, and that the seeming dust to which it is reduced includes blocks capable of sweeping away large trees, if such occurred in their course. During the early part of the summer three or four such discharges may be seen in an hour."

In all the times I have walked over Wengernalp, I have never witnessed such a spectacle. Once there was a distant rumble that made me inspect the mountain opposite for evidence of tumbling debris, but nothing more. I think it's simply a case of there now being so much less snow and ice that the daily discharge is no longer brought on by the sheer weight and volume of ice reacting to the warm sunshine. What once would "much enhance the interest of a visit to the Wengern Alp" is now a rare event, although the walk from here up to the pass at Kleine Scheidegg is still one of

The line from Grindelwald up to Kleine Scheidegg opened in 1893

the best in Switzerland (for non-walkers, that is). Dedicated Swiss hikers most likely think it is something for old ladies.

We get off at the top of the WAB line in Kleine Scheidegg, the crossover point for trains to and from Grindelwald and Wengen. It's an odd place, where half the world comes to eat, drink and change trains, but it's really in the middle of nowhere. Except that it's at the foot of the Eiger and in the heart of the area that every Victorian visitor wanted to see, hence the great train links. The BOB and WAB lines were built for tourists, as simple as that. When they opened in 1890 and 1893 respectively, there was no other reason to go to those places. They were, and still are, only financially viable because of the thousands of tourists wanting to enjoy the landscape of the Bernese Oberland and not take all day to get there. A main road eventually made its way up to Grindelwald but Wengen remains car-free, as does Mürren on the opposite side of the Lauterbrunnen valley. Even in the age of the automobile, some places prosper without cars.

In June 1907, an article entitled "A Wonderful Railway Excursion" appeared in *The Traveller's Gazette*, the Thomas Cook newspaper that had replaced *The Excursionist*. It extolled the virtues of the train trip over Wengernalp for a certain segment of the travelling public:

> We may remark that it would seem to be an ideal railway journey for honeymooners. It gives them a rest. For the most affectionately disposed Algie and Angelina could not possibly be absorbed in anything but the grand and glorious scenery.

The price of the return trip from Interlaken to Grindelwald via Wengen was then more than a bob or two: 18/6, about £60 in today's money, or two-thirds of the cost of that same ticket now.

A plate of *Älplermakkaroni* – a dish of macaroni and diced potatoes in a creamy cheesy sauce, served with apple purée – while sitting in the sun with a view of the Eiger: heaven at 2061m up and my normal indulgence when at Kleine Scheidegg. In the summer it's after a suitably hearty walk, and usually with some goats that happily trot over to lick the sweat off your arms; in winter it's to escape the endless fog that settles in the valleys. There's been a hotel here since 1840 and it hosted all the great Alpine climbers before their attempts on the North Face of the Eiger; some of them made it back down to stay another night. Guests – and the media – followed every moment of the life-and-death climbs from the terrace with telescopes; an Alpine version of gladiatorial combat, with an ogre replacing the lions.

However, the railway doesn't stop here, thanks to the vision of a businessman from Zurich who loved both trains and mountains, so decided to combine the two. Adolf Guyer-Zeller planned to build a modern miracle, an electric line from Kleine Scheidegg up inside the Eiger and then on underground to the summit of the Jungfrau, a daunting 4158m above sea level. The idea was ambitious to say the least, and not universally popular – one politician wanted reassurance that the mountains would not be sacrificed for money – but the Swiss government gave the go-ahead and

*Excavating the tunnels of the Jungfraubahn was scenic
but dangerous work*

construction started on 27 July 1896. The 9.34km Jungfraubahn railway (nearly all of which is underground) would take 16 years and cost 16 million francs to build, although it didn't quite reach the summit of Jungfrau and Guyer-Zeller died in 1899, long before it was completed.

The engineers and mechanics were Swiss, but most of the miners were Italian, clearing the land with picks and shovels and carrying electricity pylons on their shoulders. They had to work on Sundays, handle dynamite in cramped conditions and sleep three men to a bed, all for 5.20 francs a day, from which 2.30 francs were deducted for food. Perhaps that's why there were six strikes and the management had to restore order with the threat of armed force. The camp at the edge of the Eiger glacier, where the workmen lived all year round, was cut off from the world each winter, although the work carried on inside the mountain. All the provisions had to be delivered before the snow arrived and had to last until spring. The company archives reveal the annual shopping list:

12 tons flour
1,500 litres of wine
2 tons potatoes (for the Swiss)
800kg macaroni (for the Italians)
3,000 eggs
400kg coffee
50,000 cigars
4 tons meat
30 tons coal

The perishables were stored in the crevasses of the glacier. Even while the men were working on the upper stretches of the line, the first sections opened as tourist attractions. Galleries were cut into the face of the Eiger so that eager passengers could gaze out across the glaciers, or venture out onto wooden walkways perched on the edge of the icy abyss.

On 1 August 1912, when the station at Jungfraujoch officially opened, it was planned as another one of the stations en route to the top. In the end it became the Top of Europe: at 3454m up it was Europe's highest railway station, a record it still holds. The summit of Jungfrau, with a lift inside the mountain, was never reached, due to the onset of war and a lack of funds, although that doesn't mean the line was a failure – exactly the opposite. It was the crowning moment of the trains-for-tourists craze that had swept across Switzerland for four decades and was an instant hit, with 38,705 passengers in the first year, a figure that had grown to 833,000 by the line's 100th birthday.

Catch the train today and it's like travelling in a mobile United Nations, with barely a Swiss voice to be heard. No wonder the announcements come in multiple languages. The two Eiger stops on the way up are still there, letting people trot off and see the views, though these days there's plexiglass to prevent the gales coming in and people jumping out.

After 50 minutes inside the mountain, it's quite jarring to step out into the open air at Jungfraujoch, perched on the saddle between the Mönch and the Jungfrau. The light is blindingly bright, the air bitingly cold and your feet feel distinctly heavier than your head. For me, the trip up to Jungfraujoch isn't just about the panorama from the top, as wonderful as it is; neither is it about being up at Europe's highest train station, which makes some people giddy with excitement. For me, it's the trip itself and all that it took to achieve that. Thanks to the brains of Adolf Guyer-Zeller and the guts of his workforce, we can take one of the world's most amazing train rides up inside one of the world's most famous mountains. That would be an remarkable achievement today, let alone 100 years ago, but let's not forget the human cost.

Thirty men died building this pinnacle of tourist engineering. And that's all it was, and has ever been: a tourist attraction. So it's rather sad to see so many of today's visitors rush past the new, and long overdue, memorial to those who gave their lives so that we could live our dreams. A procession of simple wooden blocks, each engraved with a name and date(s), lines one of the tunnels at Jungfraujoch station. All but one of the names are Italian, one Adolf among the Paolos, Giovannis and Angelos. The first death was in 1898, the last in 1912; many have no birth dates, but where they are given it shows how young the men were – for example, Virginio Furlotti was only 18 when he died in 1908. Modern visitors might grumble at paying almost 200 francs for a return ticket from Interlaken (without a rail pass), but if they stopped to think of what it actually took to build the line, there would be no complaints.

Even without going all the way up to Jungfraujoch, there's a great view of the whole Grindelwald valley to be had from Kleine Scheidegg. In the shadow of mighty peaks that loom over the village from all sides, everything else seems to be tiny. Spread out at the mountains' feet is the wide, bowl-shaped valley of undulating green ridges dotted with a few farms and traditional chalets between the holiday homes and hotels. It couldn't be more Swiss if it tried. No wonder the Victorians were so keen to get up here, possibly inspired by the writings of John Ruskin, art critic, poet, traveller and scientist, a gentleman who had a view on everything. For instance, this was his opinion of the Swiss:

They were assumed to be either romantically virtuous, or basely mercenary, when in fact they were neither heroic nor base, but were true-hearted men, stubborn with more than any recorded stubbornness; ... proud, yet not allowing their pride to prick them into unwary or unworthy quarrel; ... You will find among them no subtle wit nor high enthusiasm, only an undeceivable common sense, and an obstinate rectitude. They cannot be persuaded into their duties but they feel them; they use no phrases of friendship but they do not fail you at your need.

Miss Jemima loves to quote a bit of Ruskin, but here she prefers to focus on his opinion of the natural splendour of the Alps:

"Nearly all the highest peaks stood like children set upon a table, removed, in most cases, far back from the edge of the plateau, - as if for fear of their falling; while the most majestic scenes in the Alps are produced, not so much by violation of this law, as by one of the great peaks having apparently walked to the edge of the table to look over, and thus showing itself suddenly above the valley in its full height. This is the case with the Wetterhorn and Eiger at Grindelwald."

Those two mountains certainly dominate the Grindelwald horizon. As the 3970m star of page and screen, the Eiger needs little in the way of introduction. It was first climbed by Irishman Charles Barrington on 11 August 1858, with the invaluable help of two Grindelwald guides, Christian Almer and Peter Bohren. That in itself wasn't anything too momentous, as the likes of the Jungfrau and Wetterhorn had both been conquered long before, although Barrington apparently went home after one summer in the Alps and never returned, the mountaineering equivalent of Harper Lee. What has made the Eiger iconic is its infamous North Face, a vast expanse of vertical black rock, which finally fell to human conquest in 1938 after witnessing countless men falling to their deaths in futile attempts to master this beast of Mother Nature. It's no wonder that the German name for it, *Nordwand*, is often changed to *Mordwand*, or Wall of Death.

In comparison, the Wetterhorn is a gentle giant that adds a photogenic backdrop to Grindelwald although, like any of the Alps, it has seen climbing calamities. Luckily, Winston Churchill did not join their ranks when he reached the top in 1894. If he were now lying alongside William Penhall in a Swiss country churchyard, the world might be rather different. However, the Wetterhorn is famous for cable cars rather than climbers. In 1904 construction began on the world's first aerial passenger cable car, the plan being to take visitors up to the summit in a series of four cars. This was the era in which such outlandish projects seemed achievable. The first section opened to the public on 27 July 1908, having cost 390,000 francs to build; its cabins weighed 4100kg, without the 16 passengers, and the 400m height difference was bridged in a single span. It was truly a wonder of modern technology – for about six years.

The First World War stopped construction and the project collapsed from lack of customers. In the 1930s the line was dismantled, although the disused upper station can still be seen on the side of the Wetterhorn. Even in Switzerland things don't always go to plan. As in Leukerbad almost 100 years later, over-confidence can sometimes lead people down the wrong path, although it's a shame to lose such an important piece of the transport history jigsaw.

Tourism put Interlaken and Grindelwald on the map. These two resorts have entertained thousands of guests over the years not for *what* they are – neither is that pretty in itself – but for *where* they are. The lakes and mountains of the Bernese Oberland have been such a magnet to visitors from a certain island nation that you could almost rechristen the region the British Oberland. It was this tourist trade that helped the region develop, providing the impetus for railway lines and grand hotels, as well as jobs for the local population. It is still the main employer today, and indirectly ensures that many other businesses thrive. As a woman from Interlaken

A postcard showing the railway stations of the Jungfrau region, including the ill-fated Wetterhorn cable car on the far left

Tourism said to me, "What future would there be for the younger generation without tourism? At least 50 per cent would leave for the cities to find an apprenticeship or a job. Without tourists, the town would not survive."

There has been a price to pay for 150 years of mass tourism, however. Both resorts have some awful eyesores that scar the scenery with their incongruous designs and unattractive construction, although it would take more than a couple of concrete blocks to ruin this landscape. Nevertheless, in being so out of keeping with their surroundings, they will hopefully act as a lesson to future planners: this is what happens when you let money talk instead of common sense. As for those train lines and cable cars that were constructed purely as tourist attractions, building them today would be almost unthinkable, in terms of both the financial and ecological cost. Green was not a Victorian colour; that century was all about man defying nature with technology, no matter what stood in the way.

Few people resisted the march of progress, but there were some who did, either out of fear of the unknown (altitude sickness in mountain trains or the corrupting influence of tourists) or for love of the countryside (ruining Alpine pastures or scaring the cattle). As we will see, those who wanted to protect the natural and cultural heritage of Switzerland soon made themselves heard.

Yet compared to some other parts of the tourist world, for example the Spanish Costas, this region hasn't fared too badly. It might have seen the birth of international tour groups, but it hasn't yet had to endure the mass invasions and mega-hotels of the Mediterranean. While this was Europe's first playground, that was at a time when the games were refined and respectable, when snow and scenery were enough to keep the masses happy. They have since moved on to louder, larger resorts, where Sex on the Beach is not just a cocktail, but the British have kept coming to their Swiss second home. For example, in the mid-1960s there were direct flights from London to Interlaken (with British Eagle), and in the late 1980s Brits were still the most numerous hotel guests in Interlaken, outnumbering even the Swiss. However, in 2012 Britain only managed No. 8, overtaken by the likes of India, Korea, China and Japan. The British century (and a half) in Switzerland is over; the Asian one has just begun.

The glaciers once reached so far into Grindelwald that there were fears the village would be crushed by ice

SEVEN

LAND OF THE FROZEN HURRICANES

*[In Grindelwald] most of the children are beggars –
occupations arising from the influx of strangers into the
valley, which has exercised an injurious influence upon
its morals and ancient simplicity of manners.*
                                                  —Murray Handbook

One benefit of spending your whole life in the same village is that you can remember all the changes, big and small. No need for then-and-now photos or old maps, you can simply close your eyes and picture how it used to be. In a village like Grindelwald there are undoubtedly a few people whose memories are long and strong enough to do that (it's the kind of place that is hard for some to leave behind) and we are lucky enough to find one of them in the local museum. Christian Kaufmann is many years away from being a candidate for Switzerland's oldest citizen, but Grindelwald was still a very different place in his childhood. From his chair behind the ticket table, he points to the far side of the room, over behind the displays of sepia photos:

> This was the school and I sat at a desk in this corner
> every day and looked out of the window across to the
> glacier.

The village school has long since relocated, leaving the handsome wooden building behind the church to find a new role. And former pupil Mr Kaufmann is the perfect man to be the curator. As for the glacier, that has shrunk back up its narrow valley so that it can only be seen from certain spots in Grindelwald. Stand in the immaculate churchyard, where gravestones for fallen climbers sit among those of the villagers, and you can still see the head of the glacier and a slither of ice trailing down from it. That's a far cry from when Miss Jemima was here; at that time the two glaciers, Upper and Lower, were within a mile of the village, and there were fears that Grindelwald would be crushed by the advancing ice. As Murray says:

> Its two glaciers, which, as they descend into the very
> bottom of the valley, below the level of the village, and
> almost within a stone's-throw of human habitations,
> are more easily accessible here than in other parts of
> Switzerland. ... Between the three mountains the two
> glaciers issue out. They are branches of that vast ice

> *field or ocean of ice ... occupying the table-land and
> high valleys amidst the Bernese Alps, and, being pushed
> downwards by the constantly-increasing masses above,
> descend far below the line of perpetual snow.*

From Kleine Scheidegg you can no longer see any trace of the
glaciers, nor do they appear on the half-hour train ride down to
Grindelwald, so far have they retreated. The train line skirts along
the bottom of the Eiger so that the mountain towers ominously
over the panoramic glass windows. Miss Jemima followed roughly
the same route, although for her it was a three-hour walk down:

> "The footpath was very rough and stony and in some parts steep;
> nevertheless we scampered down over the stones, after the manner
> of the goats, leaping rents and clearing the ground at a famous
> speed."

And she wasn't wearing shorts and trainers. By the time they reached
their hotel they had begun "to feel very tired". I'm not surprised. We
are staying in the same place, or at least its modern incarnation; of
the original, there is nothing left. In fact, the story of the village's two
historic hotels, the Adler and the Bär (Eagle and Bear respectively),
is the history of Grindelwald tourism in miniature.

The Adler came first, in around 1800, and then the Bär, both built
to cope with the steady influx of tourists. Old pictures show them
as typically Swiss wooden buildings, like overgrown chalets, and
they would eventually be run by the same family, the Boss brothers. They are the only Grindelwald hotels mentioned by Murray
("both tolerable, prices rather high") and Miss Jemima stayed in
the Adler for one night. That burnt down in 1897, but rose again,
only to be demolished in 1982, having been bought by the Sunstar
group. In its place stand two modern concrete buildings, one in
1980s chalet style and less horrendous than the other, in classic
1970s multi-storey car-park style. Both sore thumbs are easily visible from far away, but from the inside looking out, it's not nearly
as bad. There are views of the Eiger and also a tasteful interior that

Hotel stationery from the old Aigle Noir, or Schwarzer Adler

is plush, modern and almost characterful. All that remains of the Adler, once the oldest hotel in town, is the name of one of the hotel restaurants, Adlerstube.

The Bär had an equally traumatic history. It was the first hotel to open for a winter season, starting a trend that made Grindelwald a must-do for snow-seekers. Fire destroyed that old Bär in 1892, along with half the village and the English church; it was rebuilt on a far larger scale as the Grand Hotel Bear, a true palace hotel with three wings, three hundred beds, a ballroom, and three ice rinks purely for its guests. It became the place to stay during the summer or winter season, but also met a fiery end (thanks to a carelessly discarded cigarette in 1941) and the age of grand hotels in Grindelwald was over. Today there is no trace of the Bear; its location now hosts the community sports centre and tourist information.

These two hotels were part of Grindelwald's transformation from village to resort, witnessing the growth from local hardship into international recognition. It has probably changed more than any place this tour has taken us so far. Back in the 1860s it was still a village "consisting of picturesque wooden cottages,

Grindelwald with the Wetterhorn and Upper Glacier

widely scattered over the valley", while the inhabitants were "chiefly employed in rearing cattle, of which 6000 head are fed on the neighbouring pastures", according to Murray. For centuries this had been a fairly isolated spot, up at 1034m, with very independently minded people who had revolted against being ruled by Interlaken and resisted the Reformation. Then the first tourists and mountaineers, mainly British, "discovered" it, forcing the valley to connect with the outside world and cater for the visitors.

It didn't change much at first: in 1874 the *Cook's Tourist's Handbook to Switzerland* was still describing it as "a romantic village, inhabited principally by herdsmen; the cottages are very Swiss, and the villagers very civil". It was the arrival of the steam train that changed Grindelwald for ever. The BOB line opened in 1890 and the mountain village was almost instantly turned into an international resort. By 1900 there were 18 hotels (with 1250 beds); six years later there were 30. Today there are 48, making Grindelwald the fourth-largest resort in Switzerland (in terms of number of hotel beds); tourism accounts for 92 per cent of the local income. Now the cows are far outnumbered by tourists.

The two rivers of ice were Grindelwald's main tourist attraction, so of course Miss Jemima got up early on that Tuesday and set off through the hayfields and fir trees to clamber across the Lower Glacier. That would be impossible today – not just because of the far greater distance involved, but also the greater attention to safety. No one these days would attempt what they did:

> "The surface of the glacier was less shattered into forms and spires, but more crevassed than the Mer de Glace. ... Due provision for descent has been made – namely, a couple of fir planks, with bars nailed across to serve as steps, on which explorers are to hop down, regardless of the yawning crevasse beneath. True, there is a handrail, which when compared to the massive surroundings was more like a lucifer match than a balustrade. We afterwards learnt that this handrail was more a guide to steady the eye than the hand. But it was only a mountain ladder, and here was a splendid chance for the Club and kindred travellers to display their courage and ability. Some of the ladies, however, thought it better to contemplate its wonders from a distance rather than a gain a mournful notoriety."

She ends by remarking that the greatest wonder was that the gentlemen all managed a "safe descent and ascent of that glacial hen-roost ladder". I have to say I would have voted with the ladies on this one and admired the ice at surface level, rather than end up like Monsieur Mouron, a pastor from Vevey. While surveying a glacial crevasse in 1821 he leant on his alpenstock, which promptly split and he fell 250m down into the depths. It took 12 days to find his broken body, although his watch was retrieved intact. Then there's the tale of Mrs Arbuthnot who was walking up to Schilthorn, a mountain above Mürren, when she sat on a rock for a rest during a storm. Sadly the rock was composed mainly of iron, which attracted a lightning bolt and electrocuted the poor woman on the spot.

The ice is no longer an hour's walk away but more like a day's hike, and even then it's very inaccessible. Instead, modern tourists

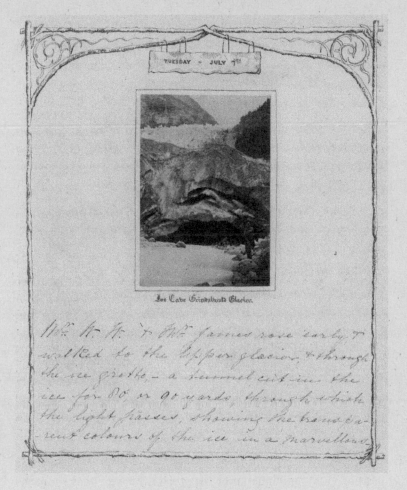

The Junior United Alpine Club hiked out to a glacier

can stroll along the deep gorge carved by the glacier, either following it from above and looking down into the depths, or walking through it at ground level. Neither is quite the same as hiking over the top, but each is spectacular in its own way, so I decide to do both – although not on the same day. This time we'll take the low road through the gorge and I'll come back to do the high

199

road along the top, which requires more time and better weather. Today's cloud and sporadic drizzle are no hindrance to walking along a path already dripping wet and partly underground.

Whereas Victorian visitors could hike out across the glacier, we can do something they never could: walk beneath where the ice once slid and ground its way down into the valley. The Glacier Gorge is testament to the power of ice in motion; water running underneath the glacier, carrying heavy loads of moraine, eroded its way down into the bedrock, creating this ravine. Its 100m high walls are littered with striations and potholes gouged out by hurtling stones and rushing water. Giant boulders of alien rock sit stranded after being carried and dumped far from home, while pink and green Grindelwald marble, quarried locally until 1903, adds a splash of colour here and there.

Our route is along a slippery boardwalk anchored into the cliff face about two metres above a churning torrent of filthy water that crashes and splashes beneath our feet – the meltwater from the remnant of the glacier. The ravine is so narrow in places that the walls seem to touch and the boardwalk has to disappear into drip-infested tunnels, where the echo of thundering water drowns out our voices. It might be summer outside, but down here it's still the ice age; another great example of nature's air-conditioning. After one kilometre the gorge widens out but comes to a dead end, and there's still no sign of the glacier. Nevertheless, through a dark V of rocks, we can glimpse the bright white Λ of a mountain before we have to turn around and retrace our steps.

After the dark, damp low road, the high road is all sunshine and fresh air – and much more taxing on the legs. Many months after being at the bottom, I pretend I'm Swiss and take a Sunday walk along the top of the gorge, roughly level with where the surface of the glacier once was. A little red cable car whisks us up to the Pfinstegg restaurant perched 360m above Grindelwald on the side of the Mettenberg mountain. From here on, we must pretend to be mountain goats and scamper along a stony path at the edge of the cliff. Vertigo sufferers need not put this on their must-see list, as Murray made clear:

It is not good for timid persons, as the path skirts some formidable precipices; but it is taken by ladies, who may ride on horseback for the first three quarters of an hour, and be conveyed the rest of the way in a chaise à porteur.

There's no chance of anyone carrying me today and no chance either of seeing "a most interesting view of the bristling minarets of ice, rising in the most various and fantastic shapes". They have long since melted away into the river of dirty dishwater far below. Instead, there is a giant cleft in the rock with our path on one side and the eastern flank of the Eiger on the other. It's not a place to miss your step, so I keep stopping so that I can safely inspect the tortured rock formations and deep grooves that scour the cliff face. At one point the rock on the opposite side of the ravine looks much newer and paler, with no scars scratched across it. This part has only been exposed to the elements for a few years: in 2006 a whole section of the cliff crashed to the ground, sending two million cubic metres of rock into the gorge. With the ice gone, there is nothing to hold back the walls; and with the permafrost melting, that cliff collapse won't be the last.

On our side of the gorge we pass a strange formation in the rock: a double-sided depression that looks spookily like a giant sat down heavily, leaving his bottom imprinted in the stone. Directly opposite us, in the eastern wall of the Eiger, is a small hole through which we can see blue sky. Twice a year the sun shines exactly through that hole, known as Martinsloch, and down onto the church in Grindelwald. The local legend is that there was once no gap between the mountains here, and so no proper outlet for the glacial meltwater. That regularly built up to such a degree that it crashed down into the valley below, destroying farms and lives. A local man named Martin, who happened to be rather large, came to the rescue. He sat with his back against the Mettenberg, placed his feet and staff against the Eiger, and pushed with all his might. Not only did he separate the mountains to create a safe passage for the water, he left his imprint on both sides of the new valley.

These days things are more practical: a tunnel was recently built to relieve the water pressure from the melting glacier and prevent a sudden flood that would devastate Grindelwald. I think I prefer the story of a giant bottom and a hole made by a stick.

Ninety minutes later we reach our goal, the restaurant at Bäregg, 388m higher than the start of the path at Pfinstegg. It's time for lunch in the sun, at tables with red-and-white checked cloths, sitting beneath a fluttering Swiss flag and with a view of the end of the glacier. As at Mer de Glace, it's not a particularly pretty sight. It's dramatic, yes, with its cradle of jagged mountains and folds of snow-covered rock, but there's no sparkling ice or sculpted pinnacles. This is the dirty end of things, more grey moraine than white ice.

The footpath carries on up to the Schreckhorn Hut, another three hours (and 800m in altitude) further on. That route is marked in the blue and white denoting an Alpine path, or one for serious hikers and climbers only. I'm happy to stay where we are, especially once I notice where the path has had to be moved up and back away from the encroaching cliff edge. It's bad enough that the restaurant, itself new after the last one succumbed to the changing landscape, seems to teeter on the edge of nothingness. All this is because the glacier has retreated 1.6km from its peak in the 1850s; once there was ice 200m thick, now there is nothing. In 1861 it seemed that "both the Mer de Glace, under Mont Blanc, and the Grindelwald Glacier, appear to have shrunk, and sunk considerably below the level they once attained; but this may be merely temporary, or even only their dimensions in summer, when most reduced". Lord Byron called the Alpine glaciers "frozen hurricanes", but in some cases they are now merely a frozen summer breeze. And to think that men used to cut 100 tons of ice a day from the tongue of this glacier, transport it to Interlaken and sell it to customers as far away as Paris and Vienna; a trade killed by the First World War and the invention of artificial ice.

Ice was an important factor in Grindelwald's growth, although not only in the shape of its two glaciers. It was the flat expanses of the white stuff that helped the resort become one of the main places for Brits to enjoy a winter break. In 1900 Grindelwald had

16 ice rinks for tourists. The Grand Hotel Bear had the largest (at 25,000ft², or about a third of a football pitch) and was the headquarters of the Grindelwald Skating Club, an English creation that catered for the growing winter sports craze. By 1905 Thomas Cook was offering a 10-day skating tour to Switzerland for ten guineas, full board.

In resorts like Grindelwald there wasn't just skating but also curling (with its own British-only club) and gymkhanas organised by the Amusements Committee. They were a jolly wheeze to keep the punters happy, with such pursuits as potato collecting (pick up the spuds and put them in a basket as you skate around) and egg blowing, where the men had to blow eggs across the ice and the women rolled them back with wooden paddles. There was also a winter version of a three-legged race, dubbed the *Rennen der Lahmen* or Race of the Lame: one man and one woman, each with one skate and one snowshoe, racing hand in hand across the ice. Those Victorians certainly knew how to amuse themselves, although some were not amused by Continental skating practices.

In his entertaining book *Switzerland and the English* (1944), Sir Arnold Lunn recounts:

> *The English skater keeps his unemployed leg rigidly to his side, and sweeps over the ice in long sweeping curves. Not individual display but combined skating is the ideal of the English school. ... It is a pity that four Englishmen skating a "combined" need more space than fifty foreigners waltzing in the degenerate Continental style. In the days of our Imperial power, nobody dared to question the English skater's demand for Lebensraum.*

He then catalogues the decline of standards on the rinks of Switzerland as if they were part of the British Empire: "The foreigners increased, and their latent opposition was fanned into open revolt by degenerate English traitors to the noble ideals of Anglican skating. They even asked for a band on the rink. On the *rink!*" It might as well have been the end of the world.

And of course, there was tobogganing and bobsleigh racing. For a while Grindelwald was home to the world's longest bob run (4.2km) and three trains a day ran between the village and the upper start of the run. It eventually went the way of the ice rinks, dismantled during the Second World War as the fad faded, in contrast to Graubünden. There it lives on, fittingly enough as it was in St Moritz that the Brits invented the bobsleigh, allegedly by tying two sleds together before sliding down a mountain. And it was the British who created the famous Cresta Run in the winter of 1884–85. No one else would have had the crazy idea of hurtling head first down a tube of ice at 120km/h while lying on a flimsy toboggan.

In fact, St Moritz was where winter holidays were born in 1864. The story goes that hotelier Johannes Badrutt bet four of his English summer guests that they would enjoy St Moritz in winter as well. If they came and didn't like it, he would refund their travel costs; but if they liked it, they could stay for as long as they wished as his guests. The four returned to St Moritz at Christmas – and ended up staying until Easter. So began the annual winter British invasion of the Alps.

Grindelwald was proclaimed "one of the best known Swiss centres for invigorating winter sports" in *Sunshine and Snow*, Thomas Cook's very first winter sports brochure. That 1908 pamphlet featured eight Swiss resorts, including Adelboden, which was then a two-hour sleigh ride from Frutigen, for those who wanted to escape "England's dullest months". Winter sports were sold on their health benefits rather than simple fun, as if there was still something decadent about taking a non-summer holiday:

Winter sport exhilarates and rejuvenates; it generates a glow of pleasure in the mind, which acts powerfully upon the whole physical organisation, while all the time the nerves and muscles are directly braced up by the keen, dry air, tempered by bright, genial sunshine.

There was also a skiing programme, such as the run down from Männlichen: a four-hour ascent from Grindelwald for a 30-minute ski back down. That makes queuing for a ski lift seem not so bad after all. Or how about a three-hour ascent up to the Grosse Scheidegg, a two-hour ski run down the other side, a boat to Interlaken and a train back to Grindelwald?

However, there was no après-ski malarkey in those days – and definitely no sick people. "It should be noted that no visitors who are suffering from any form of tubercular complaint are received at places dealt with in this booklet", the pamphlet warned. Instead, St Moritz tried to attract "the fair sex" with a ladies' curling club (the sport not the hairstyle) and phrases such as "lovers of pretty shops will find much to tempt them".

All the featured hotels were "specially fitted up for the comfort of guests during the winter, with central heating and everything of the most up-to-date character, including a good orchestra". It's nice to see that warmth came before waltzing. And they weren't only dancing inside: the winter season in Grindelwald included a challenge cup for combined figure skating, two prizes for ice waltzing and one for ladies' skating. It's not clear if there was a band on the ice.

A week at the Grand Hotel Bear in that first winter season cost £10 5s 0d (about £600 today), including second-class train travel from London, room (with lights, service and heating), full board and 56lb of luggage. Passengers could leave Charing Cross at 2.20pm and arrive in Grindelwald at 3.10pm the next day, having caught a boat, travelled through the night and changed trains four times. The same train journey today takes ten hours with three changes, in Paris, Basel and Interlaken.

By 1911 the brochure emphasised the healthy aspect even more: it was now called *Health, Sunshine and Snow*, which is possibly why Davos and Leukerbad were now included. Adverts for things like "best Swiss knitted underwear" show how quickly companies had responded to the winter sports phenomenon. Debenham & Freebody were selling clothing for skating and skiing that was "proof against snow, sleet, rain and cold winds". Outfits had to be stylish as well as practical, so for 45 shillings (or £130 today) women could buy a full-length knitted sports coat "in the new cable stitch; perfect fitting. In 50 colours." Presumably it wasn't meant to rival Joseph's technicolour wonder, with all 50 shades in one garment. But not everyone was rigged out in winter gear. *The Traveller's Gazette* noted that "Gentlemen may often be seen in the full enjoyment of exhilarating outdoor exercises in their short sleeves, and even ladies gracefully disporting themselves in their summer blouses." How shocking.

Accident insurance for mishaps "whilst participating in the Sports" appeared in 1921, though it doesn't spell out if that covered injuries sustained while egg blowing. I can imagine there were a few, including cheeks frozen to the ice. By 1924, those with an extra £17 (or £380 today) to spare could fly to Zurich instead of slumming it on the train, and then go on to any one of 20 Swiss winter resorts. Three times a week Imperial Airways ran a biplane service with 12 wicker seats, taking 7½ hours each way, though that included an hour for lunch in Paris en route.

Skating might have started the winter craze, but it eventually had to play second fiddle to the trendy new sport of downhill skiing, even if the skaters looked down their frozen noses at the skiers, or "plank-hoppers" as they called them. While skiing arrived in Switzerland with the Norwegians, it was the British who were instrumental in turning it into a sport. Brits may not have any high mountains or know how to cope with snow, but faced with a combination of the two, they knew just what to do: launch themselves down a slope while strapped to two thin strips of wood. It was exactly the kind of risky activity the Swiss liked to avoid, so it was up to those wacky Englishmen to show them the way. First they had climbed the mountains, then they were sliding down them. What would they think of next?

The irony is, of course, that the Swiss became much better at both sports. Britain has never won an Olympic skiing medal, although it came close at the Salt Lake City Games of 2002. Alan Baxter won bronze in the men's slalom (a race first created by an Englishman), but lost his medal after testing positive for traces of methamphetamine. In contrast, the Swiss Olympic Team has won 55 medals in alpine skiing, as the various types of skiing down hills (including the enigmatically named Super G) are known collectively.

Skiing came to Grindelwald in 1891, thanks to Mr Gerald Fox and his ash-wood skis with leather bindings, while in 1894 Sir Arthur Conan Doyle (of Sherlock Holmes fame) skied from Davos to Arosa. However, it was perhaps Sir Arnold Lunn who was the biggest British influence in Swiss skiing, not least because he invented the modern downhill slalom and was one of the founders of the Kandahar Ski Club in Mürren in the 1920s. He also created what is now one of the world's oldest downhill races, the Inferno, a daunting 15.8km run from Schilthorn down to Lauterbrunnen. His book, mentioned above, is fascinating not for its overview of skiing history, but for its glimpses into a world long since vanished – a world where formality was the norm, at least until the First World War, and a world that Miss Jemima and other Brits abroad at that time would have recognised:

> It would have been unthinkable for an Englishman not to dress for dinner at any of the leading winter sports centres during the first decade of the century. Such luckless guests as had lost their luggage en route slunk about with miserable and apologetic mien. It wasn't their fault that they had to dine in their ordinary clothes. We knew that. Still they were under a cloud ... I remember one miserable outcast whose registered luggage did not arrive for a week. Everyone was kind to him, but he lost caste. He was slipping. He knew it. We knew it. The head waiter knew it. And then the cloud lifted. His luggage arrived. I shall never forget the expression on his face, when he appeared for the first time in evening dress. He looked like a man who has just been cleared by court-martial of a disgraceful charge.

There were those who "made it a point of honour not to dress for dinner", but they had a valid excuse. They were members of the Alpine Club, who couldn't be expected to bother with dress clothes after hiking across glaciers. Practicality beat formality for once, not to mention the contempt many mountaineers had for skiers: "mountains are things to be reverenced and not treated as slides". Lunn laments the passing of the age of evening wear:

> In 1939 the revolt against form had gone so far that hotels which were still fussy about evening dress were finding it necessary to provide dining accommodation for those who could not be bothered to change into ceremonial garments. The English began to show a distaste for evening dress in Alpine hotels when ski-teachers began to dress for dinner.

Dress codes weren't the only minefield; there was the etiquette of the evening dances: "Young people who had tobogganed together usually addressed each other not as Miss Smith or Mr. Brown but as Miss Mary or Mr. Bobby, which was considered to mark a real advance in intimacy. To dance more than twice with the same partner was faintly compromising."

Sir Arnold also had a unique insight into the world of winter sports because his father, Sir Henry Lunn, was "the first tourist agent to discover the possibilities of the winter Alps". His stroke of genius was to market the trips as something for the elite, even though his tours were disparaged by that class as downmarket. Ski holidays were arranged via the Public Schools Alpine Sports Club, so that Lunn's Tours (which later became Lunn Poly) never had to appear on a luggage label. It wasn't a Club for plebs: "The principal qualification for the Club Members was a public school or university education." As incredible as it seems, some of the best hotels were reserved exclusively for those members, with other clients unable to book rooms there during the season, including the Swiss themselves. Arnold Lunn was himself astonished at a situation "under which Swiss citizens were excluded from many of the best hotels in the most popular winter resorts unless they were members of a British club". It would be unthinkable today.

The best part of Lunn's book describes his father's attitude to foreigners:

> *My father had travelled widely, but had never made the slightest attempt to master any foreign language. He was always happy in America because the Americans spoke English, and he had a real affection for many of the Swiss, but he had no interest in foreigners as such, and looked forward to a distant Utopia when all foreign nations would learn to speak English. ... He never felt the need to master enough French or German to ask his way to the station.*

The same could be said of many a British tourist then and now.

After lunch at the Bär Hotel in Grindelwald, Miss Jemima travelled in

> "the landlord's bulky carriage to Interlacken. We had a magnificent ride and arrived in time for the steamer to Giessbach, with a little surplus for the fracas with the porteur, who, at the landlord's instigation, was bent on making an overcharge."

The trustworthiness of landlords and charges for extras are topics that exercised nineteenth-century travellers. Cook stated: "I am not disposed very strongly to recommend an inferior class of hotels, where parties often spend as much money as in the first-class establishments, the tariffs of which are well understood." By that he meant the small-print charges that appeared as if by magic on a hotel bill, something Murray also warned against: "The practice is now general of the waiter rushing into your room before you and lighting the wax candles without consulting you." The wax is emphasised as the norm was tallow candles, cheaper and made from animal fat.

He goes on to list the usual charges at first-class hotels as a guide to "protect [travellers] from extortion and imposition on the part of those innkeepers or couriers who may be disposed to take advantage of them". Such extras include breakfast (1.50 francs), a candle (1 franc), a night light (50 rappen) and a foot bath (50 rappen; "unreasonable but usual"). And of course there's service – "One franc a day is usually given to the servants, and is almost always added in the bill. This includes all the servants except the porter, who expects something extra." Murray continues: "Swiss inns have, in general, the reputation of being expensive, and the innkeepers of being extortionate; of late years, however, great improvement has taken place." His last words of advice are:

> It is often supposed, and perhaps correctly, that two sets of charges are made – one for natives, or Germans, and another for the English; on the principle that the latter have both longer purses and more numerous wants, and are more difficult to serve.

English purses may be shorter now, but I wonder if we are still so demanding. I hope not.

The extras are now internet usage and the minibar, as well as the "tourist tax", often still called a "kurtax" or cure tax, revealing its roots as an old-fashioned levy on visitors coming for curative treatments. The cures might have gone, but the complaint is still there. While not everywhere has a tax, those communities that do can set their own; for example, in Grindelwald it's 2.10 francs per adult per night. So why not always include it in the room price, like sales tax? Guests must pay it, so adding it on to the bill is a nasty sting in the tail.

We pay our dues and leave the Sunstar, née Adler, to stroll down the hill to Grindelwald station. The BOB arrives up from Interlaken and is as packed as a rush-hour tube on the London Underground. Everyone piles out, most of them dashing across the platform to the waiting WAB train for the trip up into the clouds. That leaves us with a whole train to ourselves as we clatter down beside the churning Schwarze Lütschine to Interlaken. Having caught an early train, we have enough time before our boat for a visit to

*Before the train arrived in 1890, Interlaken Ost was simply a
semi-rural boat station*

the Interlaken hotel where Miss Jemima and friends stayed. "We
rejected the famous Jungfrau as also the Belvedere and we had no
reason to regret our decision", she wrote, praising "the comfortable rooms of the Hotel du Lac, with its exquisitely clean, curtained
little bedrooms".

The Hotel du Lac is still there, on the riverbank beside Ost station and the boat dock, but it was full when we tried to stay (1
August and all that). Instead, we pop in for a chat with the owner,
Ernst Hofmann, whose family has been in charge for almost 130
years. He's an affable chap, with excellent English, and is happy
to share what he knows about the hotel's history. That it has been
in his family for so long is down to his great-great-grandparents
being in the right place at the right time.

In the 1880s they were working in the posh Bellevue Hotel in
Bern, a famous meeting point for politicians and businessmen in
the capital, and they heard snippets of the big changes coming to

*The Hotel du Lac, Interlaken with the current owner's
great-great-grandfather, Peter Hofmann, at the
front entrance*

Interlaken. They decided to act before it was too late and in 1888 bought the then-bankrupt Hotel du Lac, beside the little-used Zollhaus station, as Interlaken Ost was then known. It was a good move on their part. Back in 1874 the Bödelibahn had been extended from Interlaken out to Bönigen, on the western shore of Lake Brienz, where passengers could change to the boats across the lake. That had made the area around Zollhaus a tourist wasteland and the large hotel near the station didn't survive the downturn. However, just as had been rumoured, all that changed with the opening of the BOB in 1890 and the relocation of the boat dock from Bönigen to right beside Zollhaus in 1891. Interlaken Ost was born.

Peter Hofmann had been installed at his hotel for three years by then, and was well prepared for the tourist onslaught that followed the opening up of the Oberland. By 1904 he could afford to add an extra storey and a tower to the hotel, so that it became the building we know today.

Frustratingly, no records survive from before the Hofmanns took over; another dead end for me in the search for Miss Jemima in Switzerland. Instead, Mr Hofmann fishes out the oldest surviving photo of his ancestor with his hotel, from 1898. Peter Hofmann is standing there, hand on hip and watch chain looped across his waistcoat, at the entrance of a fairly substantial building even before the extension: four storeys high, plus one room in a central gable, and nine windows across, each with double shutters. This is no palace hotel with domes and doormen; it's a simpler, more traditional affair, as the sign implies: "Hotel et Pension du Lac". Today, despite the tower and pink walls, you can see the original structure at the heart of the current building, with even the gabled room still there, minus its mini-A-frame roof. This is definitely a hotel that builds on its traditions rather than changing them with each passing fad.

"About half our guests are English-speaking," Mr Hofmann explains, "and half of those ones are British. They come for more than two days and we have a nice atmosphere every evening in the hotel. We don't want to lose that by taking large groups who only stay a day or so and never eat in the restaurant."

That is of course the dilemma facing every hotel in Interlaken, and across much of Switzerland. The economic crisis and strong Swiss franc have meant that visitor numbers from traditional European markets have decreased sharply in the past few years. For example, in 2008 the Germans and the British were the top two nationalities visiting Switzerland, with 2.3 million and 825,000 arrivals respectively; in 2012 they dropped to 1.8 million and 660,000. In their place are increasing thousands from India, Brazil, Russia, the Gulf States and above all China. In 2008 Chinese tourists were the same in number as those from Norway and Sweden combined; now they are the fifth largest foreign market with well over half a million arrivals, an increase of 350 per cent in four years. Most of them come in groups, and want to eat Chinese food and see Switzerland in two weeks. That might be good news for the watch shops, where the Chinese spend a lot of money, but it isn't always great for the hotels. As Mr Hofmann says:

Interlaken used to be a big village with some grand hotels. It was a resort with some character. Now it's more groups, more beds, more mass tourism. It's more like a regional centre than somewhere to come on holiday. Other hotels have changed to take in the large groups, so lose their character and maybe close the restaurant. We don't want that.

You could see him as Canute trying to hold back the tide, futile resistance to the wave of the future. Or it could be a brave attempt to stop Interlaken selling its soul and becoming an Alpine Costa del Sol, albeit with Asians instead of Brits. The town already has more Chinese, Halal, Korean and Indian restaurants than many Swiss cities, with even the venerable Café Schuh serving an Asian dish of the day. In trying to survive economically, it is in danger of spoiling the very reason it was attractive in the first place: its inherent Swissness.

The same complaint could be made of that first deluge of tourists in the late nineteenth century, who prompted the building of all those hotels and railways. That wasn't tourism for the quainthearted. They wanted hotels with bathrooms and ballrooms; they wanted Paris in the Alps – and they got it. Luxury as well as landscape became synonymous with Switzerland, so that both are now a fact of life in the twenty-first century. Nevertheless, enough of the traditional aspects of Swiss life survived, particularly once some Swiss reacted to the endless development. It remains to be seen how Switzerland will cope with the latest cycle of tourism.

Another lake, another boat. Today it's Lake Brienz, about half the size of its Thun counterpart, and the MS *Brienz*, a modern incarnation of the paddle steamer that once bore that name but sadly now without paddles or steam. We don't mind as, after two days on strike, the sun finally makes an appearance, almost exactly as the captain gives a double whoop-whoop blast on the horn, and we set off on our zigzag route across the lake. My contemplation of the water is broken by my mother.

Paddle steamers, such as the DS Brienz, were a vital transport link and still criss-cross the Swiss lakes today

"Listen to this." She is reading the journal again. "Miss Jemima wrote, 'The afternoon was a lovely one and we much enjoyed our quiet sail on the lake.'" She puts the book down and sighs. "She took the words right of my mouth. 150 years later and it's still just as beautiful."

I can only nod in agreement.

Lakes Thun and Brienz are in effect two bulges in the course of the River Aare, which is incidentally the longest river entirely within Switzerland. Only the Rhine, which starts in Switzerland, is longer, but that mighty river is shared by more than one country; the Aare is 100 per cent Swiss for all of its 295km until it meets the Rhine. However, that's where any similarity between the lakes ends. Not only is Lake Thun larger and its shoreline more developed, but its water is clearer and bluer; Lake Brienz has that typical glacial-lake look going on, as if someone has mixed milk with turquoise ink. And it's not just the Aare washing down tons of deposits from the mountains: the Lütschine constantly spews out its glacial load into Lake Brienz. At Bönigen the boat glides past the long, thin stream of greyish liquid laden with debris and detritus that intrudes far into the lake before dissipating into the larger mass. Nevertheless, by the time the water has flowed down the Aare to Lake Thun, all the sediment has settled, leaving only crisp Alpine water.

Miss Jemima's destination that day, so therefore ours, soon appears in front of the boat, a small wooded hillock of land sticking out from the southern shore of the lake. From this angle, there's a gap halfway up the expanse of leafy green covering the whole shoreline, a hole filled by possibly the best example of collective conservation in Switzerland: the Grand Hotel Giessbach. In 1978 this historic hotel closed and was going to be replaced with a "jumbo chalet", a plan that prompted environmental campaigner Franz Weber to leap into action. He created the "Giessbach for the Swiss People" Foundation, which bought the hotel estate for three million francs after a national fundraising campaign.

It has been painstakingly renovated, with period furniture and authentic décor, making it one of the few hotels where we can experience hotel life from the Belle Époque era, although with en suite bathrooms and television. Even if Miss Jemima hadn't stayed there I would have been tempted to stop for tea on the terrace, but her itinerary means staying the night. It's the most expensive night of this whole journey and one I had to book months in advance to be sure of a room, but it's a unique opportunity to live like a Victorian tourist for a few hours. Our boat sidles up to the hotel's boat house and we step off onto the dock, and back in time.

A little red carriage with five compartments and green curtains sits waiting to carry us up to the hotel, 105m above us. This is Europe's oldest public funicular, opened on 21 July 1879 and still using the original carriages, which explains the hard wooden seats and open sides. Each compartment is slightly higher than the previous one, meaning that the whole carriage slants at a permanent angle, although the seats are level. The driver ensures that all the small doors are shut and latched, then we're off at the stately

GIESSBACH

Giessbach's funicular still runs today but its first grand hotel burnt down in 1883

speed of 1.5m per second; in other words, about five minutes later we reach the hotel. It's the kind of luxury nineteenth-century grand hotels could afford, and indeed needed to build if they were to attract guests. Miss Jemima had to walk up from the lakeside, but that was in 1863, before Giessbach was a hotel for the rich and the royal.

Twelve years after her visit, Giessbach became the latest spot in Switzerland to sport a grand hotel, designed by the same architect as the Victoria-Jungfrau in Interlaken, Horace Edouard Davinet. Sadly, this hotel bankrupted him and he died a poor man in 1922; his grave stands in the hotel grounds. His five-storey palatial creation, topped by domes and known locally as "the Louvre", survived only eight years; its upper floors were destroyed by fire in October 1883. The phoenix that emerged from the ashes was more angular, with pointed gables and witch's hat towers, more Swiss chalet than

French château. From the outset it had the latest gadgets, such as electric lighting and water closets, plus a darkroom for photographers and three concerts a day. This is the building that was nearly torn down in the 1970s, and it's our home for the night. It may not look as refined as its predecessor, but its creamy white walls and blood-red shutters make a memorable impression against the backdrop of woods and water. The interior looks like the set for a period drama, complete with parquet floors and dangly chandeliers, and plaster cherubs popping up all over the place.

I feel a tad underdressed in my shorts and T-shirt, and am beginning to wonder if there's a Lunn-style dress code for dinner. Luckily, smart casual is smart enough for Giessbach and most places these days, except the Palace Hotel in Gstaad where gentlemen still have to wear jackets. Someone should tell them it's no longer 1913.

Up the hill behind the current hotel is the old one, almost as large but built in the 1850s in a simpler chalet style. It looks like the prototype for so many faux-rustic Hilton Garden Inns, except that it's the real deal. Today it serves as the staff quarters, but back in 1863 it was "said to afford the best quarters in the Bernese Oberland", according to Murray. However, there was no room for the Junior United Alpine Club:

> "Our application for beds at the large and fashionable hotel was ineffectual, the hundred and fifty it contained being all engaged. But an offer was made that our party might occupy a chalet that stood on the grounds, without fear of intrusion from other travellers. This arrangement fell in so charmingly with our ideas of novelty and romance that we immediately appropriated rooms, through whose lattices twined the pendants of the vine and over whose carved balcony clung the tendrils of the Virginian Creeper."

The real reason people came to Giessbach wasn't the lake views, as beautiful as they are, but the waterfalls, a chain of cascades that tumble down the adjacent hillside, creating an idyllic woods-and-water setting. Miss Jemima liked them:

"Although inferior in height to some others, it surpasses them in beauty, and in the adjunct of a rich forest of firs through which it breaks its way. The Giessbach is one of the prettiest of falls, about 500 feet in height. There is nothing wild about it; indeed, with its immediate surroundings of green turfy knolls and dark woods, it had the effects of a park scene."

And she was right. These falls are not as dramatic or tumultuous as others in Switzerland, but they are infinitely more accessible. A stepped path climbs up alongside, leading to a gallery behind the curtain of water, then back down through the woods and under the tall stone pylons of the funicular. It's easy to see how enchanted visitors would have been (and still are, I confess) – especially once you consider the nocturnal extravaganza that used to be laid on every night, much to the audience's delight:

"At ten the bell rang to summon the company to the region of the hall. At a signal of a sky-rocket, each of the six leaps, from being shaded in the dusk were instantaneously illuminated by coloured lights. The lower fall poured rubies, the one above emeralds, above that amethysts, then the topaz mounted to the next storey, and lastly crystals showered their gems in succession. The colours were then reversed as they lighted the beautiful scene. ... The effect was magical."

There are no such kaleidoscopic displays on offer today, although the lower falls are lit with plain yellow lights. Instead, we can enjoy an outstanding dinner, with fish from the lake and meat from Brienz – the hotel tries to be as sustainable as possible, using local farms and suppliers – and possibly the best service I have ever experienced in Switzerland. It's a joy to stay in a place where the staff smile and actually seem to enjoy their jobs.

Miss Jemima's chalet night was very similar to ours in Kandersteg – "It seemed laughably like sleeping in a tea-chest. You had wood as your zenith, wood for your nadir and on north, south, east, and west, wood encompassed us." There's no tea chest for us tonight, but a somewhat palatial room looking out across the lake so that we can watch it darken to inky black as the sun goes down. And we get a perfect night's sleep, safe in the knowledge that our boat will not depart until 10am. Being tied to public transport timetables can often be frustrating; today it's a luxury, as we have no other way of leaving Giessbach. So we can linger over a sumptuous break-fast buffet, by far the best yet, and enjoy a memorable place. Miss Jemima waxed lyrically about it:

> "It was a positive Swiss Elysium that evening at the Giessbach, and we were quite willing to give ourselves up to the delusion for those few hours that we were really the possessors of chalet, grounds and waterfall."

Or as my mother put it, "Expensive, but worth every single penny."

For Miss Jemima, today's journey was one of the longest and most convoluted of the whole trip. Here's what lay ahead: boat to Brienz, diligence over the Brünig Pass to Alpnach, boat to Lucerne, boat to Weggis, and finally a four-hour hike to the top of Rigi. They got up at 5am and arrived at 10pm, although that did include four hours' sightseeing in Lucerne that they somehow contrived to squeeze in around lunch. No wonder she talks of a "sense of fatigue" by the time they reach the summit in the dark.

The first part of our journey couldn't be easier. We ride down in the funicular, take a paddle steamer for the ten-minute glide across to Brienz and arrive in time for the train at the adjoining station. The fact that the whole Swiss transport system functions as one inte-grated network never ceases to amaze me. Timetables and tickets for trains, boats, buses and cable cars all run seamlessly together, no matter how many different companies are involved. And it actually works, so that the system generally operates like clockwork.

Look at the map and there's an obvious route for a road to link Canton Bern with central Switzerland: the Brünig pass, which at 1008m high was a challenge, but not an insurmountable one. Harder to overcome were the political and financial hurdles. Bern's neighbouring canton Obwalden had neither the will nor the way to contemplate any construction. In the end the Swiss government provided the funds, on strategic grounds, and the increasing demands from tourist traffic supplied the motivation.

The new road was only two years old when the Junior United Alpine Club travelled over it in a coach and horses, and Miss Jemima was suitably impressed:

> "This road, like the one over the Dala, has won for the Swiss the character of being the best roadmakers in Europe. It is wide and supported by granite buttresses, and in one part is overhung by a shelf of rock which projected entirely across the road."

Murray was more taken with the views, and not just the more prominent one of the Haslital and Bernese Alps to the south. He looked north as well: "a charming and first-rate view is obtained along the entire valley of Nidwalden, backed by Pilatus, with the Lungern See for a foreground, forming altogether one of the most delicious scenes in Switzerland". Of course he meant Obwalden when he wrote Nidwalden, but it's easy to get the two muddled up (the former means "above the woods", the latter "below the woods"); Ob- and Nid- were once known together as Unterwalden, one of the three founding cantons of Switzerland.

Miss Jemima went by carriage; we can experience the same views over the Brünig in one of Switzerland's prettiest train rides. The Golden Pass line, linking Lucerne with Interlaken (and then on through Gstaad to Montreux), may not have the wow factor of some other mountain train trips, but its gentle beauty makes it hard not to like. And it's so very Swiss, with cows in the fields, boats on the lakes, snow on the mountains and big windows on the trains.

The Brünig Line opened on 14 June 1888 and was conceived as a way of linking Bern with the Gotthard line to Italy (this was long before the Lötschberg Tunnel), although it's yet another route that was built principally for, and sustained by, tourism. That's partly because the narrow-gauge line (the only one to be run by

It was a tight squeeze for the original Brünig train line

the national rail company, SBB) wasn't that suitable for cargo, and partly because it was a part-time line. It was a summer-only service for the first 15 years, and the final stretch to Interlaken wasn't completed until 1916; before that passengers had to change to a boat in Brienz. Although it serves the towns and villages along the way, it's still an important tourist route, with the Golden Pass line marketed as one of the four principal panoramic train rides in Switzerland. If only you could travel along the whole line in one trip, without having to change trains, I'd like it even more.

Before we climb up and over the pass, the train takes a half-hour detour along the flat U of the Aare valley to the town of Meiringen. This is not strictly necessary geographically speaking, but politically and economically it was essential to the line being built. The more direct route would have left Meiringen stranded and unable to entice tourists off the rails and onto old-fashioned wheels. Today trains still pull into Meiringen before returning back along a short stretch of the same track and heading upwards.

Other than its unusual train arrangements, Meiringen has two claims to fame. It is said to be the birthplace of the meringue, hence the name of that dessert, although this is much disputed. Any proof that an Italian chef named Gasparini had his sweet moment of inspiration here was lost in two disastrous town fires in the late nineteenth century. Easier to verify is the connection with Sherlock Holmes. The town's old English church is a Holmes museum, including a very authentic recreation of the parlour at 221b Baker Street, and outside stands a bronze statue of the man himself, in a suitably thoughtful pipe-in-mouth pose. And this is all because he died at the nearby Reichenbach Falls.

Sir Arthur Conan Doyle visited Meiringen in 1893 and decided to use the imposing falls as the site for the struggle to the death between Holmes and Moriarty. The spot where they plunged from the ledge into the foaming water is marked by a star, even though Holmes didn't actually die. The public outcry, and lure of money, led Conan Doyle to resurrect his most famous character ten years later. As for the great "death" scene, it perhaps wasn't even his idea. Peter Lunn, son of Arnold, once told the story of that summer in 1893, when Conan Doyle was staying with his grandfather, Sir Henry. The conversation turned to the problem of Sherlock. "My grandfather said 'Push him over the Reichenbach Falls', and Conan Doyle hadn't heard of them so he showed them to him," Lunn reported. Meiringen has been silently thanking him ever since.

The Reichenbach Falls are much bigger and louder than those at Giessbach, and here too a little red funicular with open sides and wooden seats (this one dating from 1899) hauls visitors from the valley floor up to the top. Perhaps it was built to cope with the rush of visitors to the falls after Holmes brought them worldwide fame, so what better way to enjoy the short journey than with Conan Doyle, in *The Final Problem* (1893):

> *It is, indeed, a fearful place. The torrent, swollen by the melting snow, plunges into a tremendous abyss, from which the spray rolls up like the smoke from a burning house. The shaft into which the river hurls itself is an*

immense chasm, lined by glistening coal-black rock, and
narrowing into a creaming, boiling pit of incalculable
depth, which brims over and shoots the stream onward
over its jagged lip.

Come on 4 May (the date of that fictional fatal struggle in 1891) and
there will undoubtedly be a few hardy souls in Victorian costumes
around to mark the anniversary – not just someone in a deerstalker,
but also a Watson, a Mrs Hudson and a Moriarty too.

From the Brünig Pass it's downhill all the way to Lake Lucerne,
along a route that passes a chain of smaller lakes. The first, Lake
Lungern, used to be considerably larger, but a creative solution
to the lack of usable farmland and waves of rural emigration
resulted in the water level dropping 18m. After almost 50 years'
construction, and much discussion (which divided the village of
Lungern into the Wets and the Dries), a 420m tunnel opened in
1836, carrying gallons of water downhill and exposing acres of
new land. There were some unforeseen after-effects, such as land-
slides, but the village gained useful land to farm in an otherwise
fairly inhospitable area. Switzerland may have been an adventure
playground for tourists, but it wasn't much fun for the locals in
spots like this.

Murray complains that the lake is no longer so beautiful, but it
looks picturesque enough to me, framed by quintessentially Swiss
soft green fields and deep green hills. And there are plenty of large
lakes dotted all over Switzerland to keep the Wets satisfied.

The train trundles on down through the gently undulating
countryside and tidy little towns with their Catholic churches
topped by golden crosses. Miss Jemima wrote of this landscape "its
character is peaceful and pleasing, but not grand" and she wasn't
wrong, although she had the advantage seeing it in sun, which
"shone with its usual Swiss force". The Swiss sun was clearly rather
strong for their sensitive British constitutions, as Mr William noted,
"It is so hot in the middle of the day that it is foolish to do anything
but rest." In contrast, after a promising start our weather is going
downhill faster than we are, so by the time we reach Sarnen, the

capital of Obwalden, there is more grey sky than blue. Obwalden, one of the smallest cantons in terms of both area and population, is literally at the heart of Switzerland: just south of Lake Sarnen is the geographical centre of the country, a spot called Älggialp that hosts an annual ceremony to honour the Swiss Personality of the Year. And some people think the British have strange customs.

At the stroke of midday, the Swiss family sitting across the aisle from us get out their lunch and start munching away. You can bet that thousands of people are doing exactly the same in homes and restaurants all across Switzerland. Whether it's a sit-down meal or sandwiches on a train, most Swiss like to eat at noon no matter where they are. Schools close, building sites fall silent and offices empty in time for everyone to eat their lunch, or midday meal as it's called in German: *Mittagessen*, or in the Swiss German dialect *Zmittag*. We remain resolutely British and don't join in. Not because we had a giant breakfast, but simply because all I have in my bag are some Ricola herbal drops. Lunch will have to wait until Lucerne.

Miss Jemima had to switch to the boat at Alpnach and was "glad to change our mode of travelling from land to water, from the smothering diligence to the lake steamer". We can stay on the train thanks to the Lopper Tunnel, which when completed in 1889 finally linked Lucerne with Brienz. A far more impressive feat that year was the opening of the train line up Mt Pilatus, which towers over our heads. This is the world's steepest rack railway, with a maximum gradient of 48 per cent, an achievement made possible by a revolutionary horizontal cogwheel system. That was the brainchild of Colonel Eduard Locher of Zurich, who also created a company to raise the capital needed for the line. No government money was involved. Why build a 4.6km railway up a barren rocky mountain? So that tourists could stand on the 2132m summit and admire the splendid panorama of the Alps without having to walk or ride up. They have been doing so ever since, to the tune of 350,000 passengers a year these days. The Pilatus railway might have seemed like a crazy idea, but it has been paying dividends ever since it opened for business on 4 June 1889.

If we are to follow Miss Jemima, we have now four hours to see the sights before our boat across Lake Lucerne. Our first stop is the bank of blue lockers beside the platform. Swiss stations nearly all have luggage lockers, which is nothing short of miraculous to me. I grew up in Britain during the 1970s and 1980s, when lockers were seen as potential bomb depositories for the IRA, so I cherish being able to store my bags for the day without being thought of as a terrorist.

We have no time to think about life and liberty – we are off in pursuit of happiness, Lucerne style. I'm not entirely sure that our first stop is the best place to start the quest, though. We are going to see the saddest monument in Switzerland.

EIGHT

QUEEN OF THE MOUNTAINS

It would never do for us not to ascend the Rigi. It would be like going to Rome and not seeing the Coliseum or going to Naples and not seeing Pompeii.
—Cook's Tourist's Handbook to Switzerland, *1874*

Die Luzern-Rigi-Bahn von Vitznau nach Rigi-Kulm.

Europe's first mountain train has been climbing up Rigi since 1871

Once upon a time the men of Switzerland were armed with more than a red penknife and their trips abroad were not to see the sights. These men were mercenaries, hired by kings and emperors across Europe to fight their battles and conquer their enemies. It hadn't always been like that. For the first 200 years of Switzerland's existence the Swiss fought their own battles, invaded neighbours, and generally behaved as badly as any other country. They regularly trounced the Habsburgs and it was the much-feared Swiss soldiers who crushed Burgundy in 1476, sealing the fate of that once-powerful duchy. However, defeat by the French at the Battle of Marignano in 1515 prompted the Swiss to have a change of heart and they decided no longer to fight against anyone – except if they were paid to do so. While the country became neutral, its men were anything but. They fought for whoever who would pay the price – France, Britain, Austria, the Netherlands, Spain – and not just as individuals but in whole battalions from the cantons.

This was the perfect solution to two big Swiss problems: too many men, too little money. Manpower was one of Switzerland's biggest natural resources and earners of foreign currency, particularly for the poor rural cantons. And shipping the men off to fight abroad meant fewer mouths to feed at home and less testosterone swirling around looking for an outlet. Let them die earning a crust abroad rather than from hunger, or civil war, at home. It was a win–win situation, except for the men who lost their lives.

The French kings were particularly fond of their Swiss boys in red, both as a force of up to 25,000 on the battlefield and as a personal guard. And it was exactly that guard who were massacred during the French Revolution. Most of the 900-strong force were killed on 10 August 1792 during a heroically futile defence of the Tuileries Palace, the Paris home of Louis xvi. Many others were taken prisoner and guillotined in the ensuing chaotic months. One who escaped, because he was in Lucerne on leave, was Captain Karl Pfyffer, and he decided to erect a memorial to his fallen comrades. He started collecting money in 1818 and travelled to Rome to engage the famous Danish sculptor Bertel

Thorvaldsen. On 10 August 1821 (the 29th anniversary of the massacre) the monument was unveiled. The sculpture, carved into the cliff face of a disused sandstone quarry, is 6m high and 10m long. It is one of the most photographed spots in Lucerne, and one of the most forlorn. It is the Lion Monument.

> *The Lion lies in his lair in the perpendicular face of a low cliff – for he is carved from the living rock of the cliff. His size is colossal, his attitude is noble. His head is bowed, the broken spear sticking in his shoulder, his protecting paw rests upon the lilies of France. Vines hang down the cliff and wave in the wind, and a clear stream trickles from above and empties into a pond at the base, and in the smooth surface of the pond the lion is mirrored, among the water lilies.*

That was how Mark Twain described what was then, and now, a much-visited place. Murray noted, "There is a quiet solitude and shade about the spot which is particularly pleasing and refreshing." And he's right, even on a day like today when visitors stream through the gates as if on a conveyor belt from the ten tour buses parked nearby. There are Chinese couples consulting their guidebooks, American students listening half-heartedly to their teacher, Indian families posing for photos, and countless cameras or smartphones being held aloft to capture the fallen beast for ever.

Amid the sea of tourists and waves of chatter, my mother and I stand still and silent, transfixed by the sight of a dying lion. And we aren't the only ones to be moved motionless by the world's saddest sculpture. Others too are simply looking, absorbing every tiny detail of the lion: the outstretched paw, his slight frown, the fatal wound and a half-open mouth, as if he's taking his last breath while we watch. My mother wipes away a tear and we retreat to a nearby bench.

Listening to the conversations ebbing around us, it's clear that few people know what the monument commemorates, perhaps because the inscriptions are in Latin, although the ignored info

The Lion of Lucerne has been a tourist attraction for almost 200
years, as illustrated by this postcard from 1904

boards nearby provide all the necessary background. The general
consensus is that it's a tribute to the Swiss struggle for independence. If only it were that worthy. As poignant and majestic as it is,
the Lion Monument is a memorial to men who sold themselves for
money and to republicans who died for an autocratic monarch. It
remembers valour and honour that were sacrificed for a lost cause
and financial gain. That makes it even sadder.

Mercenary armies were abolished in the new Swiss federal constitution of 1848, although existing contracts were still honoured
(how very correct) until the government banned all forms of fighting for money in 1859. The sole survivor of the bloody practice is
the Pope's Swiss Guard, which has been protecting his Holiness
since 1506. To serve in Rome, the men must be under 30, over 1.74m
tall, single and have completed their Swiss military service. Being
both Swiss and Catholic are somewhat essential as well. If they
qualify on all grounds, then they get to wear the jaunty striped uni-
forms, which were not designed by Michelangelo in the sixteenth

century but Commandant Jules Repond in the early twentieth. He used Raphael's frescoes and the Medici colours as inspirations for an outfit that looks like it's been around for centuries.

The Lion Monument was one of the "lions", or essential sights, on Miss Jemima's whirlwind tour of Lucerne. If you think many of today's tourists rush around in a hurry, then take a look at what the 1863 group had in mind:

> "We had but four hours in Lucerne, and in those four hours a respectable dinner had to be taken in a respectable manner, the Cathedral to be done, the gabled frescœs of the Bridges to be examined, the feudal wall and its four watch towers to be inspected, and of course Thorwaldsen's Lion would feel slighted if forgotten."

In the end, they managed it all except the wall and its towers. First they marvelled at the "most brilliant" altarpieces in the cathedral, more commonly called the Hofkirche. Its tapering twin towers have been one of the symbols of the city since 1633, when the church had to be rebuilt after burning down on Easter Sunday. Then our group hurried to the "beautiful picture of fidelity and resignation amid heroic suffering", as Miss Jemima wrote of the Lion. In the ten minutes before dinner, they inspected the famous covered bridges that cross the River Reuss. Here too, fire has been part of the story.

The long wooden Chapel Bridge used to be the principal link between the old town on the right bank of the Reuss and the new one on the left. It was built in the fourteenth century and formed part of the city's defences, along with the sturdy stone water tower that stands beside it. Pride of place under the roof were 111 triangular religious paintings, but over half of them, and most of the bridge, were destroyed in a blaze on 17–18 August 1993. Today's structure is a reconstruction, although I wonder how many of the snap-happy visitors realise that as they stand and click in front of it. Most never know that the city's surviving medieval covered bridge, the Spreuerbrücke or Mill Bridge, is only a few metres downstream.

Before Lucerne's road bridge was built, the steamboats docked right beside the old town at the Schweizerhof Quai

There used to be an even longer wooden bridge, the Hofbrücke, which stretched all the way along the lakeshore to the Hofkirche. It might have been splendid, but it didn't fit in with the needs of a Victorian city, so was dismantled in 1852 to make room for a new lakeside embankment, boat docks and a road bridge across the river. That was finished in 1870 and, as in Geneva, has marred the waterfront ever since. I envy Miss Jemima seeing Lucerne without its ever-present noise and pollution. The one saving grace of the traffic-laden waterfront is that the old town was spared modernisation. It's as beautiful as ever, a time capsule where elegant murals adorn the buildings and fountains sit in uneven cobbled squares. The only drawback with being so attractive is that the place is usually heaving with people all year round, particularly during Carnival and the uncomfortably named Blue Balls Festival, which is all about music, in case you were wondering.

With our time running out, we grab a sandwich and an ice cream beside the river before heading back to the station. That too was the victim of a calamitous blaze – what is it with Lucerne and fires? – when the glorious domed building, which wouldn't have looked out of place in Paris, came crashing down in flames on 5 February 1971. Only the front portal remains as a monument to past splendour, with the angular modern replacement station lurking sheepishly in the background. Directly opposite is our paddle steamer, the oldest working example in Switzerland. What better way to sail across Lake Lucerne than on the good ship *Uri*, in service since 1901 and still going strong?

As we cast off, the long-threatened storm breaks and the heavens open, forcing us to huddle under the overhang from the upper deck (the rarefied level for first-class passengers), along with a Belgian family and their Australian friend. It would probably have been drier to swim. My mother fishes out a packet of Ricola (cranberry flavour) from her handbag and passes them round. I'm only glad she didn't have room for a Thermos in her suitcase or we'd all be drinking a hot beverage together. How very British.

The multi-fingered lake that sits at the centre of the country, both geographically and historically, is known locally as Vierwaldstättersee, which is why most English speakers stick to the simpler Lake Lucerne. The official translation would be Lake of the Four Forest Cantons, referring to its role as the birthplace of Switzerland. It was along its southern shores, in Rütli meadow, that three men swore an oath of allegiance in August 1291, so founding the confederation that would develop into Switzerland. Those first three cantons bordering the lake (Schwyz, Uri and Unterwalden) soon became four with the addition of Lucerne, so giving the lake its name.

If that wasn't enough, the area also plays host to the story of William Tell, a citizen of Uri who stood up to the Austrian Habsburg rulers. He was given an impossible challenge by Gessler, the new Austrian bailiff in town: shoot an apple off the head of Tell Junior. Our hero was handy with the crossbow so did exactly that, but was arrested anyway and sent to prison on the far side of the lake. As he and his captors crossed the water by boat, a storm descended

Lucerne, its lake and Rigi – and its ill-fated domed railway station on the lower right

on Lake Lucerne and Tell jumped to freedom. It's all a myth, but one that became a Swiss legend thanks to a nineteenth-century play written by a German and a toe-tapping tune written by an Italian.

In Miss Jemima's day the tourists didn't flock here for a slice of Swiss history (and they probably still don't today); they came by the thousand for the perfectly picturesque scenery of Switzerland's second largest lake: "you will not see a more beautiful lake in your life" was the view of *Cook's Tourist's Handbook*. The crooked cruciform shape of Lake Lucerne means that the rugged shoreline is never far away, as if the mountains are reaching down to dip their toes into the clear water. And one such peak is Rigi, known as the "Queen of the Mountains", though it would never win a beauty contest – at least not in Switzerland, which is spoilt for choice in terms of attractive peaks. There are several more impressive, more dramatic or more graceful mountains to choose from. And in a country that can claim 48 named peaks over 4000m high, Rigi is

Vitznau was chosen as the start of the Rigi Bahn after Weggis decided against it

a mere hillock at 1797m. So what is the attraction? Why do 1.25 million passengers every year still climb aboard the Rigi Bahn, the mountain railway that runs to the summit?

Simple: they want to enjoy the 360-degree panorama from the top, which is definitely worth the ride: Rigi sits resplendently detached from nearby mountains, surrounded on almost every side by water and with clear-day views across the whole Alps – "All around, the splendour of the world" was Goethe's comment in his diary. There is also what lies beneath passengers' feet: Switzerland's first mountain train. Its revolutionary cog wheels and toothed track made climbing the mountain possible for more than just men and mules; women were often carried up in sedan chairs, including Queen Victoria in 1868.

The line was built on this mountain not only because Rigi isn't as steep or as high as others, but also because it was already top of Switzerland's must-do list for every traveller in the mid-nineteenth century. See a glacier, tick. Buy a watch, tick. Watch the sunrise from on top of Rigi, tick. Conquering Rigi with rails was a key moment in developing both the train system and the country as a whole. It marks the moment when Switzerland truly became the playground of Europe.

The quickest way to reach the foot of Rigi was by boat and back in 1863 the Junior United Alpine Club sailed on the aptly named SS *Rigi*, which, in a stroke of good fortune, can still be seen at the Swiss Transport Museum in Lucerne. Built in 1848, the steamer is the oldest surviving means of motorised transport in Switzerland – and is remarkably small and plain. An open wooden deck, a single black funnel, two little huts for the captain and stores: all very minimalist compared with the ostentatious Belle Époque steamers (such as the *Uri*) that are floating palaces of polished brass and refined saloons. The SS *Rigi* is but one of the many fascinating exhibits at Switzerland's most-visited museum, along with a Wetterhorn cable car and a parade of trains, planes and automobiles. You don't have to be a petrol-head to enjoy the wealth of transport history on display there. Miss Jemima would probably find it rather amusing to see the ship she sailed on preserved as a historical object.

Among the passengers on board that day with her were

> "guides who had taken a passage on the boat for the purpose of securing a party for the ascent of the mountain. We engaged the most honest-looking to carry our satchels on his upright frame, packed on after that ingenious fashion of adhesiveness known only to Swiss guides and porteurs."

However, having a guide didn't stop them being harassed after docking and deboarding in Weggis, a small village that was a traditional starting point for the hike up Rigi. Their experience is so un-Swiss to modern sensibilities that it's worth reliving:

> "We landed at Weggis, and if each man, boy and mule-keeper who attacked us had been a wasp and each word a sting, Weggis had possessed our remains. We were literally infested by, dogged and danced around by these importunates! Our efforts and ruses

> to evade them were numerous and varied. The last hopes of the applicants were only finally crushed by la plus jolie dame announcing we had been up Mont Blanc! That was too much for even a Rigi man to equal. They fell back speechless before such climbers, and finally allowed 'la plus jolie dame' and the mountain Amazons to pass unseized."

Change the place names and it could easily read like a modern tourist's account of visiting India or Egypt. It certainly is not Weggis today, where apartments now sell for 1.5 million francs, nor modern Switzerland, where even in the most touristy of places people are rarely harassed by touts and hawkers. The Swiss developed politeness and wealth at the same time. As prosperity increased, the urgency of survival through selling something disappeared, as did the hard sell; the richer they got, the softer their sales techniques. They're so soft that sometimes in Swiss shops you're lucky if the staff even acknowledge your existence; I often feel like apologising for interrupting their chatting or daydreaming. But rather that than this:

> "Again, we are reminded that tourists are the staple commodity in the twenty-two cantons of Switzerland as another band of parasites would feed upon us, or rather feed us, as they dangled bunches of cherries in our faces with the cry of 'Vingt centimes! Vingt centimes!' These cherry vendors regard us as their legitimate prey – they industriously reap a good harvest in their Rigi farms as they try every art and device to make us purchasers."

And they were certainly persistent. A few hundred metres further on, Miss Jemima's enjoyment of the scenery came to an abrupt halt:

> "'Vingt centimes! Vingt centimes!' again rings in our ears, putting to flight our dreams of history, of valour, of poetry and beauty. This was too much for Miss Eliza's equanimity, who was roused to evoke such vilification of the enemy as her refined vocabulary could furnish."

Whatever Miss Eliza said, however colourful her language, it did the trick and the group was then left in peace to climb their mountain, only having to bear the stares of a "goitred ogre" who stood guard beside a cherry tree.

When Mark Twain walked the same walk (and famously took three days rather than three hours to finish it), he was faced with boys singing a rather different tune and handled them in typical Twainish fashion:

> The jodling (pronounced yodling – emphasis on the o) continued, and was very pleasant and inspiring to hear. Now the jodler appeared – a shepherd boy of sixteen – and in our gladness and gratitude we gave him a franc to jodel some more. So he jodeled and we listened. We moved on, presently, and he generously jodeled us out of sight. After about fifteen minutes we came across another shepherd boy who was jodling, and gave him half a franc to keep it up. He also jodled us out of sight. After that, we found a jodler every ten minutes; we gave the first one eight cents, the second one six cents, the third one four, the fourth one a penny, contributed nothing to Nos, 5, 6, and 7, and during the remainder of the day hired the rest of the jodlers at a franc apiece, not to jodel anymore. There is somewhat too much of this jodling in the Alps.

The Junior United Alpine Club tackled the hike much more seriously, employing various measures to keep up the pace: a quick step, beating time with their alpenstocks, linking arms and eventually that faithful standby, "diligent plodding". As Mr William wrote, "It took us four and a half hours ... you may be sure we were well tired when we reached the top at half past nine o'clock."

The group was taking a well-beaten track, a path that had been widened in 1819, with the help of inmates from Lucerne's prisons, to accommodate sedan chairs and donkeys, and upgraded again 20 years later to allow horses. This was all to make it more comfortable for the tourists – around 50,000 a year at that time – flocking to pay homage to Queen Rigi. This deluge of visitors sustained jobs such as porters, guides, luggage carriers, horsemen and delivery boys (bread was taken up on foot, starting at 2am so that hotel guests at the top could enjoy it fresh for breakfast), all better paid than farming. Not forgetting the beggars and yodlers, as even that was preferable to starving (such as in the famine of 1816–17). By 1863, a horseman earned ten francs for a trip up Rigi, and that at a time when the average farm worker was on less than two francs a day; no wonder they fought for every customer. The arrival of a boat in Weggis often led to undignified scuffles and such chaotic scenes at the dock that the authorities had to introduce minimum standards and fixed rates. All of that – the jobs, the fights, the money – disappeared when the train line opened in 1871.

As in Neuhaus and Frutigen, the train killed the tourist trade for those left behind, but in Weggis the story could have had a different ending. The village was given the chance to be the starting point for this new technological wonder but had refused, scared of what it meant for their horsemen, chair carriers and others. Too much competition was not a good thing; they wanted to keep their share of the pie for themselves, but in trying to do that they ended up giving it all away. The train line started further along the lakeshore, in Vitznau, and Weggis died for a while, deprived of the oxygen of tourism.

One history book on Rigi quotes the reaction of a local man who returned at that time:

> Back in my home town, the abandoned almost dying Weggis! Abandoned by tourism, Rigi tourism gone, the barely-awakened hotel industry in its final throes, neglected farming, bleak earning potential, that was the sign of those times.

The local council put it more succinctly – "Ever since the Rigi Bahn is in service, tourism between Weggis and Rigi has almost come to a standstill" – but the village eventually bounced back and today has an air of genteel prosperity about it. It also has a modern cable car up the mountain.

The Rigi Bahn was "one of the most novel features in mountain climbing", according to the Cook Handbook. It was also an instant success. The starting capital was raised in Zurich in a few hours and investors saw a healthy return: shares with a nominal value of 500 francs in August 1871 were worth 1350 francs a year later. That was mainly down to the line carrying 60,000 passengers in its first summer, despite the three trains being slow and small, which meant ridiculously long waiting times. At peak periods, passengers catching the first ship of the day from Lucerne would have to queue in Vitznau until 3pm to get on a train. They must have been foreigners, as no Swiss would ever stand in line for that long, even for a train ride. And after all that waiting, at first they couldn't even reach the summit by train. That was only possible in 1873, not through lack of demand or failures in technology, but because of the Swiss political system; in other words, cantons.

Rigi sits across the border of Cantons Lucerne and Schwyz, with the summit squarely in the latter. When it came to building a railway, each canton granted its concession to a different company and the race was on to see who would finish first. The Lucerners won when their line from Vitznau opened on 21 May 1871, after a slight delay caused by the Franco-Prussian War, which had prevented the delivery of enough rails. However, that line could only run as far as the cantonal border at Staffelhöhe, where passengers had to get out and walk the last few hundred metres. The Schwyzer line, coming up the back of the mountain from Goldau, wasn't completed until 1875, although those canny Schwyzers built the top section first. After that part opened in June 1873, they rented the tracks to their rivals, so earning money from the others running trains to the summit. As for the Vitznau line, it had to increase to ten locomotives to cope with the demand. The two lines merged in 1992, although you can still see their origins in the different liveries: red trains for Vitznau, blue and white for Goldau.

There were other schemes to transport visitors up Rigi, which at the time probably didn't seem any more outlandish than a

The 1864 air railway: one of the weirder plans to transport people up Rigi

mountain railway. In the book *Rigi: Mehr als ein Berg*, there's the great story of a Dr Schnyder, who planned a line using the recently unemployed porters and guides as ballast. Twice a day, 44 men would walk up and so act as a counterweight to haul the tourists up. While he was serious, it never happened. Or consider the slightly less bizarre Luftbahn, or air railway, with giant hot-air balloons carrying 200 passengers and tethered to a guide rail. That never got off the ground either.

The train killed off the horse and chair trade up the mountain, not just because it was trendy and exciting but because it was also quicker and cheaper. In 1871 it cost 5 francs for a one-way ticket, 7.50 francs for a return (which is roughly what the train driver earned per day). Compare that to the three porters, at 6 francs each, needed to carry someone up in a sedan chair, plus an extra porter for the luggage, or 10 francs for a horse and guide, and that was just for the upward journey. So while some jobs disappeared at the bottom of the mountain, many others were created by the hotel boom on the mountain. This was not only at the summit, known as Kulm, but all the way up at Kaltbad, Scheidegg and Staffelhöhe. Rigi became one giant dormitory, at least for a few decades. In a way, the story of the Rigi hotels is a mirror of tourist development in Switzerland: small at first, then a boom, followed by long-term growth and coping with the down times.

In 1816 Joseph Bürgi opened the first guesthouse on the summit, with a grand total of six beds. Within a couple of years, he was accommodating over 1000 guests each summer, so he expanded again and again to cope with the demand. By the time Miss Jemima arrived there were two hotels, together sleeping 330; more in peak season when the owners rented out the staff rooms to cope with the demand. Murray warns:

> During the height of summer, when travellers are most numerous, the Kulm inn is crammed to overflowing every evening; numbers are turned away from the doors, and it is not easy to procure beds, food, or even attention.

Miss Jemima stayed in the newest addition, the Regina Montium (or "Monstrum" as it was dubbed), with its 25m long dining room that could seat 200 at one sitting. Rooms cost 4 francs a night including lighting and service, breakfast was 1.50 francs and dinner 3 francs (altogether 8.50 francs for an overnight stay, or about 120 francs in today's money). Then came the railway, and the age of the palace hotel.

The Grand Hotel Schreiber made the others on the summit look like little summerhouses in its garden. Its huge, opulent design came from a familiar hand, that of star hotel architect Edouard Horace Davinet whose work we saw in Interlaken, and it took 2½ years to build (having to bring everything up by train didn't help). Five storeys high with 300 beds, it looked like a French château that had been airlifted onto the summit, complete with billiard room, music rooms and two restaurants. But there weren't many toilets. The original floor plans show that even such a grand hotel had very few: a typical bedroom floor had 38 rooms, with 64 beds in total, and 4 WCs. The hotel opened on 7 June 1875 and cost 20 francs a night, including food and drink, which was the same as a

week's wages for the average hotel worker. The Schreiber brothers wanted the highest quality available, so they employed Cäsar
Ritz, a Swiss hotelier from Valais who was still 13 years away from
transforming the London hotel scene. One Ritz story that made
the news around the world is recounted in the book *175 Jahre Rigi
Kulm Hotel* by Felix Weber:

> *Forty Americans arrived during a freak summer snow-
> storm expecting warmth and sustenance. The hotel's
> heating had failed, so Ritz hauled four palm trees out of
> their giant copper tubs, which he promptly filled with
> oil and lit to warm the dining room. Forty big stones
> were also heated and distributed to defrost diners' cold
> feet while they ate. The cold starter was replaced by hot
> bouillon with egg, the ice cream changed for flambéed
> crepes. Ritz, and the hotel, gained nothing but praise.*

In 1890 there were over 2000 beds available at all the Rigi hotels.
Then again, there were over 150,000 visitors a year. Rigi was the
tourist centre of Switzerland and its development showed no signs
of stopping. This was the Belle Époque, the era when Swiss tourism could do no wrong, the age of mountain trains and cable cars,
posh hotels and wealthy guests. And the Schreiber was the crown
on the head of the Queen of Mountains.

Such luxury came at a price, however. The monthly transport
bill for bringing food up to the summit was 2300 francs in August
1903 (about 31,000 francs today). That's not surprising once you
see that month's shopping list:

> *14,100 bread rolls*
> *141 kg crackers*
> *1,730 kg bread*
> *5,760 eggs*
> *4,500 litres beer*
> *2,752 kg meat*
> *37 ox tongues*

334 kg fish
1,980 kg chicken

At the other end of things, there was the "Rigi Disease" (aka diarrhoea, or maybe Rigi's Revenge), which continually plagued many guests, and even typhoid, which recurred as late as 1932. It took a while to realise that the sewage from the highest hotels was polluting the water of those at the bottom. That was a very real side-effect of building too many hotels in a confined space with no infrastructure.

As we have seen all across Switzerland, the golden era ended in the summer of 1914. Neutral Switzerland stayed out of the Great War but its visitors stayed at home, with their only trips abroad being to the trenches. Swiss holidays were off the agenda, as one example shows. In 1913 a total of 2.3 million passengers sailed on the Lake Lucerne paddle steamers; such a figure (the same as the current annual tally) would not be reached again until 1928, by which time it was almost too late for the Rigi hotels to recover. The original Kulm hotel burned down in 1935 and the remaining two started to fall apart. With so few guests, it wasn't worth repairing the holes and rain soon leaked into all the rooms. Other grand hotels at Kaltbad and Scheidegg either went up in flames or were pulled down.

By 1952, the giant Kulm hotels were unkempt and unsightly, and so large that they ruined the view from the summit, so they were demolished and all traces of grandeur were wiped off the mountain. In their place one smaller hotel was built, in the traditional style of an Alpine hospice, such as at the Great St Bernard Pass – and that's where we will spend the night, having booked in advance, just as Miss Jemima did: "Our beds had been secured by telegram from Lucerne." I sent an email.

From Vitznau up to Rigi Kulm only takes half an hour by train, but it is 30 of the most enjoyable minutes in Switzerland. As soon as you board the red carriage, it's immediately clear that this is no ordinary mountain train – not because it was the first one in Europe, but simply because of its size: it's as wide as a normal train carriage. The Rigi Bahn runs on a standard gauge (1435mm), whereas other rack railways in Switzerland use narrower ones, for example 1000mm for the BOB or 800mm for the Pilatus Bahn. If that means as little to you as to me, suffice to say that there's none of that feeling squashed and uncomfortable that you get on most mountain trains; plenty of cat-swinging space on this line. The train chugs up behind the village church, then seemingly through people's back gardens, so it's no real surprise when we stop to let off a woman with her bulging bags of shopping. It's almost like a community bus and is often the only way to reach the hillside houses other than on foot.

Once clear of the village, we climb on through the fir trees, with patches of blue water popping up here and there in the background. The higher we go, the better the views across the lake to craggy Mount Pilatus. A couple of walkers get off at Grubisbalm, where a sign advertises an eco-hotel; super view, but really in the middle of nowhere.

Ever upward we go to Kaltbad, the main stop on the mountain even though it's only halfway up, at 1433m. This once used to be a rail junction, with a line going off along the southern ridge to Scheidegg, 6km away. Despite opening at the height of Rigi's popularity in 1875, the line was bankrupt within three years, only to be resurrected before finally being dismantled in 1942. Not every tourist venture was a success, although the old route now makes a pleasant walk. Today it's the cable car from Weggis that ends at Kaltbad, but there's also a post office and village shop among the clutch of buildings.

The village began as a curative centre, where patients would bathe fully clothed in the cold natural springs ("Kaltbad" means cold bath) and then sit in the sun until they dried. That sounds like a way to catch your death rather than be cured. Far more relaxing is the warm water of the fancy new spa designed by the latest Swiss über-architect, Mario Botta, with his trademark curves, stripes and acres of stone. Above stands its ugly sister, the concrete block of a hotel that replaced the last of Rigi's palace hotels. On the night of 9 February 1961, the 111-year-old Grand Hotel Kaltbad burnt down, killing 11 people in the process. One survivor was a young waiter named Erich von Däniken, who most likely thought that aliens started the fire and had the idea for a certain book that became a bestseller.

We wait a while at Kaltbad, ostensibly for any passengers transferring from the cable car, but actually so that a teenage boy riding in the train driver's cab can dash off to a house up the street, disappear inside for a minute, then sprint back down to climb back on board. It may be a tourist line, but the locals make great use of it. Ruth Reinecke-Dahinden, one of the many children who grew up in Kaltbad, recently wrote a book, simply called *Die Rigi*, about her mountain home. Between the old photos are great details such as the Grand Hotel Kaltbad having cows milked directly outside the hotel so guests could have fresh milk. I couldn't resist contacting her, to hear her stories of life on Rigi. Listening to her, it's clear how the hotel boom gave farming families in the nineteenth century a crucial extra income from working in the laundry or gardens, or as dishwashers and waiters. For better or worse, tourism changed the face of Rigi for ever.

A couple of hundred metres higher is Staffel, where the blue-and-white train from Goldau arrives on the neighbouring track and races us to the top. We win, and pull into Kulm station, 1752m above sea level. The final 45m are only accessible by a footpath, but are an essential final step in order to see all 360 degrees of the panorama. Only then is it possible to appreciate why so many thousands have come over the centuries: the Queen of the Mountains is surrounded by the best scenery in central Switzerland, ringed by lakes and with the whole Alps punctuating the horizon. Such a shame that some idiot plonked a giant communications tower on the mountain top; how to spoil a view in one easy lesson.

On the way down from the summit I notice something peculiar. Rigi isn't one big lump of rock; it's a granular mass of thousands of stones that have clumped together. The technical term is conglomerate, which is essentially a big word for thousands of pebbles stuck together by strong gluey cement. It looks as if it would fall apart if you stamped hard on it, but of course it doesn't, although this is not the most stable of rock formations. In September 1806 a vast section of Rossberg, a nearby mountain of conglomerate, slid down into the valley below, wiping out Goldau along with 457 people. It was one of Switzerland's worst natural disasters, and still traumatic enough for Murray to devote four pages to describing the event in detail more than fifty years later.

With perfect timing, we enter the hotel as the clouds race in. Within a few minutes, the view has vanished into a dense mass of swirling grey and it's not long before the rain is lashing down. But this is no passing storm like before and two hours later the rain has still not let up, giving us a grand view of nothing at supper in the panorama restaurant.

Luckily we have something to keep our minds off the damp outdoors: chatting to the hotelier. Renate Käppeli's family has owned the hotel since its modern incarnation opened in 1954, and she is more than happy to show off the oversized gilt mirrors, which once graced the walls of the Schreiber, the palace hotel that was pulled down in the 1950s after a crusade against it from the conservationists.

The Schweizer Heimatschutz, or Swiss Heritage Society, was founded in 1905 with the aim of protecting both the architectural and environmental heritage of Switzerland. Its foundation was a response to the decades of endless development in the Swiss Alps, where nowhere seemed safe from hotels and railway lines. The final straw was a plan to build a train line up to the top of the Matterhorn; you might as well turn Heidi into a prostitute at the same time. Plans aborted, national icon saved and a new voice found, one that made itself heard loud and clear. After the Second World War, the society had plenty to say about Rigi Kulm, with its dilapidated hotels and plethora of souvenir stands spoiling the view. It was time they went.

A public campaign selling chocolate coins (this is Switzerland, after all) raised 330,000 francs for the restoration of Rigi to its natural state. The Regina Montium and Schreiber hotels, so long a symbol of the triumph of tourism, were dismantled and replaced with a more sombre, more Swiss creation. On the 50th birthday of the Heritage Society, a giant bonfire on top of Rigi reduced the last remains of the hotels to ashes. The soul of Rigi had been saved – only for it to be sold a decade later in the form of a radio mast. Tearing down a century of history to restore the view is one thing; ripping it down to make way for something far uglier is pointless. Tourism, for all its faults, is part of Switzerland's history, its heritage, and has helped make the country the way it is. Who knows, without the tourists the Swiss Heritage Society might not even have the money to be guardians of anything, let alone sell the family silver to the highest bidders.

Ruth Reinecke-Dahinden told me that the demolition of the old hotel was very painful for her and her family to witness, a sad moment in Rigi's history. As tempted as I am to ask Frau Käppeli what she thinks, I demur and instead ask if there happen to be any records from the nineteenth century; I have yet to see any proof that Miss Jemima was in Switzerland. The hotels she stayed in have suffered a string of calamities since she was there: Geneva – now a watch shop, Chamonix – now a casino, Sion – vanished, Leukerbad – demolished, Kandersteg – burned down, Interlaken – bankrupt, Grindelwald – burned down, Giessbach – demoted, Rigi – demolished. This is my last chance to find her in a visitors' book – and there's a glimmer of hope from this penultimate stop on the tour.

"We have guest books dating back to 1816," says Frau Käppeli with a smile.

My heart jumps. I almost get carried away with the prospect of seeing Miss Jemima's name in a guest book from a hotel that no longer exists; then the other shoe drops.

"But we keep them down in our archives in Schwyz."

So near and yet so far.

My mother's sigh is as defeated as my face, which always betrays any disappointment (I'd be a useless poker player). Our hostess tries to explain.

"*Die Bücher sind heilig,*" she says, switching to German. This literally means "The books are holy", but fear not, dear English reader, I won't force you to test your German any further. Suffice to say, Frau Käppeli promises to go down to Schwyz soon and see who signed the book on 9 July 1863. Patience is a virtue, apparently, but right now I'm not feeling that virtuous.

It's early to bed for us. The rain is still driving down, meaning that our planned star gazing away from the city lights is off the agenda. We also have to get up at an unhealthy hour to watch something that happens every day, although our sunrise on Rigi is in serious danger of being a washout.

Saturday, 5am. Complete silence. And that means only one thing: fortunately, there will be no rain on our parade today.

Miss Jemima described her rude awakening after barely five hours' sleep:

> "At three o'clock the winding notes of the arousing horn were heard, its blasts approaching nearer and nearer as each corridor was in its turn blown up. Truly this was an effectual awakener, as blow upon blow, blast after blast, was twisted out of that bark-bound hookah."

Instead of an alphorn I have my mother. We can get up slightly later than Miss Jemima, thanks to the advent of summer time, which Switzerland introduced after the rest of Europe. Back in 1977, the Swiss government brought in a new summer time law, proposing that Switzerland follow other European countries, particularly neighbouring France and Italy, by having daylight saving between March and October. The farmers weren't happy (or at least their cows weren't) and they forced a referendum on the issue. The cows won: in May 1978 the Swiss voted against summer time. The government leaflet advocating a Yes vote was great, not least because one argument was that television and radio times wouldn't be in sync – you'd come home from work to find that you'd missed your favourite show. Much of German-speaking Switzerland watches German television and all the programme times would be wrong.

Nevertheless, in Switzerland there's one thing more important than cows, and that's trains – and train timetables. Once Germany

Sunrise on Rigi was the highlight of many Victorian trips to Switzerland

and Austria had both introduced summer time in 1980, Switzerland became a little time warp in the centre of Europe for six months of the year. Some might argue that the Swiss are always one step behind the rest of Europe, but being one hour behind all its neighbours proved to be a logistical headache for the train timetablers. So the government brought back the summer time law, and on this occasion the cows lost.

And thank goodness for that, as it means we can lie in until 5am. Clear skies might mean a visible sunrise, but also very fresh air. We both don almost every piece of clothing we have with us and head outside into the dark, silent night – alone. It was rather a different story 150 years ago, when seeing the first rays of sunlight from Rigi was the highlight of a Swiss tour, so it was busy, very busy, as Miss Jemima wrote:

> "We counted about a hundred and fifty early risers, most of whom wore the miserable expression that would find words in

Dr. Watts' moral song 'You have waked me too soon, I must slumber again.'"

We are precisely two people, with a whole mountain to ourselves. Evidently, watching the sunrise from Rigi is no longer a must-do for today's tourists. Most likely I would never have thought to come up for it if Miss Jemima had not brought me here, though I'm grateful she did. In a world where travel has become so fast and crowded, there's something rather special about simply watching the sun rise over the mountains. This is one of the few times when Miss Jemima had to share the experience with countless strangers and one of the few times when we have managed to do it alone; a reversal of fortune for which we had to wait the whole trip.

"The vastness of that mighty panorama was impressively sublime and in hushed silence we gazed on that serrated belt as daylight awoke on its three hundred miles of mountains, valleys, lakes and villages."

Miss Jemima's view of a Rigi sunrise has scarcely changed at all. The lights of Lucerne and Zug are twinkling away far beneath our feet, the only signs of life in an otherwise empty blackness. As the first glimmers of light appear on the eastern horizon, so too do the misty layers of the landscape. Ridge after ridge, each paler than the one below, pop up out of the shrinking darkness and the sheets of water around us fade from black to blue. The streaks of cloud and airplane tracks burst into flame as the sun finally appears, making the snow-covered mountains blush and the wisps of fog disappear. As the crisp daylight inches along the valley floors, the green fields emerge from the night, filling the whole panorama with summer colour. The final flourish of this dawn spectacle is the shadow of Rigi creeping its way over to Pilatus – a huge grey pyramid stretching across the lake and almost touching the craggy summit opposite.

Thank you, Miss Jemima. Without you I would never have seen such a memorable Swiss sunrise; or been so bloody freezing while enjoying it. Mr William had a similar opinion: "quite the grandest thing we had seen and worth a great deal of trouble ... it was bitterly cold."

"At our eight o'clock breakfast we were almost alone", wrote Miss Jemima after sunrise that morning. Fifteen decades later, but at exactly the same time, we are sitting in the empty dining room of almost the same hotel. But after that, whereas the Junior United Alpine Club had no choice but to walk down to the lakeside town of Küssnacht, we can take the first train of the day, following the Schwyz line to Goldau before changing to a regular train there. The blue-and-white carriages roll into view and the driver hops out to unload the milk and other supplies for the hotel. Short of using a helicopter, it's still the only way to get goods up to the top.

For the return journey the train acts as delivery and postal service, carrying sacks of postcards and packages – and two passengers – down to the bottom. The Rigi Kulm hotels used to print their own stamps (until that became illegal in 1883) and thousands of cards and letters went from there all around the world. The postcard business boomed: in 1873 only 22,000 cards were sent abroad from Switzerland; 10 years later the figure was 2.6 million and by 1900 it was 15.7 million. The funny thing about postcards in those days is that there was almost no room to write a message; you had to squeeze it into a small blank space, typically under the picture or a triangle across one corner (as the Lion postcard on page 231 shows). That's because the address and stamp filled the whole of the reverse side.

The weather gods smiled on us today, but not everyone is so lucky. As the Murray Handbook says, "Fortunate are they for whom the view is not marred by clouds and rain, a very common occurrence, as the leaves in the Album kept in the inn will testify." The Album means, of course, the guestbook – I can only hope the gods will be as kind when it comes to finding a certain name in said guestbook. Fingers crossed.

We could have taken a train straight through from Goldau to Lucerne, but in an effort to follow Miss Jemima more exactly, we get off in Küssnacht am Rigi and switch to the boat. As pretty as it is, Küssnacht is not exactly on the Lake Lucerne tourist trail, but is known across the rest of Switzerland for two events. After escaping his captors during the storm on the lake, William Tell caught up with the baddy Gessler in a leafy lane near Küssnacht and killed him; the Tell Chapel in the Hohle Gasse reputedly stands on the exact spot of the deed. More artistic is the Klausjagen festival every December, which celebrates St Nicholas with a procession of 200 or so people wearing huge transparent mitres, each lit internally with a candle.

Other than that, Küssnacht sits in sleepy splendour at the head of the most easterly finger of the lake, with a boat only every two hours. Even on this Saturday in summer, it's refreshingly quiet: no groups, no hordes, just locals enjoying a coffee in the sun. There's the usual smattering of handsome old buildings that populates almost every Swiss town; missing out on two world wars ensured that Switzerland did not have to suffer the destruction of its architectural heritage (at least not from bombs and bullets). Apart from the lakefront being dominated by a car park, it's a perfectly pleasant spot to wait for a boat, in this case a sleek catamaran that whisks us over the water to Lucerne.

Whereas it took Miss Jemima & Co. most of the day to travel from Lucerne to Neuchâtel, we can manage it in under two hours. After all those mountain trains, the ride from Lucerne seems so gentle and so lush. We skirt round the Emmental region, where the holey cheese comes from that is synonymous with Switzerland, even though there are many other types of Swiss cheese and few of them have holes. By the way, the holes (technically called "eyes") are really trapped CO_2 released by bacteria added during the final stages of production.

Each round of Emmental weighs up to 120 kilos and each kilo requires 12 litres of milk. That demands an awful lot of cows. No wonder Canton Bern has more cows than any other canton, and most of them seem to be in the fields outside our train window. This is agricultural Switzerland at its most typical, a chocolate-box image: not only cows but farmhouses with geraniums in every window box, barns with roofs the size of tennis courts, a lumpy landscape covered in what appears to be green velvet, and a not-so-distant backdrop of the Alps. It's a Swiss version of the Cotswolds, only with bigger hills and fewer sheep, and pretty enough to make you want to yodel. That is, until you reach Olten, where prettiness goes out the window.

To be fair, Olten has an attractive old town tucked away inside the modern outskirts, much like every town in Switzerland. The problem is that all most people see of Olten is the train station and the railway lines, none of which is worth writing home about. As Miss Jemima said, "Olten is a central junction, where lines cross." It would be rather like sending a postcard home from Crewe.

This is the focal point of the Swiss train network, the X where the main north–south and east–west lines cross, the 0 from which all distances were once measured (though that has since moved to Basel; Olten is now at the 39.29km mark). In Switzerland, all trains lead to Olten – or at least they did, thanks to Stephenson and Swinburne, those English engineers who mapped out the national network in 1850. Intercity trains from Bern to Zurich no longer stop here, but in the early days everyone did: going from Zurich to Lucerne by train meant changing in Olten and travelling along two sides of a triangle. No wonder the journeys took so long, although having slow trains, cheaply built lines and small engines didn't help either. For example, the only direct train service from Zurich to Geneva travelled at an average of 30km/h and stopped at 35 stations along the way.

At least the Swiss trains were comfortable; Mr William wrote that "the second class are superior to our first class". Only about 5 per cent of carriages were first class and many Swiss couldn't afford to travel in anything but third, with its hard wooden seats. Tourists generally chose the upholstered comfort of second, as we have done today. It's not plush, but it's definitely not wooden and it's perfectly comfy – and clean. After a change in Olten, of course, we finally reach Neuchâtel, a place that sounds so much more romantic in French than German (Neuenburg) or English (Newcastle). This was the last stop in Switzerland for the first conducted tour of 1863, which means that for us the end is nigh.

Lakeside Neuchâtel was Miss Jemima's final stop in Switzerland

Carved from a slab of butter. That's how the novelist Alexandre Dumas described Neuchâtel, although cheese might be a more apt description for a Swiss city. Either way, the buildings of the old town are a gorgeous deep golden colour that looks even warmer on a sunny day, with the light reflecting off Lake Neuchâtel. Throw in a distant view of the Alps and the castle on a hill (hence the town's name, though it is no longer new) and you have a picture of Swiss urban happiness. This was not the motive for this being the final stop on Miss Jemima's tour, nevertheless; that was down to two practical reasons: taking the shortest route home, along the newly opened train line to Pontarlier in France, and buying a watch. Canton Neuchâtel has been the centre of the Swiss watch industry for centuries, ever since the watchmakers of Geneva moved out of their overcrowded city into the Jura mountains.

Up to the mid-1600s, Geneva had been the capital of Swiss watchmaking, thanks to Calvin banning jewellery, which forced city craftsmen to turn to a new trade. They formed the world's first Watchmaker's Guild and established a reputation for precision and beauty. However, Geneva wasn't big enough for all of them, so many

moved to the hills between Lake Neuchâtel and the French border.
Today, the area is known as Watch Valley and the likes of Omega,
Tissot, Swatch and Tag Heuer are all made here. Back in the mid-
1800s the town of La Chaux-de-Fonds, up behind Neuchâtel, was
the sixth largest town in Switzerland, only marginally smaller than
Zurich. After a fire in 1794 it had been rebuilt on a grid pattern and
designed specifically for the watchmakers' needs. As Murray says:

> The chief manufacture [of the canton] is that of watches
> and clocks, of which 130,000 are exported annually: the
> central seat of it may be said to be the valley of Chaux
> de Fonds and Locle; but much is done in the town of
> Neuchâtel.

Fast forward 150 years, and whereas Zurich has grown by over
2000 per cent, La Chaux-de-Fonds has only trebled in size, although
it's still making watches, and lots of them. Switzerland now exports
30 million watches every year, with a value of 19 billion francs.
Its watches are synonymous with quality and accuracy, even if the
whole industry did have to be saved by a cheap plastic version in
the 1980s. There was no trendy Swatch for Mr William back in
1863, who wrote, "I have bought a watch for £7 and like the bargain very well". That's about £525 today, or rather more than the
average Swatch, but substantially less than a Rolex.

As neither my mother nor I need a new watch, we amble happily round the town centre instead. A drink overlooking the lake,
a peek into the Collégiale church, a taste of Bleuchâtel, one of the
few blue Swiss cheeses around, and generally being rather lazy.
It's our version of Miss Jemima's relaxed agenda:

> "This morning was to be one of leisure, the first of the kind in our
> programme, so a breakfast earlier than eight a.m. was not enforced.
> We spent it loitering through the town."

It seems that this is a town for doing little more than walking and
watching. Thomas Cook did exactly the same on his way back to

England after leaving his group the week before; and he was much encouraged by what he saw:

> Amongst those numerous promenaders of all ages, both sexes, and all seeming grades of society, there was no rudeness, not the least resemblance of immoral or ridiculous behaviour. The reputed simplicity and morality of the Swiss character was well sustained and abundantly confirmed by a two hours' ramble and close observation on the banks of the Lake of Neuchâtel.

I'm happy to report that we saw no signs of "immoral or ridiculous behaviour" either, although I fear our standards might be somewhat lower than Mr Cook's. What he would make of the prolific graffiti I dread to think.

At the time of Cook's visit, Neuchâtel had not long been Swiss. Renowned for reputedly having the best French speakers in Switzerland, Neuchâtel was also once a political anomaly, as it was part of Prussia. For many years it was a canton within the Swiss Confederation but at the same time a principality belonging to the King of Prussia, an odd state of affairs that arose out of the tangled web that was Europe in centuries past. When the Princess of Neuchâtel, Marie of Orleans, died in 1707, the people had to elect a new ruler from among the many claimants to the throne. They chose Frederick I of Prussia, because it was more important for him to be Protestant than to speak French. Napoleon briefly took over and then it was back to being a Prussian principality in 1815, even though Neuchâtel had by then officially become the 21st canton of Switzerland.

This unusual situation of being Swiss and Prussian lasted until 1848, when a bloodless revolt in Neuchâtel created a new republic. The royalists didn't give up without a fight, one that almost caused a war between Prussia and Switzerland until an international conference sorted things out. No princes, no Prussians, Neuchâtel has since then been a totally Swiss republic.

Both of us are feeling somewhat weary after our 5am start – it really is a challenge keeping up with these Victorians. Even Mr William commented in one letter home that he was "surprised that the ladies have all stood it so well. I should not like to have to work so hard for much longer tho' it is very enjoyable for a short time and we are delighted with our visit." We have yet to find a hotel in Neuchâtel, as the one where Miss Jemima stayed, the Bellevue, no longer exists. A modern replacement seems less than appealing.

"How do you fancy sleeping at home tonight?" I ask my mother, meaning my home in Bern, not hers in Hampshire.

"Oh, I'm so glad you said that. I was thinking exactly the same but didn't want to say anything. It feels a bit like cheating."

We agree that it's not strictly following the rules, but we can live with that. So we decide to return to Bern and the comfort of home. It's exactly two weeks since we were in Newhaven waiting for this trip back in time to start, but somehow it feels like so much longer. Almost every day has been far busier than a normal holiday, always on the move, changing hotels, seeing the sights, hitting the heights and generally rarely stopping. There's also the small matter of someone having made a mistake when booking a flight. A lapse of concentration meant that I booked my mother's flight back to London for tomorrow morning, one day too early. Even seasoned travel writers make basic mistakes. It could have been much worse: I could have left my passport at home, turned up at the wrong airport or checked in a day too late, all of which have happened to former colleagues over the years.

Miss Jemima and friends left Neuchâtel at 4pm, with an overnight train journey to Paris ahead of them. Twenty hours later they were back in the French capital for their extended city sightseeing tour, but our heroine confesses that they did not completely enjoy the experience:

> "Whilst we were pleased with our peep at Paris, it must be admitted we saw it rather disadvantageously. Reaction from the excitement of Swiss travel and the weariness induced by rapid

journeyings came upon us just when we most needed great powers of endurance to bear the fatigues of sightseeing in a great city."

At last, she succumbs to being human. I was beginning to wonder if there was something in the water back then that gave them such stamina. And she admits that Paris could not compare "with the wonders of mountain scenery by the side of which any scene of man's device is paltry". When, on Thursday, 16 July 1863, our intrepid travellers finally returned to London, they were most evidently pleased to be home:

"The memory of our three weeks' holiday has many bright spots, but none in their way more precious than the happiness we experienced in setting foot on an English shore, and hearing again our mother tongue."

Mr William also looked back on the tour in his last letter home. "I am very glad we came. Apart from the great pleasure we have had, the experience it gives is really very valuable. I should have no difficulty in going about anywhere now and we are so much better informed on many subjects."

It really was character-building stuff for him, and his sister, much as it had been for the first Grand Tourists and would be for teenage InterRailers many decades later. The times and transport change, but the results remain the same. And as her journal ends, Miss Jemima reflects a little on the tour and all that the Junior United Alpine Club had experienced:

"It is to the Swiss rambles that we look back with the greatest pleasure, apart from the recollection of a pleasant companionship that has served to enliven many subsequent hours. ... We had acquired a wider knowledge of human nature, habits of self-reliance, and valuable lessons of our own ignorance that amply repaid us all for the fatigue and inevitable annoyance attendant on foreign travel."

At supper that evening, my mother and I raise a glass to a long-gone lady who has been our constant companion and guide for the last 14 days. Without Miss Jemima, we would most likely never have stayed at the Giessbach hotel, watched the sunrise on Rigi, walked along a glacial gorge or sat in the rain waiting for Mont Blanc to appear. We have followed her route and her time-table, albeit with modern means of transport and far more pairs of underwear. And for the most part, the Switzerland she saw is still recognisable today. Yes, the towns have grown as the glaciers shrunk, the toilets have improved as much as the trains, and prices have risen with standards. But the landscape is as beguiling as ever; it was the main reason they came 150 years ago and the reason people will keep on coming. Some things never change, no matter what.

Many months later I am back on the Rigi Bahn, riding through a winter wonderland of trees laden with so much snow they look like they're disguised as cauliflowers. A few days earlier I got an email from Renate Käppeli about one particular entry in an old guest book. She may have found something, so I'm returning to the Kulm hotel to see what she has uncovered in the archives. I can barely sit still now that the summit of Rigi is in sight; I can't wait to see the book. Will Miss Jemima be in there? I do hope so.

The battered brown guest books may be sacred, but they are also crammed full – for that one day in July 1863 there are four big pages of swirly Victorian script to decipher. I can practically hear the quills scratching across the creamy, ink-blotted paper as I run my finger down the list of names of now-dead visitors from Berlin and Rotterdam, Boston and Savannah, Lausanne and Zurich. Every third one seems to be from London, Cheltenham or Saffron Walden, making the search that much harder.

And then there they are, at the top of the day's last page.

W.W. Morrell, York, England
Miss Morrell, Selby, ditto

They really were here. After following her for so long, I have finally found her. The hotel where they slept has gone, but this tiny record of their visit has survived 15 decades among thousands upon thousands of other tourists' names. I'm not usually that keen on signing hotel guest books; they always seem either pointless or egotistical. From now on I will sign one everywhere I stay.

I almost kiss Frau Käppeli, but Swiss decorum gets the better of me. Instead, I skip down to the train and smile my way back home. And I send my mother a text:

"Found: one lady from Yorkshire, answers to the name of Miss Jemima."

The Morrells' guestbook entry from Hotel Rigi Kulm, 9 July 1863

AFTERWORD

"Kings and cockneys may be excellent people in their way. But they have in common the property of being very objectionable neighbours at an hotel." Sir Leslie Stephen's caustic observation is interesting, not just for the fact that it came at a time when the h of hotel was still silent in English, as in French (so was preceded by "an"), but also on the matter of class. He did not want to share the Alps with the common man or a nobleman; it was a place for gentlemen, preferably of the upper-middle class, who knew how to dress for dinner but didn't expect a valet to do it for them. Thomas Cook ruined all that by becoming travel agent to kings and cockneys and everyone in between. He prompted a mixing of cultures and classes never seen before on such a scale. Switzerland was soon a playground for the whole of Europe.

It began as an affordable tour for a group of English people in search of a new adventure; it mushroomed into an industry that accounts for 5 per cent of global GDP thanks to one billion international tourist arrivals in 2012. That's one billion people going abroad In a single year, with Switzerland, the birthplace of mass tourism, accounting for a mere eight million of them. It's a small fish in a very big pond.

So what happened between then and now? What became of the main players in the tale I have just told – Thomas and Jemima, and Switzerland itself? It's time to see how that first tour changed a country, created a global brand and conjured up an incredible surprise for me.

In 1863, Switzerland was slowly edging towards prosperity and stability, although the challenging topography and piecemeal politics meant that wealth was concentrated in a few places. As we have seen, many rural areas were relatively poor, with people supplementing small farming incomes with handicrafts. Cantons and communities were distinct entities, isolated from each other by

In 1874 Thomas Cook produced his own guidebook to Switzerland, featuring ships, trains, coaches – and camels.

distance and by attitude, while federal government was as young and weak as a new-born lamb. The railways changed all that. With the advent of trains and tunnels, Switzerland could be one nation for the first time, geographically speaking. It no longer took days to reach Ticino from the northern cities and Valais wasn't cut off by its mountain borders any more. Trains also made it possible to travel around the whole country in winter, not only for tourists but for everyone. The weather, like the Alps, had been conquered. Even travelling in the lowlands became comparatively quick and easy, giving the Swiss – or some of them – the chance to explore.

Railways ushered in an era of faster, cheaper mass transport – 25 million passengers in 1880, 240 million in 1910 – but for many Swiss it was still out of reach financially. What was affordable for British visitors was a luxury for locals. Transport history centre Via Storia reckons that most of those 240 million passengers were tourists and the small layer of Swiss society with money, but the middle classes could at least contemplate a trip for the first time; not often or far, but a possibility, although in third class most likely, as first class was double the price, and mountain trains were even more expensive. Someone from Zurich might manage a day trip once a year to Lake Lucerne or to another Swiss city, one that had probably been an economic rival until then.

At that time, Swiss industry was as fragmented as its politics, with no one city dominating the economy. This decentralisation, due to the lack of good transport links but also to the political system, meant that the country specialised into many mini-economies. Different areas concentrated on particular goods, normally those of high value to overcome the crippling transport costs and limited terrain. For example, St Gallen had its embroidered textiles, La Chaux-de-Fonds its watches, Basel its silk ribbons, Alpine regions their cheeses. It wasn't a perfect system, nevertheless. Incomes were low, hours were long and some local economies became dangerously dependent on one trade. In 1913, the embroidery trade in St Gallen employed half the population, and exported more in value than the watch industry, so when it died with the loss of overseas markets in the First World War and the advent of cheap foreign competition, the blow was devastating to the local economy.

The railways integrated Switzerland into a single market, psychologically and economically. Products could now reach their customers quickly and cheaply, whether that was watches going abroad or carrots to the cities. And it was tourism that helped finance the railways. Outside the heavily populated lowlands, few lines would have been viable without the money coming in from tourists. A train to Grindelwald made no economic sense other than to take visitors up to the mountains, and probably still doesn't. How long would the famous Glacier Express survive as a normal line? None of the towns along its route is big enough to support such a remote train service.

Tourism was from the outset the grease that oiled the wheels of the trains that united Switzerland. It became a perfect circle of life: tourists made the railways viable and financed new lines, which brought in more tourists, which made it feasible to raise more capital to build more lines. And all the time the economy as a whole was benefiting from improved transport and bigger markets. Tourists also bought watches and chocolate to take home, so spreading the word about Swiss quality products. Furthermore, the new art of photography made the mountains seem so much more realistic, and inviting, than an oil painting, motivating ever more tourists to see them in person.

It's almost as if the Swiss economy had been waiting for something to kick-start its race to success. While all the elements were in place, a vital link was missing; that is until tourism made the railways viable in such a difficult environment, when it was full steam ahead on every front. A look at some of the Swiss companies founded in the decades after 1863 says it all: Nestlé foods 1866, Schindler lifts 1874, Maggi foods 1884, Victorinox penknives 1884, Sandoz pharmaceuticals 1886, Laufen bathrooms 1892, Roche pharmaceuticals 1896, Kuoni travel agents 1906. Switzerland transformed into something closer to the country we know today, not quite as prosperous but well on the way. A knack for innovation helped, giving us products like cellophane, tin foil and stock cubes

– all Swiss inventions from the early 1900s. Then came the two world wars, which turned everything upside down. Nevertheless, the Swiss economy survived both traumas largely unscathed and filled the void left by shattered economies elsewhere. Immigration from southern Europe provided cheap labour, Swiss attention to detail ensured high quality, and the trains delivered access to a worldwide market, so the money rolled in.

All through that meteoric development, tourism has been the backbone of the Swiss economic miracle, providing a bedrock of income that helped sustain development elsewhere. The Alps had been a perilous place and a hindrance to progress, but they quickly became Switzerland's greatest resource and the key to its success. Industrialists in Zurich could invest in ever grander hotels and ever higher railway lines, knowing that they would reap the rewards. Ruskin may have bemoaned the "consuming white leprosy of new hotels and perfumer's shops" and castigated his fellow Britons for having taught the Swiss "all the foulness of the modern lust of wealth", but there's no denying that tourism transformed the countryside economy. In 1870 there were 38,000 people working in the hospitality and transport sectors; in 1900 that had rocketed to 118,000, many of them in rural areas. Such growth was sustainable only because the tourists kept on coming.

Switzerland had a total of 9300 hotel beds and 2.9 million overnight stays in 1863; ten years later those figures had more than doubled, and by 1913 there were 211,000 beds and 23.8 million overnights. Such a peak would not be reached again until the 1950s. Today the levels are higher, 245,000 beds and 35.5 million overnights, but the latter figure includes much larger numbers of Swiss domestic tourists. A hundred years ago that was only a fifth of the market, now it's more than twice that. One sure sign that the Swiss are richer than they once were is that they can afford to holiday at home. In 1863 a hotel breakfast cost the same as a day's wages for a Swiss farm or factory worker; in 2013 it's probably not even an hour's worth of work time.

The luxury element has not been lost either. The tradition of palace hotels offering every possible comfort lives on in Switzerland, which has 93 five-star hotels, or one for every 85,000 inhabitants; in comparison Germany has 125, or one for every 650,000 people. In the past these grand hotels were the first to have electric lights, lifts, central heating and indoor toilets, because their guests expected it, and such modern comforts soon trickled down into Swiss towns and homes. Today these top (that is, expensive) hotels undoubtedly help the bottom line, which is tourism's healthy contribution to the Swiss economy: 35.5 billion Swiss francs, half directly in hospitality and transport, half indirectly in goods and services. Then there are the 275,000 people directly employed in tourism, and probably almost as many dependent on it. Someone has to make the chocolate!

It's not all roses, though, as the recent referendum on holiday homes shows: under the new rules no community can have more than 20 per cent of its housing as second homes. This was a clear reaction to overdevelopment, overpricing and overcrowding, although most of the tourist regions voted against it. Should the countryside or the economy be protected? That conundrum was being debated a century ago when they built the Jungfraubahn, and will probably never be resolved.

For all its drawbacks, tourism has helped Switzerland to prosper and will continue to do so. A growing middle class, increased personal wealth, improved transport links and the lure of the Alps – those are exactly the conditions that in the nineteenth century transformed Switzerland into the world's first mass tourist destination. They are the same reasons that Chinese, Indians and Brazilians are today arriving in their thousands. The countries have changed, but it's the same scenario as 150 years ago. Thomas Cook's legacy lives on, not just in the 680,000 British visitors who still find their way to Grindelwald and beyond, but in the countless other nationalities who join them there.

However, there is one big difference. Today's tourists can organise everything, or have it done for them, before they even leave home. That first tour was remarkable for its lack of planning and preparation, not really the sort of package tour we know now, where you pay up front with, at the very minimum, your travel and accommodation included. Things were much more ad hoc and relaxed than that, at least at the beginning, so they could easily have gone pear-shaped. Switzerland's transport system was not as developed as in other countries and outside the main towns there was little in the way of infrastructure. It could have been a disaster, a thought that must have been on Cook's mind the whole time.

He needn't have worried. The first conducted tour was so successful that a second tour followed in August, during which Cook wrote:

> I am in Paris surrounded with some 500 or 600 enterprising Tourists, and am expecting an addition of 400 or 500 more tonight. Already a party of 100 has started for Switzerland, and I expect to follow them to-morrow with 260 to 300 more.

In the end there were over 200 Tourists (Cook always gave them a capital T as they were on his Tours) in his Swiss party travelling on from Geneva on that second trip, so he had to divide the group for the Circular Tour to Mont Blanc. Half followed the same route he had taken in June (as we have seen with Miss Jemima), ending up with a boat across Lake Geneva; the other half were sent round in the opposite direction, starting with the boat and ending with carriages from Chamonix – another extraordinary logistical triumph. As for Cook, he then ventured off to Lucerne, Interlaken and Bern, surviving on a "hash of bad French, worse German and broad English". Language difficulties aside, his readiness to explore more of Switzerland so soon, with a view to adding those destinations to his tours, is perhaps proof that he realised what he had unleashed: an appetite for all things Swiss.

A third conducted tour followed, so that by the end of that summer 2000 people had travelled with Cook to Paris, with about 500 of them going on into Switzerland. This set the (snow)ball rolling, and it soon became an avalanche. In May 1864, the season began again and Cook was already offering four different tours in

Switzerland. The first, starting in Geneva, was the familiar Mont Blanc circular tour from the year before, where ladies were provided with mules from Chamonix to Martigny (or vice versa) when travelling in either first or second class (for 45 francs or 40 francs respectively); gentlemen only got a mule in first class. The other three routes had starting points in Lausanne, Basel and Neuchâtel and included Lucerne, Bern, Lake Thun and Lake Brienz in various combinations on their itineraries.

Two more circular tours were added the following year, designed to be combined with any of the existing ones. Within a few years nearly all of Switzerland was covered by one of Cook's many circular interconnecting touring routes. Customers would choose which route they wanted to take to Switzerland (by 1905 there were 13 possible permutations between London and Lucerne, for instance, all with different prices) and then which tours to add on, with tour tickets valid for one month and bundled together as a booklet of coupons. Cook was simply a facilitator, who made the trips possible, and his Tourists were, in effect, the first InterRailers. They chose their tickets and off they went, many of them doing their own thing without a Cook conductor to guide them and using regular train services rather than specially chartered ones. Such leeway was immensely popular, as Cook himself recognised:

> One great element of success in a system of tours is freedom, without loss on the value of the tickets ... it is not necessary that all travel together; holders of the tickets may go alone if they prefer, and they can leave the prescribed line at any point they choose.

People loved the flexibility of tour coupons, and the affordable prices, so it was only a matter of time before Cook introduced the same system for hotels. By 1868 customers could buy hotel coupons in advance at a fixed rate in England and then use them as they toured. This made life much easier: no quibbling over the bill, no fiddling with foreign money, no fretting about quality. And for hoteliers it meant assured business, as the tourists were tied to using specific hotels. For example, *Cook's Tourist's Handbook to Switzerland* of 1874, his first real guidebook, listed 47 hotels across the country that accepted Cook's coupons, including the Victoria in Interlaken, the Adler in Grindelwald, Giessbach and Rigi Kulm. One coupon cost eight shillings (or £30 today) for one night, including a *table d'hôte* dinner and a non-meat breakfast, no matter which hotel. Unused coupons could be refunded on return to England. It was as simple as it was successful, as was the "circular note", introduced in 1874 so that customers didn't have to carry lots of money around. This was a credit note that enabled tourists to obtain local currency in a safe and easy way, having paid Cook for the note in London. In other words, it was an early form of a traveller's cheque.

Cook's first high-street shop opened in London's Fleet Street in 1865, selling tickets along with anything else a Tourist might need, and offices abroad soon followed. The same year saw the publication of his *Guide to Cook's Tours in France, Switzerland and Italy*. Priced at one shilling and sold separately from *The Excursionist*, it gave practical advice as well as marketing the tours. It distinguished between an Excursion (a special trip at very reduced prices) and a Tour (a wider, more circuitous range using regular public transport). What is fascinating is how quickly the advertisers had seized on this new market. This guide, coming barely two years after the first tour, has a clutch of adverts touting waterproof coats "readily carried in the pocket", a Tourists' Telescope "well-adapted for Swiss Tourists" and the Alpine Boot "specially adapted for Mountain Excursions".

There was also this notice from the Swan Hotel in Lucerne:

> *The Brothers Haefeli gratefully acknowledge the extensive support which they have received from English Visitors and Tourists, and beg to intimate that, encouraged by past success, they have now added another large establishment, which will enable them to provide accommodation for greatly increased numbers.*

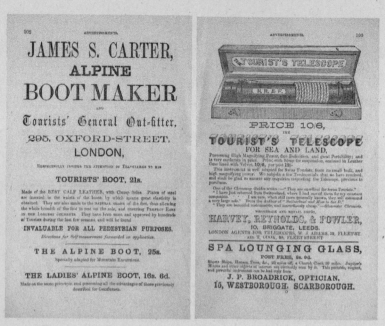

All sorts of things were advertised in the Cook guidebooks

As we have seen, this wasn't the only sign of the Swiss reacting quickly to the sudden influx of visitors (and money). Even Cook himself seemed surprised at both the size and speed of his success: "That which took *teens* of years in Scotland seems to have been acquired at a single bound in Switzerland." And it was just the beginning.

On the back of the Swiss success came tours to Italy and Germany, this time more profitably, and then Cook expanded ever further, into Egypt, Palestine, India and North America: the first Cook's Tour there in 1866 took nine weeks and covered 10,500 miles. The market blossomed into much more than two-week trips to the Alps, and a world tour eventually took place in 1872–73. Thomas Cook became synonymous with tourism all around the globe.

He also realised that not everyone wanted to tour around; some people simply wanted a holiday abroad. So by 1900 "Popular Holiday Tours" were on sale, less luxurious than conducted tours and, in effect, what we now think of as a package holiday. For example, the five guinea tour to Lucerne offered second-class travel from London and a week in "good comfortable hotels", including a *table d'hôte* dinner and meat breakfast every day. All for £5 5s, or about £300 today, and "the only advertised five guinea tour to Lucerne on which no booking fee or extra charge of any kind whatever is made". Also on offer was a week in Interlaken for seven guineas, with the chance to buy all your tickets for the mountain trains of the Bernese Oberland in advance. No wonder they were "popular" with every class of passenger.

Thomas Cook (the man) died on 18 July 1892, but the company carried on under the steady hand of his son, John Mason Cook, who had long been a partner in the business. When he died in 1899, it went to his sons and all seemed well for a while. Thomas Cook & Son was the travel agent of the British Empire and even war didn't stop things at first. In December 1914, *The Traveller's Gazette* advertised Christmas in the South of France or along the Swiss Riviera: 18 days in Nice or Montreux for £21 15s in first class. Escorted tours to Paris were running as late as September 1915, which seems incredible: the world was at war but it was business as usual for holidays abroad, although that didn't last. And then in 1928 the grandsons simply sold the whole company.

Every last part of the Cook empire was sold to the Companie Internationale des Wagons-Lits, operators of the Orient Express, before being nationalised in 1948 to become a government-owned travel agency. By 2001 Thomas Cook had been re-privatised and bought by the Germans, who very sensibly kept the brand name the same. A merger with MyTravel and flotation on the Stock Exchange made the company British again, trading as the Thomas Cook Group. It is the second-largest travel company in Europe, but faces an uncertain future competing with online booking, budget airlines and DIY packages. Nevertheless, amid the falling share prices and job losses there is Thomas Cook Signature, a programme that can be seen as the direct descendant of the conducted tours. Perhaps that's where the future lies – in tailored holidays from the world's oldest – and most trusted? – tour operator.

That was how it all started, with personal service and reliable products from a trusted source.

Before Switzerland, Thomas Cook had spent ten years trying to find the winning formula for overseas tours; after Switzerland, it only took him ten years to conquer the whole world. Or, as he put it, "Now-a-days, everybody may travel, everybody ought to travel – in fact, everybody does travel." The Swiss conducted tour wasn't the first step, or in the end the biggest, but it was the one that worked, the one that truly started mass tourism – and the one that made Cook into a brand that is still recognised around the world. So much of what we take for granted about modern tourism can be traced back to Thomas Cook and his conducted tours. If Switzerland had not been a success for him, maybe we would not have the tourist industry as we know it, from city breaks to fly-drives. Or perhaps it would all have developed eventually in some form, one way or another.

Is the world a better place for mass tourism? Who knows? Environmental cost against economic benefit, pleasure for the masses versus luxury for the few, development or depopulation. Switzerland has seen both sides of every argument, and maybe managed to come out with a positive balance overall – maybe.

It wasn't only Thomas Cook that enjoyed an explosion in customers, it was the guidebooks as well. For the likes of Murray, Baedeker and Cook's own guides, the 50 years after that tour were to be golden ones, with more and more destinations coming under their scrutiny. No one left home without a guidebook in their bag. After the First World War, it would take another 50 years for the guides to recover the lost ground and discover a new market of package tours and backpackers. However, 50 years after that, their future is not so rosy.

The Murray Handbooks carried on being a British travel institution long after Miss Jemima had used hers. But in 1901 the rights were sold and they were later reincarnated as the Blue Guides, with a Switzerland edition appearing in 1923. These are still going today. As for John Murray Publishing itself, that stayed in the family until 2002 when John Murray VII sold the company to Hodder Headline, now part of Hachette UK.

Thomas Cook's guidebooks continued in various guises until the summer of 2013 when the company pulled the plug on publishing. It could no longer compete with rivals such as Lonely Planet and Baedeker, itself still going strong after all this time, or the new threat: the mountain of online information. That could eventually kill off paper formats completely, and not just Cook's guidebooks.

Murray, Baedeker and Cook – all these guidebooks played an integral role in the development of tourism, giving people the courage to go it alone and explore a wider world. They were criticised from the start for creating a herd mentality, for damaging the local economy by making tourists less reliant on local knowledge and for ruining the very places they sought to extol. These were all true, perhaps, but not everyone was rich enough for a personal courier or brave enough to set off alone. Many were quite content to be part of a group, see the main sights and send some postcards. It is clear that Miss Jemima loved every minute of her tour, even if she barely interacted with the locals. Who knows, without the much-disparaged guidebooks and tour groups, all those people might simply have stayed at home. Would that have made the world a better place or them better people? I doubt it.

Mass tourism, via either groups or guidebooks, has been blamed for everything from overdevelopment to undermining the locals. Such criticism is nothing new. In 1870 the Reverend Francis Kilvert wrote, "Of all noxious animals, too, the most noxious is a tourist. And of all tourists the most vulgar, ill-bred, offensive and loathsome is the British tourist." He was most likely talking about people on a Cook's Tour, people like Miss Jemima. However, would she qualify as a tourist today? I'm not so sure.

She travelled as part of a group, mainly because it was the only affordable choice for her, and she consulted her guidebook, much as backpackers use Lonely Planet or internet forums today. She saw the Lion of Lucerne, but she also rode a donkey over an Alpine pass; she wanted a nice cup of tea, but she drank the local water (which she pronounced to be "delicious"); she walked up Rigi, but she hiked across glaciers. And while it wasn't quite Stanley going down the Congo, it was still an adventure, a pioneering new form of intrepid travel with no set itinerary, no pre-booked hotels and no real plan other than to see Switzerland in a fortnight. To modern sensibilities Miss Jemima was, in effect, more a self-sufficient traveller than a mollycoddled tourist. She was an independent, indefatigable lady with a dry sense of humour, boundless energy and an eye for detail, as well as the desire to go home after three weeks away.

That said, travel snobs today would probably dismiss her as a tourist who went around in her own bubble, not a real traveller at all. Worse than that, she created a template for all who came after her. And following in her footsteps, it's difficult to avoid doing the same, thanks to the relentless schedule of constantly moving. You get so caught up with seeing the sights, finding hotels and enjoying everything that you end up in a world of your own. So neither Jemima nor I sat and chewed the fat with the old men of the village; nor did we hike up to a remote hut to see cheese being made. However, that didn't spoil her evident delight in everything Swiss, or make her trip any less worthwhile. Is being moved by a much-visited stone sculpture any less valid an experience than going off to meet a mountain woodcarver? As for watching the sunrise from Rigi, that was once such a touristy thing to do but has become almost the opposite. It's so out of fashion that only the dedicated few do it any more, so it could now be considered an authentic Swiss experience.

Tourists and travellers are two sides of the same coin living in a symbiotic relationship of mutual contempt but actually dependent on each other. Without the infrastructure of tourism, being a traveller would be much harder work and much more expensive; without the frontier spirit of travellers, tourists would be trapped in the same old places, not knowing where the next new destination is. In the end there's no big difference. Tourist, traveller – many people are both, even on the same trip. Miss Jemima certainly was – Tourist by name, traveller by nature. What is important is that she had the chance to travel, thanks to Thomas Cook. That perhaps is the legacy of her trip and his work: the world became more accessible so that everyone could see it, not only a privileged few. And to the locals every visitor is a tourist, no matter how long they stay, how they arrived, what they see or how they view themselves. We are all tourists once we start to travel.

One tour, two trips, 150 years apart, but how great was the change in between? Some things are very different now – we travelled at a faster pace, we had our own bathrooms and showered every day, we could enjoy milk chocolate for elevenses – but when you look at the two trips together, in fact not much has changed. Miss Jemima would still recognise her tour, even with the improvements in transportation and sanitation, and still be familiar with most of the places along the route, not merely the never-changing mountains, but also the view across Lake Thun or Lucerne's old town. Despite ugly blemishes, such as the radio mast on Rigi or the concrete blocks in Grindelwald, the twentieth century was kind to Switzerland. Interlaken has grown, but it's still a small country town that happens to have a lot of hotels, while the Swiss love of tradition has helped preserve many local customs. For sure, events like bringing the cows down the mountain or Swiss wrestling matches have become tourist attractions, but they are still cherished as part of the national culture, supported not forgotten. Having tourists there too is an added financial bonus.

One thing that has certainly changed is my own view of Switzerland. Seeing it through Miss Jemima's eyes meant looking beyond the modern image of stability and prosperity, where millionaire bank accounts and punctual trains are the norm. That Switzerland is a recent incarnation. She showed me the Switzerland that was around for far longer, the one with beggars in the villages, goitres in the mountains and a ramshackle infrastructure. So while the magnificent Swiss landscape is much the same, the people living in and around those mountains definitely are not. Maybe that's why the Swiss are so careful with money; it wasn't so long ago that many of them had none. Tourism played an integral part in the Swiss success story, helping change rural poverty into national prosperity. Uncovering Switzerland's life before it won the economic lottery made me see the country differently. And I appreciate it even more – not something I anticipated from retracing a 150-year-old journey.

I also didn't expect the revelation of how adventurous those normal Victorians were. Miss Jemima put up with things that few people today would contemplate on a European holiday: 18-hour journeys in cramped trains without toilets, no running water in the hotels but sewage in the streets, an average of about four to five hours' sleep a night. As for the clothes, that just makes it all the more impressive: walking 25 miles in one day over a mountain pass while wearing hot and heavy layers of petticoats, crinoline, corset and jacket. Even with all that, the members of the Junior United Alpine Club had the time of their lives: in Mr William's words "We work very hard but are enjoying it amazingly". It was indeed hard work, both then and now, but it was a labour of love. They left full of excitement and went home full of memories; I left full of curiosity and came home full of admiration – for what they had achieved and for everything that they, and the tourists who came after them, made possible.

A PERSONAL POSTSCRIPT

Having spent so long in Miss Jemima's company, the urge to find out what became of the heroine of our story is overpowering. It's not as if she was a household name after her journal was published – that was simply for private consumption among the Junior United Alpine Club, and it's only by chance that it was found again in the ruins of a bombed building. Those two big red volumes now sit in the Thomas Cook company archives in Peterborough, safe and dry. The mystery of how and why they ended up in a blitzed warehouse in London has never been solved, but we can at least discover what happened to their author after she wrote them. It's time for some genealogical investigating.

Luckily, I have two sources who can do the digging for me. My father's greatest hobby, other than watching rugby, is genealogy and he has spent many hours tracing our family tree back through the centuries. So who better to ask when I need help with finding out about Miss Jemima and her family? And it doesn't take him long, thanks to her unusual surname and his detailed knowledge of where to look.

At last I have a picture of Miss Jemima's life, but alas no actual picture of the lady in question. That I get from my second source, Peter Williamson at Inntravel, a specialist tour operator based in North Yorkshire. The company now offers a self-guided 12-night tour following in Miss Jemima's Swiss footsteps, hence his research into her story. And here it is.

Four years after her epic exploration of Switzerland, in 1867, Jemima married John Greenwood, a widower ten years her senior who apparently had no need of a job to earn an income; he was listed simply as a "landowner" in the next census.

John brought three children from his first marriage but had one more with Jemima, a son named Robert Morrell Greenwood, born on 21 January 1868. The family was not short of money and moved to Lytham in Lancashire, then to Somerset, then finally back to Yorkshire, where John died in 1906. Jemima followed on 13 October 1909, and was buried in a small country churchyard in East Morton, near Bradford. She did live long enough to see Robert get married to Margaret Leir, and left him an estate worth £14,261, or about £800,000 in today's money. He was awarded a CBE in 1918, and died in 1947 without having had any children. There Miss Jemima's line ended, as did that of her elder brother, whose children also died without heirs.

The family name continued on through her younger brother William, although he died five years before her. The tour's paymaster, he became a bank manager in York, and was also the author of *The History and Antiquities of Selby*, which featured illustrations by Jemima. Both his sons went to work for Rowntree, the York chocolate maker that invented KitKats and was eventually bought by Nestlé, the Swiss food giant. The younger of the two sons, John Bowes Morrell, ended up as a director of Rowntree, Lord Mayor of York and a founder of York University. And it is through him that his grandchildren and great-grandchildren have a continuing link with Miss Jemima; some of them even took part in the costumed re-enactment of the tour on its 100th anniversary in 1963. Same route, same family, one century later.

So the Morrell family's part in this story ends; or does it? A few days later, my father sends me an email. He recognised one name that had popped up, that of Robert's wife – Margaret Leir from Hertfordshire – and so dug a little deeper. And then everything becomes a little spooky for me personally. Sitting on my parents' sideboard is a handsome silver teapot with the Leir family crest engraved on it. Not only that, but one of the many old family portraits in their house is of a distinguished gentleman who looks like he'd have a walk-on part in *Pride and Prejudice*. His name: Reverend William Leir, who died in 1863. Is it a coincidence? Maybe one connection but not two, and it's not as if the family name is Smith; there can't be that many Leirs in England. It turns out that the William in the portrait was Margaret's great-grandfather, who also happened to be the great-grandfather of Thomas Bewes, my own great-grandfather. Margaret and Thomas were thus second cousins or, in other words, she is a distant cousin of mine (second cousins three times removed, thanks to the huge generation gap).

Illustration by Jemima Morrell from her brother William's book, The History and Antiquities of Selby; *notice her signature bottom left*

And the teapot? That was a wedding present to William's daughter Sophia, Margaret's great-aunt, through whom I am descended: Sophia had a daughter Elizabeth, who had a daughter Hester, who married Thomas Bewes, who had a son Arthur, who had a son David, who is my father. At the same time, Sophia's brother William (a reverend like his father) had a son Charles (another reverend), who had a daughter Margaret, who married Robert, whose mother was Jemima. Simple really.

How amazing is that? I spend four years with Jemima, reading her words and following her across Europe, and end up discovering that I'm loosely related to her daughter-in-law. It was the last thing I ever expected. I never knew my great-grandfather Thomas, and he possibly never met his second cousin Margaret (or indeed her mother-in-law). Then again, maybe he did. I know some of my second cousins and went to their weddings, so met their mothers-in-law. Britain 150 years ago was very different, with only 23 million people and classes that kept to themselves, so the two might well have met. Either way, the family connection

Reverend William Leir, 1768–1863

is there, a little echo of history waiting to be heard many decades later by an unsuspecting writer.

Sadly, as both Robert and Margaret died without children, there are no fifth cousins around for me to find. I have to make do with the mother-in-law of my great-grandfather's second cousin. Perhaps it is true that everyone is connected by a maximum of six degrees of separation. It certainly worked for me and Miss Jemima.

Generations and decades apart, fate determined that we explore Switzerland together, in joint admiration at the glorious scenery. The transport may have changed as much as the nature of tourism, but the pleasure of travel has not. And maybe it never will.

Appendix I

THE WORLD IN 1863

What was the world like when Miss Jemima went abroad? Almost 50 years after Napoleon's defeat at Waterloo, Europe was for once relatively peaceful and prosperous. Great Britain had been ruled for 26 years by Queen Victoria, now in permanent mourning for Prince Albert. She would rule for another 38 and wear black for every single one.

France was royal again, having failed twice as a republic, Germany didn't exist but was a confederation of 30-odd states, unified Italy was barely two years old, and most of Eastern Europe was still part of the Austrian or Ottoman Empires.

The not-so-United States were halfway through their civil war. At the Battle of Gettysburg in July a Swiss soldier fighting for the North, Emil Frey, was captured by the South. He later became Switzerland's first ambassador to the (reunited) USA and a Swiss Federal Councillor.

Latin America was largely independent, as was the kingdom of Hawaii. Alaska belonged to Russia, Africa to Europe and Australia to Britain. China was ruled by the Qing Dynasty and India by the British Raj, then only five years old. Thailand was Siam, Iran was Persia and Sri Lanka was Ceylon.

Great Britain's population was 23 million – not huge considering it controlled half of the globe – whereas Italy had 25 million inhabitants, the USA 31 million, France 37 million and Switzerland only 2.5 million.

1863 saw the birth of a mildly popular sport: football (of the non-American kind) had its official beginnings in October, but not everyone liked the new rules. Some chose to play the Rugby school way, sticking their heads between the legs of fellow players.

And just when Thomas Cook was launching mass tourism, London Underground ran the world's first subway trains between Paddington and Farringdon. More people could travel more widely than ever before, either across the world's largest city or halfway across Europe.

1863

January
1 Emancipation Proclamation by Abraham Lincoln, ending slavery in America
1 Birth of Baron Pierre de Coubertin, creator of the modern Olympics
4 Four-wheel roller skates patented by James Plimpton in New York
8 Yorkshire Cricket Club founded in Sheffield
10 First London Underground trains run, on the Metropolitan line
13 Thomas Crapper demonstrates his one-piece pedestal flushing toilet
17 Birth of David Lloyd George, British Prime Minister
23 State funeral of Australian explorers Robert O'Hara Burke and William John Wills in Melbourne

February
3 Samuel Clemens uses the pseudonym Mark Twain for the first time
9 Geneva Society for Public Welfare creates the committee that eventually will become the Red Cross
10 Alanson Crane of Virginia patents the fire extinguisher
17 First meeting of the International Committee for Relief to the Wounded in Geneva

March
10 The Prince of Wales marries Princess Alexandra of Denmark
27 Birth of Henry Royce, British car maker
30 Prince William of Denmark chosen as King George I of Greece

April
19 Schweizerische Alpenclub (Swiss Alpine Club) founded in Olten
29 Birth of William Randolph Hearst, American newspaper publisher

May
2 Battle of Chancellorsville in Virginia
10 Stonewall Jackson dies from wounds received at Chancellorsville
21 Seventh-day Adventist Church founded in Michigan

TIMELINE

June
20 West Virginia becomes the 35th state of the USA
23 Napoleon III grants the mineral rights to the spring water at Vergèze, later re-christened Perrier
26 Thomas Cook's First Conducted Tour of Switzerland leaves London

July
1-3 Battle of Gettysburg in Pennsylvania
16 Thomas Cook's First Conducted Tour of Switzerland returns to London
17 Invasion of Waikato during the New Zealand Wars
30 Birth of Henry Ford, American car maker

September
20 Jakob Grimm dies in Berlin
29 First performance of *The Pearl Fishers* opera by Bizet in Paris

October
3 President Lincoln sets Thanksgiving as the last Thursday in November
25 Federal elections in Switzerland, with Freisinnige Linke the largest group
26 Football Association (FA) created in London
26-29 Geneva International Conference leads to the formation of the Red Cross

November
19 Abraham Lincoln delivers the Gettysburg Address
19 Swiss Re insurance company founded in Zurich
23 Louis Ducos du Hauron patents the process for making colour photographs

December
8 Clubs following the Rugby rules of football withdraw from the FA
12 Birth of Edvard Munch, Norwegian artist
18 Birth of Archduke Franz Ferdinand, heir to the throne of Austria-Hungary
24 William Makepeace Thackeray dies in London

Appendix II

SWITZERLAND IN THE 1860s

POPULATION

According to the census of 1860, Bern was the largest canton (467,141 people), followed by Zurich and Vaud. There were only ten communities with a population of over 10,000 people, and together they accounted for only 8 per cent of the total population. Today 45 per cent of the population lives in a community of more than 10,000 people, with the top ten cities making up 17 per cent of the national total.

Switzerland	2,510,494		
German-speaking	69.5%	Italian-speaking	5.4%
French-speaking	23.4%	Romansh-speaking	1.7%
Catholic	40.7%	Protestant	58.9%
Foreigners	4.6%	British residents	1202
Cows	944,000		

TEN LARGEST TOWNS

Geneva	41,415	La Chaux-de-Fonds	16,778
Basel	37,918	St Gallen	14,532
Bern	29,016	Lucerne	11,522
Lausanne	20,515	Fribourg	10,454
Zurich	19,758	Neuchâtel	10,382

LIFE AND DEATH (CURRENT FIGURES IN BRACKETS)

Life expectancy	Men	40.6 (80.1)
	Women	43.2 (84.5)
Death rate	23.6 per 1000 people (7.8)	
Birth rate	32.3 per 1000 people (10.2)	
Marriage rate	7.8 per 1000 people (5.3)	
People per doctor	1715 (500)	

EMPLOYMENT (CURRENT PERCENTAGES IN BRACKETS)

Primary sector: agriculture   57% (4%)
Secondary sector: industry   33% (23%)
Tertiary sector: service   10% (73%)

WAGES PER DAY

Farm hand, textile factory worker   1 to 1.50 francs
Bricklayer, glassmaker   2.40 francs
Metalworker, tailor   3 to 3.50 francs

PRICES

Francs per kilo

Beef	1.08	Flour	0.48
Bread	0.43	Potatoes	0.07
Butter	2.16	Sugar	1.10

Eggs	5 rappen each	Wine	3 rappen/litre
Milk	11 rappen/litre	Shirt	2.20 francs

POST AND BANKS

Post offices   2166
Letters sent
    Domestic: 25 million   Abroad: 8 million
Telegrams sent
    Domestic: 299,000   Abroad: 116,000
Post coaches
318 lines, 734 diligences and 774,000 passengers

Number of banks   291
Total deposits   542 million francs
Interest rates   4%

Appendix III

A NOTE ON MONEY

The final page of *Miss Jemima's Swiss Journal* is Appendix II, which is short, to say the least:

> "The Editor has received the following record of our excursion from a member of the Club. It is remarkable at all events for its brevity and it is therefore inserted:
> 'Account of a tour in Switzerland and France – June 26 to July 16, 1863, twenty-one days inclusive £19.17.6.'
> W.W. Morrell, Paymaster"

That amount (£19 17s 6d) is equivalent to about £1500 today and was declared by Mr William to be "very reasonable ... less than I expected". There is no breakdown of the total, but we get an idea of that from Thomas Cook's trip later that same summer.

For the return trip from London to Rigi via Geneva, Chamonix, Interlaken and Bern, Cook spent a total of £17 0s 1d (about £1300 today), of which:

Tickets	£10 8s 1d
Hotels, etc	£6 12s 0d

Within that, Cook paid 18 francs for two nights in Chamonix, including five meals a day (the "etc" in the amount above), or about £60 today. His train fare just from London to Geneva would have cost £4 13s in second class or £6 6s in first (equivalent to £350 and £480 respectively today).

Today the hotels and food add up to far more than the train tickets. Our trip cost a total of £1824 per person for 16 days, of which:

Tickets	*£426*
Hotels	*£995*
Food, etc.	*£403*

That was including a Swiss railcard, which halved all the train and boat fares in Switzerland, something in which every modern visitor should invest.

So almost 150 years later there was not a truly vast difference in costs, although if we had spent four days in Paris at the end our total might have been somewhat higher. Perhaps the biggest difference is that, sadly, it would have been cheaper for us to fly than to take the train to Switzerland. Cheaper, but not as much fun.

The Swiss franc is one of the world's strongest currencies today, but that wasn't always the case, particularly in 1863. When Thomas Cook took his first group of tourists to Switzerland, the franc was only 13 years old. The new single currency had been created alongside the federal constitution to help unify the country after a civil war.

Up until the introduction of the Swiss franc, over 8000 different coins were legal tender in Switzerland. Not only did each canton have its own currency, but money left over from the old Republic and neighbouring countries could also be used. The new Swiss franc was modelled on the existing French one, subdivided into 100 centimes, or rappen in German. For nervous British travellers there was reassurance in the guidebooks: "English sovereigns and banknotes are usually taken at inns throughout Switzerland." That's not usually the case these days.

The pound in 1863 was the pre-decimal version that is as confusing to foreigners as it is to anyone who grew up post-1971: one pound consisted of 20 shillings and each shilling was worth 12 pence. Prices were written as £ s d to show these elements (with d the abbreviation for an old penny). For example, the total cost of this first Cook's Tour was £19 7s 6d. To make things more complicated, there were other coins and amounts with their own names, all of which disappeared either before or on decimalisation:

Bob: colloquial name for a shilling

Crown: a silver coin worth five shillings (i.e. a quarter of a pound)

Guinea: a term for 21 shillings, based on a coin that no longer exists

Sovereign: a gold coin worth one pound

In terms of comparing prices then and now, there are a couple of aspects to bear in mind when reading figures quoted in this book:

Exchange rate: In 1863 there were 25 francs to the pound, a rate that remained fairly stable until after the First World War. Since then the Swiss franc has only ever grown in strength:

1945, £1 = 17 SFr

1970, £1 = 10 SFr

2000, £1 = 2.50 SFr

today, £1 = 1.50 SFr

Relative worth: What is hardest for modern readers to judge is how much all that is in today's money. For prices of goods, we can use inflation over time as a guide: a 7.20 franc train ticket would be 100 francs in today's money, while British beef at 8d a pound is equivalent to £2.40 now. As wages and prices have risen at different rates, it's maybe easier to think laterally. In the Switzerland of 1863 butter was twice the price of beef, but the farmhand working with the cows would need almost two days' wages to buy one kilo; in Britain the same worker only needed half of a day to buy a kilo of British butter. So to help your mental maths with the prices given in this book, here's a (very rough) handy calculator:

1863	Now	1863	Now
£1	£75	25 francs	375 francs
1s	£3.75	1 franc	15 francs
10d	£3	10 rappen	1.50 francs
1d	30p	1 rappen	15 rappen

BIBLIOGRAPHY

BOOKS IN ENGLISH

Michael Bailey (ed.), *Robert Stephenson: The Eminent Engineer*, Ashgate Publishing, 2003.

Andrew Beattie, *The Alps: A Cultural History*, Signal Books, 2006.

Geoffrey Best, *Mid-Victorian Britain 1851–75*, Flamingo, 1985.

Diccon Bewes, *Swiss Watching: Inside the Land of Milk and Money*, 2nd edn, Nicholas Brealey Publishing, 2012.

Diccon Bewes, *Swisscellany: Facts and Figures about Switzerland*, Bergli Books, 2012.

Margrit Bodmer-Jenny & Rudolf Gallati, *From Interlaken with Love*, Ott Verlag, 1986.

George Bradshaw, *Bradshaw's Handbook 1863*, Old House, 2010.

R. James Breiding, *Swiss Made*, Profile Books, 2013.

Piers Brendon, *Thomas Cook*, Secker & Warburg, 1991.

W. Catrina, P. Krebs, B. Moser & R. Rettner, *Jungfraujoch: Top of Europe*, AS Verlag, 2011.

Clive H. Church & Randolph C. Head, *A Concise History of Switzerland*, Cambridge, 2013.

Ronald W. Clark, *The Day the Rope Broke*, Mara Books, 2008.

Beverly Cole, *Trains: The Early Years*, H. Fullmann, 2011.

Ann C. Colley, *Victorians in the Mountains*, Ashgate, 2010.

Arthur Conan Doyle, *The Final Problem*, Strand Magazine, 1893.

Thomas Cook, *Guide to Cook's Tours in France, Switzerland & Italy*, Thomas Cook Ltd, 1865.

Thomas Cook, *Cook's Tourist's Handbook to Switzerland*, Thomas Cook Ltd, 1874.

Ed Douglas, *Mountaineer*, Dorling Kindersley, 2011.

Matthew Engel, *Eleven Minutes Late*, Pan Macmillan, 2009.

Karen Farrington, *Great Victorian Railway Journeys*, Collins, 2012.

Henry Gaze, *Switzerland: How to See it for Ten Guineas*, W. Kent, 1862.

Gérard Geiger (ed.), *1291–1991: The Swiss Economy*, SQP Publications, 1991.

H. B. George, *The Oberland and Its Glaciers: Explored and Illustrated with Ice-Axe and Camera*, Unwin Brothers, 1866.

Jill Hamilton, *Thomas Cook: The Holiday-Maker*, Sutton Publishing, 2005.

Adam Hart-Davis, *What the Victorians Did for Us*, Headline, 2001.

K. Theodore Hoppen, *The Mid-Victorian Generation 1846–1886*, Clarendon Press, 1998.

Arnold Lunn, *Switzerland and the English*, Eyre & Spottiswoode, 1945.

Jemima Morrell, *Miss Jemima's Swiss Journal*, Putnam, 1963.

Richard Mullen & James Munson, *The Smell of the Continent*, Macmillan, 2009.

John Murray (ed.), *A Handbook of Travel-Talk*, John Murray, 1858.

John Murray III, *A Handbook for Travellers in Switzerland, and the Alps of Savoy and Piedmont: 9th edition*, John Murray, 1861.

Jim Ring, *How the English Made the Alps*, John Murray, 2000.

Ralph Roman Rossberg, *The Jungfrau Region*, Hallwag, 1991.

Alan Sillitoe, *Leading the Blind: A Century of Guidebook Travel 1815–1911*, Bookcase Editions, 2004.

Jonathan Steinberg, *Why Switzerland?*, Cambridge University Press, 1996.

Edmund Swinglehurst, *Cook's Tours*, Blandford Press, 1982.

Matthew Teller, *The Rough Guide to Switzerland*, Rough Guides, 2010.

BIBLIOGRAPHY

Mark Twain, *A Tramp Abroad*, Penguin, 1998.

Christian Wolmar, *Fire and Steam*, Atlantic Books, 2007.

John Wraight, *The Swiss and the British*, Michael Russell, 1987.

Railways in the Bernese Oberland, Photoglob, 2001.

Switzerland: 1st edition, Baedeker, 1863.

The Kandersteg Story, Altels Verlag, 2001.

The Railway Traveller's Handy Book 1862, Old House, 2012.

The Rough Guide to France, Rough Guides, 2011.

UNWTO Tourism Highlights, World Tourism Organisation, 2012.

BOOKS IN GERMAN

Georges Andrey, *Schweizer Geschichte für Dummies*, Wiley, 2009.

Hans Brugger, *Die schweizerische Landwirtschaft 1850–1914*, Huber Verlag, 1978.

Bundesamt für Statistik, *Statistisches Jahrbuch der Schweiz 2012*, NZZ Verlag, 2012.

Agnès Couzy et al., *Legendäre Reisen in den Alpen*, Frederking & Thaler, 2007.

Arthur Fibicher, *Walliser Geschichte Band 3.1*, Sitten, 1993.

Roland Flückiger-Seiler, *Hotel Paläste: zwischen Traum und Wirklichkeit*, Hier+Jetzt, 2003.

Roland Flückiger-Seiler, *Hotel Träume: zwischen Gletschern und Palmen*, Hier+Jetzt, 2005.

Thomas Frey & Hans-Ulrich Schiedt, Monetäre Reisekosten in der Schweiz 1850–1910 – Wie viel Arbeitszeit kostet die Freizeitmobilität?, in Hans-Jörg Gilomen et al. (eds), *Freizeit und Vergnügen vom 14. bis zum 20. Jahrhundert* (Reihe: Schweizerische Gesellschaft für Wirtschafts- und Sozialgeschichte – Société Suisse d'histoire économique et sociale 20), Via Storia, 2005.

Rudolf Gallati, *Aarmühle Interlaken: Eine Ortsgeschichte*, Verlag Schlaefli, 1991.

Louis Gaulis & René Creux, *Schweizer Pioniere der Hotellerie*, Editions de Fontainemore, 1976.

Albert Hauser, *Das Neue kommt: Schweizer Alltag im 19. Jahrhundert*, NZZ Verlag, 1989.

Dr Joseph Hardegger et al., *Das Werden der modernen Schweiz 1798–1914*, Lehrmittelverlag des Kantons Basel Stadt, 1986.

Adi Kälin, *Rigi: Mehr als ein Berg*, Hier+Jetzt, 2012.

Christine Kehrli-Moser, *Rosenlaui*, 2012.

Markus Klenner, *Eisenbahn und Politk 1758–1914*, WUV Universitätsverlag, 2002.

Markus Krebser, *Interlaken*, Verlag Krebser Thun, 1990.

Dr Louis Largo & Peter Salzmann, *Thermen im Wallis*, Mengis Druck, 2012.

Thomas Maissen, *Geschichte der Schweiz*, Hier+Jetzt, 2010.

Ruth Reinecke-Dahinden, *Die Rigi*, Sutton Verlag, 2011.

Heiner Ritzmann-Blickenstorfer & Hansjörg Siegenthaler (Hg.), *Historische Statistik der Schweiz*, Chronos-Verlag, 1996.

Christian Schütt (Hg.), *Chronik der Schweiz*, Chronik Verlag & Ex Libris Verlag, 1987.

F.A. Volmar, *Die erste Eisenbahn der Berner Oberlandes*, Haupt Verlag, 1946.

Hans G. Wägli, *Schienennetz der Schweiz*, AS Verlag, 2010.

Felix Weber, *175 Jahre Rigi Kulm Hotel*, Familie Käppeli, 1991.

Christoph Wyss, *100 Jahre Tourismus-Organisation Interlaken*, Schlaefli & Maurer, 2009.

Ein Jahrhundert Schweizer Bahnen 1847–1947, Eidgenössisches Amt für Verkehr, 1947.

Schweiz: 9e Auflage, Baedeker, 1862.

Schweizer Tourismusstatistik, Bundesamt für Statistik, 2011.

LIST OF ILLUSTRATIONS AND PICTURE CREDITS

Front cover
Lötschberg Bergstrecke, Colombi, 1937 (BLS AG Archive)
Back cover
Die Eiserne Thurbrücke, Ansicht von Osten gegen Andelfingen, 1857 (Zentralbibliothek Zürich, Graphische Sammlung und Fotoarchiv; hereinafter Zentralbibliothek Zürich)
Traversée de la Mer de Glace (Zentralbibliothek Zürich)
Giessbach, Rudolf Dickenmann, steel-engraving, 1879 (© Collection Niklaus and Elsbeth Wyss-Burger, Unterseen)
Guide to Cook's Tours in France, Switzerland and Italy, 1865 (Thomas Cook archives)
Front flap
Miss Jemima's Swiss Journal, 1963 (Thomas Cook archives)
Back flap
Author photo (Simon Whitehead, www.threebythree.ch)

THANKS

Four years ago I first met Miss Jemima, three years ago I had the idea for a book, two years ago I set off in her footsteps, one year ago the idea became a reality. It's been a long journey to reach this point and I've had a lot of help along the way.

Without Paul Smith, the archivist at Thomas Cook, almost none of this would have been possible; or at least it would have been seriously less interesting. He knows more than is healthy about Cook history and patiently shared and discussed the finer points of nineteenth-century travel.

All the team at Switzerland Tourism in London, but particularly Marcelline Kuonen and Heidi Reisz, were a constant source of support and encouragement, not least on the long, hot days at the House of Switzerland during the London Olympics. Thanks also to everyone at the various local tourist boards and archives who have put up with my detailed questions and odd requests, especially Fabian Appenzeller in Lucerne, David Kestens in Leukerbad, Alice Leu in Interlaken, Anne-Sophie Perrin in Chamonix, Stephan Römer in Grindelwald and Doris Wandfluh in Kandersteg.

A special thank-you to Daniela Fuchs at Jungfraubahn, Anita Grossniklaus at BLS, Ernst Hofmann at the Hotel du Lac, Caroline Kälin at the Hotel Victoria-Jungfrau, Renate Käppeli at the Hotel Rigi Kulm, Didier Plaschy at Via Storia, Alice Robinson at the Zentralbibliothek Zürich, Julia Slater at swissinfo.ch, Bryan Stone and Malcolm Bulpitt at the Swiss Railways Society, Peter Williamson at Inntravel and Christoph Wyss at the Touristik-Museum der Jungfrau-Region.

And thanks to all those who helped me get this far with this project: Louise Atkinson, Joachim Biemann, Karen Davies, Christine Falcombello, Jane Fuhrimann-Greenaway, Tony Helyar, Silvia Hess, Dagmar Hexel, Carola Klein, Anthony Lambert, Michael Murphy, Catherine Nelson Pollard, Marcela Quezada, Daniel Pedroletti, Ruth Reinecke, Peter Salzmann, Janet Skeslien Charles, Beatrice Tschirren, Dirk Vaihinger, Kathy van Reusel, Christina Warren, Markus Williner.

A personal note of thanks goes to:

Helen Fields, Shelley Harris and Brian Wright for never letting me forget that writing is fun, especially at the weekend.

Anna Galvani and John Sivell for maintaining my English through Scrabble.

Zelda McKillop for hours of proofreading.

Julie Schmutz for the extended loan of an essential book.

Martin Tschirren and Beat Stoller for keeping Gregor occupied.

Simon Whitehead for making me look good on film (see www. threebythree.ch for more from him).

Without my agent, Edwin Hawkes, and everyone at Nicholas Brealey Publishing, this book would still be sitting on my computer rather than in your hands. All their essential work behind the scenes might go unnoticed by the reader, but I am forever grateful for it.

Without Gregor, and his family, I would not have stayed in Switzerland this long and would never have written one book, let alone three. He has patiently shared me with a 180-year-old woman for the past few years and rarely complained about our unusual *ménage-à-trois*.

Last, but not least, thanks to all my family, who may be far away in person but are never far away in spirit. And most of all to my parents, whose enthusiasm and support helped me believe that this dream could come true.

ABOUT THE AUTHOR

 Diccon Bewes is a full-time writer following the international success of his previous book, *Swiss Watching*. A degree from LSE in International Relations and an 18-month world trip set him up for a career in travel writing, via the scenic route of bookselling. After ten years at Lonely Planet and *Holiday Which?* magazine, he decamped to Switzerland.

Diccon spent his childhood holidays exploring Europe by car, so he has been travelling around by train ever since. . . He has survived winter on the Trans-Siberian Express, summer on trains across America and more than a decade of London Transport.

He has lived in Bern for eight years and continues to confound Swiss expectations of a British expat by not drinking tea.

www.dicconbewes.com